Louisa May Alcott

*From Blood & Thunder
to Hearth & Home*

NORTHEASTERN UNIVERSITY   1898–1998

Louisa May Alcott
From Blood & Thunder to Hearth & Home

Madeleine B. Stern

NORTHEASTERN UNIVERSITY PRESS • Boston

Northeastern University Press

Copyright 1998 by Madeleine Stern

Library of Congress Cataloging-in-Publication Data

Louisa May Alcott : from blood & thunder to hearth & home / by Madeleine B. Stern.

    p. cm.

    Includes bibliographical references and index.

    ISBN 1-55553-349-3 (cloth : alk. paper).—ISBN 1-55553-348-5 (pbk. : alk. paper)

    1. Alcott, Louisa May, 1832–1888—Criticism and interpretation.

    2. Women and literature—United States—History—19th century.

    3. Domestic fiction, American—History and criticism.

    4. Sensationalism in literature.   I. Stern, Madeleine B., 1912– .

   PS1018.L68   1998

   813'.4—dc21   97-45008

Designed by Janice Wheeler

Composed in Caslon by Coghill Composition, Richmond, Virginia. Printed and bound by Thomson-Shore, Inc., Dexter, Michigan. The paper is Glatfelter Supple Opaque Recycled, an acid-free sheet.

MANUFACTURED IN THE UNITED STATES OF AMERICA

02 01 00 99 98   5 4 3 2

Contents

Acknowledgments **vii**

Introduction **1**

Beginnings: Early Life & Career

Louisa Alcott, Trouper: Experiences in Theatricals, 1848–1880 **13**

Alcott's First Book: Tales for Ellen E. **32**

Louisa May Alcott and the Boston *Saturday Evening Gazette* **46**

An Early Alcott Sensation Story: "Marion Earle; or, Only an Actress!" **63**

Blood-and-Thunder

Some Anonymous and Pseudonymous Thrillers of Louisa M. Alcott BY LEONA ROSTENBERG **73**

Five Letters That Changed an Image: Louisa Alcott Unmasked BY LEONA ROSTENBERG AND MADELEINE B. STERN **83**

Behind a Mask: History of a Book **93**

Developing Professionalism

Louisa's *Wonder Book:* A Newly Discovered Alcott Juvenile **107**

The Witch's Cauldron to the Family Hearth: Louisa M. Alcott's Literary Development, 1848–1868 **114**

813
LOUI

The First Appearance of a *Little Women* Incident   127

Louisa M. Alcott in Periodicals   130

Louisa Alcott's Feminist Letters   144

Appraisals & Reputation

Louisa Alcott's Self-Criticism   175

Louisa May Alcott Had Her Head Examined   BY MADELEINE
STERN AND KENT BICKNELL   239

Louisa May Alcott & Frank M. Lupton   246

Louisa May Alcott at 150: A Writer's Progress   253

Index   267

Acknowledgments

"Louisa Alcott, Trouper: Experiences in Theatricals, 1848–1880" appeared originally in *New England Quarterly* (June 1943), 175–97. Reprinted by permission of *New England Quarterly*.

"Alcott's First Book: Tales for Ellen E" appeared as "Her First Book: Louisa May Alcott's Tales for Ellen E." in *AB Bookman's Weekly*, Clifton, New Jersey (November 12, 1990), 1849–60. Reprinted by permission.

"Louisa May Alcott and the Boston *Saturday Evening Gazette*" appeared originally in *American Periodicals* (Fall 1992), 64–79. Reprinted by permission of the University of North Texas Press.

"An Early Alcott Sensation Story: 'Marion Earle; or, Only an Actress!'" appeared originally in *Nineteenth-Century Literature* 47, no. 1 (June 1992), 91–98. © 1992 by the Regents of the University of California. Reprinted by permission.

"Some Anonymous and Pseudonymous Thrillers of Louisa M. Alcott," by Leona Rostenberg, appeared originally in *Papers of the Bibliographical Society of America* 37, no. 2 (1943), 131–40. Reprinted by permission of the Bibliographical Society of America.

"Five Letters That Changed an Image: Louisa Alcott Unmasked," by Leona Rostenberg and Madeleine B. Stern, appeared originally in *Manuscripts* (Winter 1985), 5–22. Reprinted by permission.

"Behind a Mask: History of a Book" appeared originally in *AB Bookman's Weekly*, Clifton, New Jersey (January 26, 1976), 411–21. Reprinted by permission.

"Louisa's *Wonder Book:* A Newly Discovered Alcott Juvenile" appeared originally in *American Literature* 26, no. 3 (November 1954), 384–90. Reprinted with permission.

"The Witch's Cauldron to the Family Hearth: Louisa May Alcott's Literary Development, 1848–1868" appeared originally in *More Books: The Bulletin of the Boston Public Library* (October 1943), 363–80. Reprinted courtesy of the Trustees of the Boston Public Library.

"The First Appearance of a *Little Women* Incident" appeared originally in *American Notes & Queries* (October 1943), 99–100. Reprinted by permission.

"Louisa M. Alcott in Periodicals" appeared originally in *Studies in the American Renaissance,* ed. Joel Myerson (1977), 369–86. Reprinted by permission.

"Louisa Alcott's Feminist Letters" appeared originally in *Studies in the American Renaissance,* ed. Joel Myerson (1978), 429–52. Reprinted by permission.

"Louisa Alcott's Self-Criticism" appeared originally in *Studies in the American Renaissance,* ed. Joel Myerson (1985), 333–82. Reprinted by permission.

"Louisa May Alcott Had Her Head Examined," by Madeleine B. Stern and Kent Bicknell, appeared originally in *Studies in the American Renaissance,* ed. Joel Myerson (1995), 277–89. Reprinted by permission.

"Louisa May Alcott & Frank M. Lupton" appeared originally in *Dime Novel Roundup* 61, no. 6 (December 1991), 102–6. Reprinted by permission.

"Louisa May Alcott at 150: A Writer's Progress" appeared originally in *Friends of the Brigham Young University Library Newsletter* (1984), 1–19. Reprinted by permission of the Friends of the Library, Brigham Young University Library.

Introduction

Published between 1943 and 1995, the essays in this collection span half a century—a long period indeed to be saturated with one subject, even so intriguing a one as the surprisingly complex Louisa May Alcott. Actually, my preoccupation with her was less continuous than intermittent, traceable to a succession of literary discoveries and events as well as to periodic resurgences of popular interest in the Concord Scheherazade.

The four essays originally published in 1943 were offshoots of two related occurrences: research on my biography, prepared during the forties and first published in 1950, and Leona Rostenberg's discovery of the Alcott pseudonym. In the course of research, playbills in the Orchard House gave substance to "Louisa Alcott, Trouper," while the Rostenberg unveiling of A. M. Barnard as Alcott's alter ego was the pivot for "The Witch's Cauldron to the Family Hearth."

The Rostenberg article, "Some Anonymous and Pseudonymous Thrillers of Louisa M. Alcott," aroused some scholarly interest along with plaudits from a few critics, including the distinguished Lawrence C. Wroth, who announced the find in the *New York Herald Tribune* on 22 August 1943, but the news was certainly not as explosive as it should have been. Interest in the course of World War II superseded interest in Louisa May Alcott's double literary life, and it would be several decades before the Rostenberg discovery triggered appropriate scholarly exploration.

My next contribution to Alcott scholarship, after publication of my biography, did not appear until 1954 and was made possible purely by serendipity. By that time I was deep into preparation of another book, one concerned with nineteenth-century American book publishers. In this connection I was examining the multitudinous entries in a volume of the *American Catalogue* that lists publications between 1866 and 1871, when my eye was caught by an anonymous work whose title was strangely familiar to me: *Will's Wonder Book,* published in 1870 by Horace Fuller as part of the Dirigo Series. If memory served, that narrative had been issued serially in the pages of Horace Fuller's *Merry's Museum* and, as far as I knew, had never appeared in book form. It was a serial written by Louisa May Alcott when, as hard-pressed editor, she had been driven to supply many of the contributions herself. Between the debut of "Will's Wonder Book" in *Merry's Museum* and its reappearance between boards, *Little Women* had captivated the national readership, exalted Alcott's reputation, and lured Horace Fuller to republish the serial anonymously and without its author's knowledge. Here, then, was another Alcott book to delight a juvenile audience and add to the Alcott canon. The vicissitudes of the manuscript and the strange history of its publication provided material for an article, "Louisa's *Wonder Book,*" issued in 1954.

Not until two decades after the discovery of *Will's Wonder Book* were the next Alcott-oriented essays published. One morning in 1974 I awoke with a brainstorm. Reprinting by then had become a cottage industry. Almost everything worth printing had been reprinted in one form or another—with one major exception—those anonymous and pseudonymous shockers by Louisa May Alcott that Leona Rostenberg and I had tracked down in nineteenth-century story papers. I determined to rectify the situation and assemble the anthology that would eventually be entitled *Behind a Mask: The Unknown Thrillers of Louisa May Alcott.*

Publication of that book, including as it did Alcott's most arresting feminist thriller, "Behind a Mask: or, A Woman's Power," originally run in *The Flag of Our Union,* as well as her prize-winning "Pauline's Passion and Punishment" from *Frank Leslie's Illustrated Newspaper,* metamorphosed public perception of America's most beloved author of juvenile fiction. Dramatizations, interviews with and television appearances by the editor, and eventually revisionist readings by scholars and critics followed.

The anthology *Behind a Mask* also led to articles. Readers were avid not only for the stories in the collection but for the history of the collection, from Rostenberg's initial discovery of the pseudonym and the detective work involved in tracing the lurid blood-and-thunder tales to the shaping of the book, its publication, and its aftermath. In the wake of my essay "Behind a Mask: History of a Book," I prepared an in-depth study of Louisa Alcott's appearances in periodicals covering of course her contributions to Leslie's paper as well as that of Elliott, Thomes and Talbot, *The Flag of Our Union*. During the same period, "Louisa Alcott's Feminist Letters" was issued, feminism being a dominant theme in the thrillers. That essay was a forerunner of an anthology that would be published in 1996 by Northeastern University Press, *The Feminist Alcott: Stories of a Woman's Power*. A year before, the same publisher had issued an almost complete collection of the thrillers in *Louisa May Alcott Unmasked: Collected Thrillers*.

The media spotlight on Louisa May Alcott in the mid-1970s was followed by the library lamp. By the 1980s the library of Brigham Young University in Provo, Utah, was in hot pursuit of works by and about the prolific and varied author, and it enlisted our aid in amassing a collection of her writings. For an Alcott exhibition held at that institution I prepared a survey entitled "Louisa May Alcott at 150: A Writer's Progress." Also during that decade scholars Joel Myerson and Daniel Shealy began assembling Alcott's selected letters as well as all her extant journals and diaries—tasks in which I participated. Naturally, the work of editing and introducing such material was coeval with my articles on Alcott's self-criticism and her relations with her publishers.

During the 1990s another, more intense resurgence of popular excitement over Louisa Alcott erupted. Both before and during that explosion my own attention focused on Alcott's earliest works, their publishing history, and their reception. An essay on *Flower Fables* traced the dramatic evolution of that endeavor; another on Alcott's work for the *Saturday Evening Gazette* during the 1850s explored the beginnings of her writer's progress; and still another discussed the nature of one of her first published thrillers. In 1995 the essay "Louisa Alcott Had Her Head Examined" reprinted a phrenological examination of Alcott that characterized her as possessing a "dual nature" and concluded that she had a "remarkable head."

That essay was written in collaboration with Alcott collector Kent Bicknell, who at the time was much in the news. Bicknell had purchased a previously unpublished manuscript by Alcott, which Random House issued in 1995 with the title *A Long Fatal Love Chase*. While that sensation novel was touted in the media, Alcott's "dual nature" was borne in upon an eager public, and interest in the Concord writer redounded.

The phrenological analysis of Louisa Alcott was prophetic. In the current decade her reputation, which from the beginning had experienced far more ups than downs, has peaked. More of her publications in periodicals have been traced, and the bibliography of her writings has expanded. *A Long Fatal Love Chase* was followed in 1997 by *The Inheritance*, rediscovered by Myerson and Shealy. Was there no end to her productivity? Apparently not. In Boston attic or Concord study she had penned sensational page-turners with one hand and domestic sagas with the other, finding time in between to indite fairy tales for children or letters on feminism.

No doubt Alcott tried her ink-stained hand at such a variety of genres because of one potent force: her developing professionalism. Experimenting not only with genre but with theme, from sexual warfare to the Civil War, from melodramas of revenge and violence to domestic sagas, from blood-and-thunder to hearth and home, the Concord spinster was motivated by an ever-strengthening thread that wove the fabric of her double—her multiple—literary life, the complexities of her character, and her productivity. And it is this thread that runs through most of the essays collected here.

We can perceive Alcott's professionalism developing from the beginning with the printing history of *Flower Fables*, whose subsidized publication netted the young author about thirty dollars. During the 1850s, when William Warland Clapp, Jr., paid five or ten dollars apiece for her tales for his Boston *Saturday Evening Gazette*, he demanded from the novice contributor the difficult combination of brevity and interest and so helped sharpen the narrative skills she was honing.

Alcott learned much from the advice of her publishers. James R. Elliott of *The Flag of Our Union* and Frank Leslie of *Frank Leslie's Illustrated Newspaper* solicited pseudonymous and anonymous thrillers for serial publication, and in supplying them, Alcott came to master the cliff-hanger technique. And it was of course her publisher Thomas Niles of Roberts Brothers who suggested that she write the story for girls that became the unforgettable *Little Women*. From all her publishers, Louisa Alcott learned elements of the professionalism that characterizes her writings.

Basically that professionalism, the growth of which entwined with her development as a writer, determined the nature, the diversity, and the continuing interest of Alcott's writings and of her self. The genres she experimented with, and especially the themes she addressed, are elaborated in these pages. Her apprentice years are here, when she began to interweave her early addiction to the theater into her stories, eventually inserting details of the stage into her thrillers, her novel *Moods*, her autobiographical *Work*, and the domestic novels. The feminism she lived as self-appointed breadwinner to a needy family also carried over into her writings, appearing early on in the guise of a compassionate sisterhood in "Marion Earle; or, Only an Actress!" and flowering in much of her later work. The feminist anger that motivated several of her blood-and-thunders is traced in these essays to its autobiographical sources, as is her espousal of other reforms such as abolition. Her complex treatment of such themes in fiction is analyzed as well—both her intertwining of realism with sensationalism and her disentangling verisimilitude from melodrama. In these essays we follow Alcott as she emerged from the days when James T. Fields informed her, "You can't write," to the days when the "inspiration of necessity" and the suggestions of her editors induced her to experiment with genres that ranged from fairy tale to shocker to domestic drama. Her working methods are here as she learns to test the public taste; her portrait and her self-portrait are unveiled—her works in progress and the progress of her work.

The groundwork for these essays includes a body of sources, many of them previously unused, many ephemeral and hence overlooked. Those sources open windows upon Alcott's background and life, her development as human being and as professional writer.

Although some of these sources have been published, they are often neglected by biographers and critics. City histories, for example, may be tedious and self-serving, but they contain colorful on-the-spot details not to be found elsewhere. Two volumes, prosaically entitled *Walpole as It Was and as It Is* and *Bellows Falls and Vicinity Illustrated*, served me well when I was researching the period in 1855 when the Alcotts lived rent-free—thanks to the generosity of Louisa's uncle Benjamin Willis—in Walpole, New Hampshire. There Louisa became a member of the Walpole Amateur Dramatic Company, whose activities were brought to life by touches of their Walpole background.

Just so, family genealogies offer touches that enliven personalities; local directories pinpoint an address; local newspapers and death records provide informative obituaries. For researching a writer's life, contemporary newspapers yield advertisements or reviews of books. In Alcott's case of course scrapbooks of such critiques could have been assembled, starting with the brief notices of *Flower Fables* in the *Boston Evening Transcript* and the *Saturday Evening Gazette* in December 1855 commenting that Alcott's first published book contained "several agreeable sketches . . . adapted to the capacity of intelligent young persons" and that her "little legends of faery land" were "very sweet."

For the essays in *From Blood & Thunder to Hearth & Home,* contemporary periodicals were always exciting sources. A run of *Merry's Museum,* for example, shaped the image of Louisa Alcott in the role of editor as well as driven contributor inserting in its pages incidents that would later appear in *Little Women.* As for *Frank Leslie's Illustrated Newspaper* and *The Flag of Our Union,* published by Elliott, Thomes and Talbot, surely no literary sleuth could turn those chipping, brittle nineteenth-century story papers in search of Alcott's clandestine blood-and-thunders without experiencing the thrill of the chase, the joy of the find, and palpitations throughout.

The search for unpublished materials was perhaps more successful when the earlier essays in this collection were written than it is today. In 1987 *The Selected Letters of Louisa May Alcott* was published, and in 1989 the complete *Journals of Louisa May Alcott* appeared. Both volumes now serve as guidebooks to a mass of previously unused material. Early on, the promise of finding revealing Alcott letters at the Orchard House*

---

*Some of the manuscript material cited in the notes as deposited in the Orchard House is now in the Houghton Library, Harvard University.

or Houghton Library was an abiding lure. Such letters often cropped up elsewhere too. While researching my biography of Alcott, I paid a visit to the bookshop of the late Arthur Pforzheimer, who generously allowed me to copy Alcott's unpublished letters in his keeping. One was especially extraordinary. Written to Jannette E. Sweet circa 1885, it gave the literary advice of a veteran Alcott, the celebrated "Children's Friend," to a novice writer, suggesting that she present her tale "in the form of a child's story, & let their impressions, words & adventures be the main thread. . . . There is enough in the facts to make a thrilling tale told briefly & dramatically. . . . Imagine you are telling it to children & the right words will come." Surely in those lines there was more than advice—there was a self-portrait. Interestingly enough, years later that very letter was auctioned off, and the firm of Leona Rostenberg and Madeleine Stern secured it for the Alcott collection of Brigham Young University Library.

Letters addressed *to* Louisa Alcott are sometimes as interesting as her own communications. Again when gathering materials for my life of Alcott, I visited an Alcott collector on New York's Horatio Street. In his possession was an extraordinary letter to her from the publisher Aaron K. Loring, extolling a "story of constant action" that teaches "some lesson of life"—recommendations that she most assuredly took to heart.

Perhaps no letters yielded more revolutionary disclosures than the five from James R. Elliott of Elliott, Thomes and Talbot to "Dear Miss Alcott," discovered by Leona Rostenberg at Houghton Library in the early 1940s. That small batch of letters, revealing Alcott's pseudonym and naming several of her secret thrillers, unmasked the spinner of tales who led a double literary life. Eventually that find introduced the reading world to a corpus of previously unknown stories of intrigue and suspense, and changed the Alcott image forever.

Among the ephemera that helped reconstruct Alcott's life and career, none supplied more authentic color than the playbills found at Orchard House and Houghton Library. Since the stage permeates Alcott's writings in many genres, such source material is particularly significant. Along with manuscript versions of "The Mysterious Page, or Woman's Love" and "The Prince and the Peasant, or Love's Trials," playbills for the Amateur Dramatic Company in Walpole and the Concord stock company of the mid-fifties provide the backdrop for Alcott's many curtain calls. While a fragmentary unpublished diary of Abba Alcott listed the members of the Concord company, a playbill of *The Two Buzzards* assigned to Louisa the part of Lucretia Buzzard, and another bill, for Sheridan's *The Rivals,* established her in the unforgettable role of Mrs. Malaprop.

One of the most intriguing extant playbills is that for "Nat Bachelor's Pleasure Trip," a play actually written by the stage-struck Alcott and performed on 4 May 1860 at the Howard Athenaeum in Boston, where the dramatist viewed her after-sketch, performed after the main presentation, from a private parlor box in the rear of the parquet.

Of all the extant memorabilia that restore Louisa Alcott's addiction to the theater, perhaps none is more delightful than the manuscript copy of "Mrs. Jarley's Waxworks" made by Alcott for her young friend Alf Whitman and now preserved in the Houghton Library. This was no doubt Alcott's favorite role: a monologue inspired by readings in Charles Dickens. The manuscript copy recaptures for us the image of Louisa Alcott in the title role, arrayed in an old black dress with a large poke bonnet on her head, clutching an umbrella and a basket and bowing before her audience as she introduced them to "the finest collection of wax 'statooary' in the known world."

One of Alcott's early stories, "Bertha," issued in the Boston *Saturday Evening Gazette* in two numbers in April 1856, brought the author ten dollars from publisher William Warland Clapp, Jr. As she wrote in her diary (*Journals of LMA,* 78), "Got $10 for 'Bertha,' and saw great yellow placards stuck up announcing it." Years later she reminisced about that triumph: "One of the memorial moments of my life is that in which . . . my eye fell upon a large yellow poster, with these delicious words: . . . ' 'Bertha.' a new tale by the author of 'The Rival Prima Donnas,' will appear in the *Saturday Evening Gazette.*' I was late; it was bitter cold; people jostled me . . . but there I stood feasting my eyes on the fascinating poster, and saying proudly to myself, . . . 'This, this is fame!' . . . That afternoon my sisters made a pilgrimage to behold this famous placard, and, finding it torn by the wind, boldly stole it and came back to wave it like a triumphal banner. . . . The tattered paper still exists."

The tattered paper is no longer tattered. Restored, it can be viewed at the Orchard House. Like all the ephemeral sources for these essays, it is a colorful piece used to reanimate a life and a career.

That life and career are still being reanimated. When the first of these essays was written, in the early 1940s, Leona Rostenberg had just discovered the pseudonym that concealed Louisa May Alcott's authorship of her daring sensational shockers. Fifty years later, when the last of these essays was published, still more of Alcott's blood-and-thunder tales were surfacing as scholars continued to trace their original appearances in crumbling nineteenth-century weeklies. Critics are still searching out the autobiographical episodes that led the author of *Flower Fables, Hospital Sketches,* and *Little Women* to create narratives about drug addiction and sexual power struggles. And in turn they muse upon the glimpses into her life and character suggested by the products of her double literary life.

Bronson Alcott recognized in his daughter an arsenal of powers. Emerson called her a natural source of stories. As these essays indicate, Louisa May Alcott developed into a professional writer who was touched by genius and kept her hand at all times on the public pulse. She is also a springboard for critical investigators, for reconstructionists, for revisionists. Between her "dual nature" and her many-faceted literary career she provokes surprise and delight, scholarship and detection. In the pages that follow, her complexities are examined, her career traced, her productivity appraised.

The story of Louisa Alcott is by no means over. A natural source of stories, she is also, and will continue to be, a natural source of exploration and discovery.

Beginnings

Early Life & Career

Louisa Alcott, Trouper

I n the barn of a two-story frame dwelling in Concord called Hill-side, on the Lexington Road, a Spanish peasant girl disguised as a page was pursuing her beloved Count Antonio, who, in all the splendor of green doublet and plush puffs, returned her affection after one desertion, one suicide, and several elaborate speeches. The green doublet had known less theatrical days when it adorned the house as a drapery; the peasant girl in actuality bore a less exotic name than Lelie; and Count Antonio did not always flourish a black velvet cap with white plumes. They were simply Anna and Louisa Alcott, entertaining themselves and their neighbors with a brilliant performance of "The Mysterious Page, or Woman's Love."[1] The curtain had risen upon Scene One of a lifetime interest in the theater.

The curtain, which had doubtless served as a sheet in a previous existence, rose often during 1848 upon scenes where counts and peasant girls endured "love's first trial,"[2] or witches concocted magic brews in caves made of bureaus and tables, and Moorish maidens and Greek slaves pursued a destiny marvelously planned for them by the youthful co-authors and co-actors.[3] Anna and Louisa were serving a dramatic apprenticeship that taught them how to assume five or six characters in the course of a single scene, how to convert discarded furniture into props with a magic carpentry, or enclose the piazza with draperies to improvise a stage, how to manage exits and entrances with skill, how to intone a "thee" and a "thou," an "oh" and an "ah" with a voice that would echo to the rafters of the Hillside barn. Nothing was too difficult, too miraculous for the Alcott side of the footlights. Revenge and death and love made a glorious trio with which to bespell a small but select audience. For was there not a spell upon the actresses themselves? Could they not declaim in ringing tones, to the accompaniment of a stamp of yellow boots, "I am no coward, Ione; but there is a spell upon me. 'Tis a holy one, and the chain that holds me here I cannot break,—for it is *love*." Love was underscored and treachery italicized against a background of red curtains and faded brocades. Art walked the stage for the sake of art, arrayed in glorified shawls and velvet robes. The barn was a barn no longer, but Spain or Greece or any uncharted spot never to be found on land or sea. The history of the green doublet was easily forgotten as it paraded the boards in its newfound grandeur. And if the witch's cauldron had its proper place on the stove as a kitchen kettle, none would be the wiser who heard Norna murmuring incantations above its steaming depths. Call Hillside a frame dwelling on the Lexington Road as long as the tongue of practicality would wag—what was it after all but one of many stages for two itinerants gone barnstorming?

There had been earlier stages also, the stage improvised on the stairs of Hillside for a Pilgrim's Progress from the Slough of Despond to the Celestial City,[4] and Louisa could recall having taken the role of a tan-cheeked Indian maid for the edification of her neighbors at Still River.[5] By the time she was eighteen, however, such performances seemed a trifle amateurish for an actress who had begun to take her career quite seriously. Glowing with the prospect of ovations, plaudits, and curtain calls, Louisa opened her diary for August 1850 to record the fact that "Anna wants to be an actress, and so do I. . . . I like tragic plays, and shall be a Siddons if I can. We get up fine ones, and make harps, castles, armor, dresses, waterfalls, and thunder, and have great fun."[6]

It was not until five years had passed, years encumbered with poverty and marked by misfortune, that Louisa at last found an opportunity for less private theatricals and a place for her name, if not in the spotlights, at least on a playbill. The denizens of Walpole, New Hampshire, however, seemed to be content with less tragical performances than those that had been offered at Hillside, for the Walpole Amateur Dramatic Company presented a repertory exclusively of comedies and farces.

The Alcotts had ventured in July 1855 to Walpole, where Louisa's uncle, Benjamin Willis, owned a pleasant farm on Main Street, near the Connecticut River.[7] Uncle Willis, a shipowner, had modernized the old colonial dwelling, built in 1791, and settled there to indulge his interest in literature and modern history. Though his wife, Mrs. Alcott's sister, had died several years before, he was kind enough to allow his relatives a home rent-free. There Louisa's father tended his garden and was inspired to feats of conversation with his country neighbors on Village Life, its opportunities, advantages, and duties.[8]

For the Alcott girls, Walpole offered more than a stroll to the post office or a ramble to Fall Mountain.[9] If Alcott found an audience for his monologues in the parlors of his neighbors, his children found a group of young folks eager to welcome them to their Amateur Dramatic Company. There was, first of all, the Hayward family—all of them related to the Bellows clan, as who was not in the village of Walpole? Mrs. Hayward[10] herself had a notable talent for reading aloud, and it was not unusual that her children should enjoy similar academic tastes. Louisa Hayward, the eldest, had a turn for the literary, and the Alcotts were delighted to find that she had an interest in composition. Being the eldest, twenty-nine years old, she found a natural place for herself as stage manager of the Walpole productions. The Alcott girls enjoyed the company of the Hayward brothers also. John and his wife could charm many an evening with suggestions for emphasizing a bit of dialogue or expanding a role in one of the current plays. Brother Waldo, just a year older than Louisa Alcott, was perhaps the most interested in theatricals. Under his reserved exterior he had a lively sense of humor, and, with his powerful, erect physique and interest in Walter Scott, could be relied upon to portray John Duck in *The Jacobite* or to offer many suggestions regarding the historical costumes called for in the play.

Besides the Haywards, there were the Kittredges, whose home, Elmwood,[11] on the west side of the Common, offered a glorious attic for rehearsals. The four children of the town's physician and treasurer, Thomas, Helen, Sarah, and Master Samuel, ranged in age from twenty to fourteen, and did not mind relinquishing the major roles to older members of the Walpole troupe, provided that they were placed somewhere on the playbill.

As scenic artist, for the productions, seventeen-year-old Alfred Howland, son of the town's moderator and lumber dealer, who desired to become an engraver or painter, was delighted to paint a backdrop for the parlor of "The Crooked Billet," where the Jacobite met his friends and enemies. Alfred's brother Henry, a freshman at Harvard Law School, portrayed Major Murray for the Walpole audience. From Harvard came also Alfred Hosmer and Howard Ticknor, who succeeded Louisa Hayward as stage manager. There were others, too—Joshua Clark, a farmer, Dr. George Blake, young Josiah Bellows, and Gill Wheelock, who, if a second bass or cornet-à-piston was required, was happy to lend his services.[12]

With a few minor exceptions, the cast was thus completed. Fifteen-year-old Abba Alcott willingly lent herself as prompter to the task of following lines and whispering cues.[13] The Walpole Serenade Band struck up between acts, and nothing was lacking.

The double bill, J. R. Planché's comic drama *The Jacobite* and J. M. Morton's one-act farce *The Two Bonnycastles,* was scheduled for the evening of Tuesday, 11 September. With Waldo Hayward's suggestions, the required costumes had been prepared for the time of George the Second. Louisa had been assigned a part that answered her heart's desire, that of Widow Pottle, the crass, ignorant, grasping, comical keeper of the inn painted so well by Alfred Howland. She had mastered the necessary dialect and could mouth a "Ragamuffin" or an "Impudent varlet" or a "Pack up thee duds" with a fine gusto. Anna, of course, was scheduled for the ingénue role of the widow's daughter Patty, who would accept the love of Waldo Hayward's John Duck with all the necessary sweetness and light.

At seven o'clock the fathers and mothers and sisters and brothers of the Amateur Dramatic Company began crowding into the hall, while the cast donned their eighteenth-century costumes, repeated their cues, and made ready for their entrances. At eight, the curtain rose on the parlor of "The Crooked Billet," and the performance of *The Jacobite* began. Anna Alcott and Louisa Hayward entered immediately, exposed the difficulties that surrounded Major Murray, and hinted at the direction of John Duck's affections. At last Louisa Alcott roared her first line from the "cellar" behind scenes, "I've told thee so a hundred times, fool; art thee deaf!" With this line, she established her character, mouthed her dialect, and prepared to take her place upon the stage. She stalked the boards with a will, cuffed John Duck, called him a "cozening varlet," deary-me'd his honor Sir Richard, and throughout Act I supplied with a keen gusto the comic relief in a play already comic enough.

In the course of Act II, during which John Duck cleared up all the problems and retrieved the Major's pardon, Louisa had time to listen behind scenes, while she exchanged her costume for the scarlet dress, black cloak, and white bonnet of Mrs. Bonnycastle, the part for which she had been cast in the second play of the evening. Her role was that of a none-too-attractive woman in "a dreadful state of agitation" after the disappearance of her husband (Dr. George Blake), last seen "rushing frantically down Holborn Hill with a carpetbag under his arm." In a zealous desire to discover whether she was wife or widow, she rushed onto the stage well supplied with asides and significant looks, and did not leave it until the comedy of errors was straightened out and the lovers were properly paired off. After the last line, Louisa, Anna, Henry Howland, Dr. Blake, and Waldo Hayward formed a semicircle to make their bows, and the curtain fell.

The performance of 11 September was typical of the bills presented by the Walpole troupe. The cast had had enough experience in theatricals to realize the limitations of amateurs and never attempted anything that was not either a comedy or a farce. Their repertory[14] consisted of such plays as *Naval Engagements, Still Waters Run Deep, The Little Treasure, Sketches in India, The Two Buzzards, The Rivals*—all except the last, contemporary comedies in the forties or the fifties. The stage manager assigned to Louisa the role of heavy comedian in comedies, most of which concerned a lady and gentleman in "a peculiarly perplexing predicament." As Mrs. Malaprop or Betsy Buzzard she found ampler parts, though similar in character to that of Widow Pottle, and throughout 1855 and 1856 she enjoyed the experience of taking many a curtain call in the lower room of the Walpole Town Hall.

Louisa had at last seen her name on a playbill. She had turned from the "tragedies" of Hillside to the comedies of Elmwood. Though she had found a character that suited her abilities, she was still uncertain whether her future was to be found in the lap of a producer or the lap of a publisher. Nothing, however, unless it was a vision of young Booth in Brutus,[15] could equal the thrill of responding to a curtain call for an itinerant who had advanced from a barn to a town hall. For an actress of twenty-four the laps of producers were broad, the dice of the gods

were loaded in her favor, and the world was still full of possibilities—
and of theaters.

Though Concord, Massachusetts, boasted no professional green
room, it offered many a henhouse or private dwelling where the ten
dramatic passions could be enacted. When the Alcotts returned to the
village in 1857, taking up their residence on Bedford Street, they brought
with them, besides their ailing sister Elizabeth, their ardent interest in
the drama. Though Elmwood had been left behind, Louisa discovered
that there was now at Concord just as practicable a setting for rehearsals
in Frank Sanborn's school.[16]

Sanborn, just a year older than Louisa, had left Harvard in March
1855 to superintend a private school in Concord. By the time the Alcotts
returned, he had proved himself sufficiently right-minded to carry on
the affairs of the school in a manner befitting the birthplace of American freedom. It was not long before the girls met the tall, dark-haired,
book-laden young man and found to their satisfaction that he entertained the desire of establishing a Dramatic Union in Concord.

In the back of Abba's diary she listed the names of the fortunate
members who constituted the Concord Stock Company of the 1857–1858
season.[17] First, of course, was Manager Sanborn. Close upon his heels
came George Bartlett, the village doctor's son, just Louisa's age, and
with a theatrical history similar to hers, for he remembered early performances of Shakespearean tragedies played before an audience composed entirely of Aunt Betsey. With Bartlett and his two brothers,
Ripley and Ned,[18] the troupe would never lack a Nick Bottom, a Mr.
Bumble, or a Robin Starveling. The names of Edith and Edward Emerson were also duly entered. To Anna's delight, another name was inscribed, that of John Pratt, the twenty-four-year-old son of Minot
Pratt, who had served during Association days at Brook Farm. Behind
his blue glasses and bookkeeper's manner, John harbored a lively wit
and was ready to take any part assigned to him, especially that of Darby
opposite Anna Alcott's Joan. John's younger sister Carrie; Helen and
Frank Wheeler; Carrie Cheney, the lawyer's daughter; Joseph Wall,
fated from birth to play the Wall in *A Midsummer Night's Dream;* Alex
Clarke, and one or two other "strolling" players completed the list—
with one important exception in Louisa's eyes. Alfred Whitman,[19] a
yellow-haired lad, carried through life the alias of "Dolphus" after a

performance of *The Haunted Man,* and became also at least half of an as yet unborn "Laurie" in an as yet unconceived *Little Women.* Young Alf Whitman had enrolled at Sanborn's school in the fall of 1857 and, boarding with the Pratts at Pickle Roost, soon found his way to Louisa's home and to her heart as well.

Preparations were in progress, permissions were obtained from authors, red heels were hammered onto shoes that would tread the boards, and costumes were converted from sarcenets and cambric curtains. In the vestry of the Unitarian Church a portable stage was erected, Abba Alcott accepted the position of musical director, and the triple performance of 1 December 1857 was soon under way.[20] The curtain rose on "The Fountain Inn" this time, and did not fall until two pairs of ill-matched lovers had sorted themselves out, both chronologically and amorously. Louisa had by this time resigned herself to taking the part of a charming young widow of forty and inimitably played Mrs. Pontifex in a puce satin pelisse. George Bartlett was her "Kingston dear" until, in the course of *Naval Engagements,* he found a younger bride. Anna was naturally given the ingénue role, while Alf Whitman satisfied himself with the part of the waiter. *The Dumb Belle* by Bayle Bernard was performed next, after which Louisa again appeared as Betsy Buzzard opposite John Pratt's Glimmer, Frank Sanborn and Anna Alcott providing the other set of lovers in *The Two Buzzards.*

This triple bill was typical of the performances of the Concord troupe, but gradually new plays were added to the repertory[21] until Louisa could boast having run the gamut of comedies and farces, from *Kill or Cure, A Morning Call,* and *Poor Pillicoddy* to *My Wife's Mirror* and *Fortune's Frolic.* Just for variety, she played Lady Somerford in *The Jacobite,* and began to cast her eyes in the direction of the Boston theaters, hoping for an opportunity to act for larger if not more select audiences.

As manager, Sanborn realized Louisa's skill in depicting characters from Dickens. Even George Bartlett, consumed as he was with plans for a Grand Dickens Cosmorama, saw fit to bow before the opinions of Anna Alcott, who had acted in *Scenes from Dickens* at Syracuse,[22] and of Louisa, who spoke Dickens almost in her sleep. What was more appropriate for the Christmas of 1857[23] than a series of dramatizations from the great man's works? From *David Copperfield* the troupe chose the discovery of little Emily's flight.

The scene is laid in an old boat & Peggotty Ham Mrs. Gummidge & David appear. Peggotty expecting Emily home & putting the light in the window Ham coming in with the dreadful tidings, the reading of the letter & Peggotty's vow—It makes a splendid scene—[24]

To this were added the Pickwick Trial and The Tetterby Family, in which Louisa played Sophia to Whitman's Dolphus. The prologue of Old Yule and Young Christmas had ushered in a lively performance to greet the new year.

But the new year was not as beneficent as the old. The doctor soon pronounced Lizzie Alcott's condition hopeless, and the girls gave up all their plays immediately.[25] On 14 March, Lizzie's death made Louisa think less of public theaters than of private woes, less of comedy than of tragedy. The Unitarian Church had other purposes now than for a portable stage, and Sleepy Hollow Cemetery was nearer than Sanborn's schoolhouse.

The footlights still beckoned, however, and by the time June slipped round, Louisa hoped against hope that Thomas Barry, manager of the Boston Theatre, would allow her to take the part of Widow Pottle before a metropolitan audience. The arrangements were conducted in the strictest secrecy; the dress would make an excellent disguise, but—alas—Mr. Barry broke his leg and Louisa quite temporarily broke her heart.[26]

After seeing William Warren in *Lend Me Five Shillings*,[27] she could not help feeling that perhaps it was acting and not writing that she was destined for—acting in private if not, just yet, in public. At any rate, if the Boston Theatre was not ready to welcome her upon its stage, Pickle Roost had no objections whatsoever. To add a merry finish to an otherwise dull year at Concord, and to brighten the spirits of John's young brother, Theodore Pratt, who was mortally ill this year as Elizabeth had been the last, Louisa played, not Widow Pottle, but Major Murray in *The Jacobite*. She wrote Alfred Whitman, in Kansas, a full account of the affair:

. . . I never could get through the first long speech . . . & utterly routed Carrie's ideas by informing her that my false name was "Charles Antwerp" a merchant of Vosdeck. . . .

We played in the Pratt parlor after a nice little tree full of gifts & goodies had been stripped, & had no stage or properties but rambled about among the audience in a . . . vague manner. . . . John Duck got under the table for a chest & the Major with a wooden sword pried up the table cloth & dragged him out. . . . Mr. Pratt read the part of the villianious [*sic*] "Sir Richard" with angelic meekness—Carrie darted in & out of Mrs. Pottles & Lady S's clothes with amazing rapidity & Annie & John did the "lovyers" to the life.[28]

Finally, the brilliant audience of fifteen applauded copiously, and Thedie Pratt's last Christmas was brightened with such jollification as the Concord troupe could supply.

A few months later, Louisa was again in an "exciting whirl" of plays, participating in "some grand doings" at the home of the Sargents.

> . . . we rummaged up two gents & with—the four Sargents—John Ab & I, we got up some startling things . . . the great Geo B was there also—. . . we made a great spread in the way of gold & damask . . . drapes &c. We had a play . . . called the "Jacobite"—John as "Duck" Kitty as Patty & the "Widder" Edward Adams Johns cousin as "Sir Richard" Geo Cabot (Parkers nephew) the famous "Major" & a nice one he was . . . having got a real dress from the theatre. . . . Ab was "Lady Somerford.". . .
>
> After the "Jacobite" the great G.B. & the greater L.M.A. did the "Morning Call" . . . Sir Edward having got up in a red velvet hunting suit & a suprising [*sic*] wig, to say nothing of top boots & an emerald pin as large as a warming pan. "Mrs Chillingtone" was troubled with a violent desire to grasp him by the wig. . . .
>
> . . . the evening wound up with a magnifique spread . . . finishing off at twelve P.M. by a general warble & flourish. The Sargents were so pleased they mean to have plays every month.[29]

And so, not altogether unfortunately, the season ended, not in the Boston Theatre, but in the Sargents' parlor. Had it ended with Widow Pottle at the Boston instead, Louisa Alcott might have told a different tale when she sat down to write a story for girls; indeed, she might have told no tale at all.

The delights of writing had, however, always rivaled the call of the stage for Louisa, and what was more natural than that she should combine her two interests and produce a "great" drama? Even before she had impersonated Widow Pottle at the Walpole Town Hall, Louisa had written a story about two actresses, for which she had received ten dollars from the Boston *Saturday Evening Gazette*. "The Rival Prima Donnas"[30] appeared on 11 November 1854, under the pseudonym of Flora

Fairfield, but there was no doubt in Concord that it was Louisa Alcott who had written the marvelous narrative about Beatrice and Theresa, two rivals on the stage and in love, one of whom sought vengeance by crushing her competitor to death with an iron ring placed upon her head. The story ended suitably with the remorse of the gentleman who had caused the tragedy and the sudden insanity of the perpetrator of the crime. Perhaps it was after Louisa had read *The First Night; or, A Peep Behind the Scenes,* a comic drama telling the same story with a less melodramatic ending, that she decided to turn "The Rival Prima Donnas" into a play.

With the help of her uncle, Dr. Charles Windship, who combined a Roxbury practice with an interest in the theater, the script was placed in the hands of Thomas Barry. After several months, Louisa altered the play for Mrs. Julia Barrow's 1857 season. After another six months had passed, in November 1856 Louisa visited Mr. Barry at the Boston to discuss the everlasting play, which was always coming out but apparently never came. The cultivated, fine-looking manager escorted the playwright all over the great theater on Washington Street, the largest and most elegant in the country. A dance floor, he asserted, could be fitted over the orchestra chairs and the house converted into a ballroom. Without waiting for the necessary alterations in carpentry, Louisa danced a jig on the huge stage, and received, besides a pass to the theater, the assurance that "The Rival Prima Donnas" would be brought out soon. Mr. Barry himself would take the part of Claude, and Mrs. John Wood, the pretty, sprightly soubrette who was turning the heads of all masculine Boston, would act as one of the Rivals, and probably Mrs. Barrow the other. That evening Louisa saw La Grange as Norma, and herself as an established playwright.

Perhaps it was because Mrs. Wood and Mrs. Barrow could not agree about which rival produced the better part, or because Thomas Barry was too busy arranging for a five-weeks' engagement of Edwin Forrest, to whose performance of Othello Louisa's pass admitted her,[31]—but whatever the reason, the largest, most elegant theater in the country was to survive without offering "The Rival Prima Donnas" to its patrons. Flora Fairfield's name still appeared boldly on the pages of the *Saturday Evening Gazette,* but Louisa Alcott's was locked in a drawer at the Orchard House, where the rival prima donnas were fated to remain for the rest of their natural, or unnatural, lives.

About the same time that the young playwright was manufacturing an iron ring for Theresa's unhappy end, she was also turning her versatile hand to a farce, in which she was certain that William Warren, one of her favorite comedians, would make a fine Nat Bachelor. Mr. Warren may have been too preoccupied with *Poor Pillicoddy* and *The Rough Diamond*, for even with Dr. Windship's mediation, he was too busy to take the part. Mrs. William H. Smith, wife of the actor-manager, was next approached; and the encouraging word came through that "Nat Bachelor's Pleasure Trip; or, The Trials of a Good-Natured Man" would be produced at her benefit.[32]

Nat Bachelor was, however, to endure several unpremeditated trials before his good nature was to be exhibited on the stage. In January 1856 Joseph M. Field, the prolific dramatist of the Mobile Theatre Company, took the farce to his native city. It was an ill-fated year, however, not only for Louisa, but for Mr. Field, for the author of "La déesse, an Elssleratic Romance," and other similar stage wonders, died in the course of it, and the theatergoers of Mobile were destined to silence on the part of Nat Bachelor. Mrs. Smith, acting at Laura Keene's Theatre in New York, still promised to bring out the farce there.

"Nat Bachelor's Pleasure Trip," accepted in 1855, was not produced until 4 May 1860,[33] at the Howard Athenaeum. Though the greater portion of the audience had come to see Mrs. W. H. Smith's benefit performance in *The Romance of a Poor Young Man*, Louisa Alcott came to see her own little after-sketch. She looked about her at the newly painted, frescoed, carpeted theatre on Howard Street, which had once been a Millerite Tabernacle; noticed Edward L. Davenport's whimsical sign, "Boys, don't smoke, and if you love your manager, turn down the gas"; and seated herself in a private parlor box in the rear of the parquet.[34] Here was a change indeed for the frequenter of the Museum pit. She glanced a little ruefully at the playbill, which announced a *"new local sketch"* by the popular authoress Louisa *Adcott,* but was satisfied that if the name was incorrectly spelled, at least it was a name and not a pseudonym.

At half past seven the curtain rose upon *The Romance of a Poor Young Man* and its "unparalleled cast," Mrs. Barrow, Mr. Davenport, and

Mrs. Smith. Through the playing of Thomas Comer's incidental music, and during the wait at the end of the performance, the playwright was consumed with an impatience that five years of anticipation had not entirely subdued. At last the farce was acted, Miss Josephine Orton, Mr. William J. LeMoyne, Mr. and Mrs. W. H. Smith exposing the trials of a good-natured man. Louisa was not completely satisfied with the performance and felt, after her experience with professional farces, that "Nat Bachelor's Pleasure Trip" was a small affair. But good Dr. Windship handed a bouquet to the playwright,[35] and if the rafters of the Howard Athenaeum did not ring with applause, at least the sketch had been acted and the authoress had tasted the pleasures of a seventy-five-cent box seat.

If by 1860 the winds of fortune were turning more toward Boston's Grub Street than to its Theatre Row, Louisa still felt that though she might never act for fame, she might very well act for charity. The annual festival of the Concord Anti-Slavery Society had already featured her as Lady Somerford in *The Jacobite*,[36] and, even before that, the Alcott girls had performed "some fine plays for charity."[37] During the sixties, opportunities never lacked for benefit performances to aid one cause or another.

At the home of the Sargents, the abolitionists often gathered for such entertainment, when, according to Abba, the Alcotts got up "some of the most successful plays we have ever had anywhere, having Wendell Phillips, Garrison & all that antislavery set one evening. . . . I had a splendid time . . . as Lady Somerford was my first & favorite character . . . I had nice lovers. . . ."[38]

The Parker Fraternity were also eager to welcome the Alcotts to their stage. The flags and pennants that waved at the Music Hall for the opening of the Sanitary Fair did not attract a more appreciative audience than Louisa's dramatization of six scenes from Dickens, which realized twenty-five hundred dollars for the same cause. To raise funds for the Concord Lyceum or the New England Women's Hospital, Mr. Clarke's Church Fair or the Authors' Carnival, Louisa dashed into Boston or Cambridge or Dorchester, playing Mrs. Pontifex or Lucretia Buzzard, if not for art, at least for human welfare.[39]

The performance that seemed most suitable for such purposes was not strictly a play, but a monologue inspired by readings from Dickens.

In an old black dress with a large poke bonnet on her head, clutching an umbrella and a basket, Louisa bowed often before her audience as Mrs. Jarley,[40] and claimed the honor of presenting the finest collection of wax "statooary" in the known world. "The collection of figures," she declared, "is elegant and instructive, classical and calm. . . . In the words of our great national poet, George Washington, 'Wax work is friend of man, it refines the fancy, enlarges the sphere of reason, cultivates the soul, therefore cherish it.' "

Cherish the waxworks they did, from Elizabeth's maid of honor, who died from pricking her fingers in consequence of working on the Sabbath, to Jasper Packlemerton of atrocious memory, who destroyed eleven wives by tickling the soles of their feet. Louisa's umbrella pointed, in many a good cause, to Martha Bangs, the insane maid who poisoned fourteen families with pickled walnuts, or to Lord Byron as he appeared in the throes of composing the ninth chapter of *Childe Harold.* Often a watchman's rattle wound up the "figgers" of Welsh dwarfs or Chinese giants, and lively airs were played as Louisa allowed the audience a brief pause so that they could get out their handkerchiefs and drop a silent tear for Little Nell. For one benefit or another, the actress poked her umbrella toward Mrs. Micawber and her twins, or toward Mrs. Pipchin, whose most successful pupil, Paul Dombey, had died "owin' to a constitutional weakness in his bones in spite of Radway's Ready Relief and Jacob's Oil Preparer." For the sake of numerous sinking funds, she announced to the world the discovery of Prof. Owlsdark, the great excavator, that Shakespeare had died in Boston and been buried on "Bacon" Hill.

The umbrella, the poke bonnet, and the black dress appeared in private and in public as the years passed, after "Mrs. Jarley" had gone to nurse the soldiers in Georgetown and returned with ideas for *Hospital Sketches,* after *Moods* had appeared, even after *Little Women* had filled the coffers of the Alcott sinking fund and its author considered herself "too old for such pranks."

For one of the last of the charitable theatricals in Concord, Louisa added yet another role to her repertory, that of the tall, spare, prim-looking female of middle age known as Miss Beswick to the readers of J. T. Trowbridge's story *Coupon Bonds.*[41] On Monday evening, 8 July 1867, Miss Beswick, with a shawl over her head, entered the Ducklow home to speak her mind to its denizens in "a pretty smart lectur'." For the benefit of Reuben, a returned soldier, played significantly by James Melvin, who had himself lost three brothers in the war, Miss Beswick cleared her decks for action and retrieved the lost coupon bonds. The Concord company now included Annie Keyes and Mrs. Jane G. Austin, the budding novelist, but George Bartlett was still on hand to play Pa Ducklow and act as manager, and Louisa was still ready to entertain so that enough twenty-five-cent tickets would be purchased to supply the demands of charity.

As the years drew on, the domestic dramas of the actress's life occupied more of her time than did those enacted in the Concord Town Hall. Yet the author did not forget her barnstorming days. In two very definite ways, she used her theatrical experiences in her writing. The melodramatic elements that appear in much of Louisa Alcott's early work may be traced to *Comic Tragedies*. "Pauline's Passion and Punishment" contains such details as forgery and brutality, themes that the writer had employed in the Hillside plays. Even the dialogue is reminiscent of "Norna" and "The Captive of Castile"—

Traitor! Shall I kill him?
There are fates more terrible than death.

The disguises and impersonations of "V.V.; or, Plots and Counterplots" are simply part of a histrionic technique learned in a Concord barn and put to use for the publisher of thrillers. Such devices as drugged coffee and mysterious iron rings remind one strongly of the elaborate machinery of *Comic Tragedies*. Similar details reappear in *Moods* (1865), where death, sleepwalking, and shipwreck suggest the violent themes of "Norna" and "The Greek Slave." In *The Mysterious Key* (1867), and *The Skeleton in the Closet* (1867), the blood-and-thunder method is employed again, with all its paraphernalia of unlocked caskets, steel bracelets, and silver keys. One need search no farther than the Hillside barn for Louisa Alcott's propensities toward melodrama. The thrillers that she launched across the pages of the penny dreadfuls had their source in the writer's early dramatic career.[42]

In a second, more fruitful manner, Louisa Alcott put to literary use her experiences in private theatricals. Whenever she wrote a story that contained any autobiographical elements, one theme was sure to concern the drama. As she remarks in *Jo's Boys*, "It is impossible for the humble historian of the March family to write a story without theatricals." The statement held true as early as 1856, when she sketched in "The Sisters' Trial" a rough outline of *Little Women*. In that tale, the actress Agnes is one of four sisters bent upon enjoying a career. Later, in *Work*, Christie was Louisa, initiated into the mysteries of the stage, led into the greenroom on the first night of "The Demon's Daughter, or the Castle of the Sun," convinced eventually that she was "no dramatic genius born to shine before the world." Christie, like Louisa, earned her laurels when Dickens's dramatized novels were played. The little episode of Lucy and the heroine was simply a humanized version of "The Rival Prima Donnas." The whole theatrical interlude was the creation of an author remembering her acting experiences.

When she sat down to write the story for girls that was to make her fortune, Louisa was quick to include in it an account of the Hillside troupe, and, taking Hagar from "The Unloved Wife," Hugo from "Norna; or, The Witch's Curse," Zara from "The Captive of Castile," and miraculous potions from "Bianca," evolved a composite melodrama entitled "The Witch's Curse, an Operatic Tragedy." Now, for the benefit of thousands of readers throughout the country, incantations were chanted over a steaming kettle by the Little Women. Louisa had taken another pseudonym, and Jo March stormed through the pages of a book that an older Jo March had once lived.

In the series of juvenile books that followed *Little Women*, a section is almost invariably devoted to private theatricals. When Jo March appeared as an aunt with a scrap-bag of stories, Louisa glorified Dolphus as one of Her Boys, and played again the part of Tetterby. Six years later, when she wrote an account of Her Girls, she described herself as "D"—"one of a large family all taught at home, and all of a dramatic turn." "D" appeared on the boards, "tried the life, found it wanting, left it and put her experiences into a clever little book." In *Eight Cousins*, charades are performed on an outdoor stage, along with scenes from "Babes in the Wood" and an "Incident in the Life of Napoleon." The sequel, *Rose in Bloom*, contains the revealing statement, "I'd rather be a second-rate doctor than a second-rate actor." Louisa Alcott had learned from her experience. Open any of the Alcott books that the firm of

Roberts Brothers was offering to the juvenile world in the 1870s and 1880s, and there will appear the "Tragedy in Three Tableaux," the Christmas plays at Plumfield, or the Owlsdark Marbles. The animated discussion about costumes, the elaborate preparations, the performance itself with one or two amusing mishaps, are all autobiographical, dating from the days of the Walpole and Concord Amateur Companies. It *was* impossible for the historian of the March family to write a story without theatricals, for when she produced her best work she took her material from her own life, and that life had included a more than common interest in the drama. Call the prima donna Jo March, or Christie, or "D"—she was Louisa Alcott reliving the days when she had worn a satin pelisse to portray Mrs. Pontifex or an old black dress to impersonate Mrs. Jarley.[43]

And in many other less tangible ways, Louisa Alcott remembered, putting into literary practice the lessons she had learned from acting in contemporary farces. Her concentration upon homely dialogue and her skill in heightening a humorous situation may be traced to no other source than the stock companies of the fifties.

Even as late as 1880, Louisa Alcott still retained her interest in the drama. That most delightful of brothers-in-law, John Pratt, had long since died, and Anna, forgetting her ambitions to shine as a prima donna, had settled down into an old woman, sober and sad, with gray hair. Mrs. Alcott would never again cry "Ankore" and clap her dress-gloves to rags. Abba's prompting days were over, for she lay buried in the Montrouge Cemetery. But in her room at the Bellevue, as spring returned to Boston, Louisa sat dramatizing *Michael Strogoff*, not for the delight of the family, or the cause of charity, or even for a task-master publisher, but simply to amuse herself, by reliving the dramatizations of earlier days. The Hotel Bellevue was a far cry from Hillside, and in 1880 it was difficult sometimes to remember the Comic Tragedies of 1848. But for Louisa Alcott, a curtain call was never to be refused, nor the demands of a stage manager denied, even when, as now, the stage manager was Time, and the final curtain would not be long in falling.[44]

NOTES

1. MS in Orchard House, Concord.
2. In "The Prince and the Peasant, or Love's Trials," MS in Orchard House.

3. In "Norna; or, The Witch's Curse," "The Captive of Castile; or, The Moorish Maiden's Vow," and "The Greek Slave," in *Comic Tragedies* (Boston, 1893).

4. Mary Hosmer Brown, *Memories of Concord* (Boston, 1926), 85.

5. Annie M. L. Clark, *The Alcotts in Harvard* (Lancaster, Mass., 1902), 32.

6. Ednah D. Cheney, ed., *Louisa May Alcott: Her Life, Letters, and Journals* (Boston, 1889), 63. Hereinafter "Cheney."

7. Thomas Bellows Peck, *The Bellows Genealogy* (Keene, N.H., 1898), 130. For Benjamin Willis, who married Elizabeth Sewall May, see Richard Sullivan Edes, *A Genealogy of the Descendants of John May* (Boston, 1878), 22; and Pauline Willis, *Willis Records* (London, n.d.), 73 ff.

8. Odell Shepard, ed., *The Journals of Bronson Alcott* (Boston, 1938), 296.

9. For Walpole, see George Aldrich, *Walpole as It Was and as It Is* (Claremont, N.H., 1880), 111; P. H. Gobie, *Bellows Falls and Vicinity Illustrated* (Bellows Falls, N.H., 1908); and John Hayward, *A Gazetteer of New Hampshire* (Boston, 1849), 139.

10. For Mrs. Louisa Bellows Hayward (1792–1878), and her children, mentioned below, see Peck, *Bellows Genealogy*, 190–91, 387–94.

11. For Elmwood and the Kittredge family, see Aldrich, 305; Franklin W. Hooper and Henry E. Howland, *Old Home Day and One Hundred and Fiftieth Anniversary* (Keene, N.H., 1903), 13; and Peck, *Bellows Genealogy*, 478–79.

12. Most of these persons are mentioned in Aldrich, *Walpole as It Was*, 122, 180; Emily R. Barnes, *Narratives, Traditions and Personal Reminiscences Connected with the Early History of the Bellows Family* (Boston, 1888), 129; and Peck, *Bellows Genealogy*, 188, 386, 400, 552.

13. See the playbill of 11 September 1855, at Orchard House, for Abba Alcott's assignment, as well as for the roles of all members of the cast.

14. The repertory of plays presented at Walpole may be established with some degree of completeness by an examination of the playbills at the Orchard House. Unless otherwise recorded, all dates of plays are those of first performance. The known list includes Charles Dance's farce *Naval Engagements*, 1848; Félix Duvert and A. T. de Lauzanne de Vaux-Roussel, *Used Up*, a two-act comedy, translated by Charles Mathews from the French of "L'homme blasé"; A. Harris, *The Little Treasure*, a two-act comedy, 1855 (Louisa played Mrs. Meddleton on 12 September 1856); John M. Morton's farces *The Two Bonnycastles*, 1851, and *The Two Buzzards*, 1853 (Louisa played Lucretia Buzzard in 1856); Thomas Morton's farce *Sketches in India* (Louisa played Lady Scraggs on 12 September 1856); Planché's *The Jacobite*, 1847; Sheridan's *The Rivals* (Louisa played Mrs. Malaprop in 1855); and Tom Taylor, *Still Waters Run Deep*, a three-act comedy, 1855.

15. Cheney, 91.

16. For Sanborn and his school, see Allen French, *Old Concord* (Boston, 1915), 151; Henry James, *Notes of a Son and Brother* (New York, 1914), 215 ff.; and F. B. Sanborn, *Recollections of Seventy Years* (Boston, 1909).

17. In her fragmentary diary for 1852 and 1854 at Orchard House, which she re-used for the purpose.

18. See George B. Bartlett, *Parlor Amusements* (New York, 1876), 8–10; *Letters of Ralph Waldo Emerson*, ed. Ralph L. Rusk (New York, 1939), VI, 30 n. 126; and *The Pratt Family* (Boston, 1889), 199.

19. See Louisa Alcott's *My Boys* (Boston, 1872), 15–16; a collection of letters from the Alcotts to Whitman, at Houghton Library; and Alfred Whitman, "Miss Alcott's Letters to Her 'Laurie,'" *Ladies' Home Journal* 18 (October 1901).

In November 1858 Whitman left for his home in Kansas.

20. For details, see the playbill of 1 December 1857, in the back of Abba Alcott's fragmentary diary for 1852 and 1854, Orchard House; and *Ladies' Home Journal* 18 (October 1901): 5.

21. The Concord repertory may be established by reference to the playbills at Houghton Library and Orchard House. The writer is grateful to Sarah R. Bartlett for the playbill of 28 January 1858. The Concord repertory includes John Till Allingham, *Fortune's Frolic; or, The Ploughman Turned Lord*, a two-act farce, 1837 (Louisa played Margery 10 February 1858); Bayle Bernard, *The Dumb Belle*, one-act farce, 1835; John Baldwin Buckstone, *The Rough Diamond*, comic drama in one act, 1841; Charles Dance, *Kill or Cure*, one-act farce (Louisa played Mrs. Brown 12 November 1857); Charles Dance, *A Morning Call*, comedietta in one act, 1851 (Louisa played Mrs. Chillingtone 12 November 1857); Charles Dickens, *Scenes from Dickens;* John M. Morton, *Poor Pillicoddy*, one-act farce, 1848 (Louisa played Mrs. O'Scuttle 12 November 1857); Thomas Morton, *A Pretty Piece of Business*, one-act comedy, 1853; John Oxenford, *Dr. Dilworth*, one-act farce; Howard Paul, *A Lucky Hit*, one-act comedy, 1854; James Robinson Planché, *The Loan of a Lover*, a vaudeville, 1834; Shakespeare, *A Midsummer Night's Dream* (the comic underplot); and E. G. P. Wilkins, *My Wife's Mirror*, one-act comedy, 1856 (Louisa played Mrs. Racket 10 February 1858).

Plays that had been in the Walpole repertory and that were also performed in Concord were *The Jacobite* (Louisa played Lady Somerford 28 and 29 January 1858 and Major Murray 25 December 1858); *Naval Engagements* (Louisa played Mrs. Pontifex 1 December 1857); and *The Two Buzzards* (Louisa played Lucretia Buzzard 1 December 1857).

22. Playbill of 19 December 1854, at Orchard House.

23. The playbill of 25 December 1857 is in the back of Abba Alcott's diary for 1852 and 1854 at Orchard House.

24. Anna Alcott Pratt to Alfred Whitman, Chelsea, 8 December [1867], Houghton Library.

25. Cheney, 96.

26. Ibid., 99.

27. Ibid., 108.

28. Louisa Alcott to Alfred Whitman, Concord, 26 December 1858, Houghton Library.

29. Louisa Alcott to Alfred Whitman, Concord, 13–15 February 1859, Houghton Library.

30. MS of play in Orchard House.

31. Cheney, 86–87, 89–90.

32. Ibid., 81.

33. Playbill, Houghton Library.

34. See Henry Austin Clapp, *Reminiscences of a Dramatic Critic* (Boston and New York, 1902), 51; Edwin F. Edgett, *Edward Loomis Davenport* (New York, 1901); and Arthur Hornblow, *A History of the Theatre in America*, vol. 2 (Philadelphia, 1919), 134, 149, 153.

35. Cheney, 121.

36. Playbill of 28 January 1858, Houghton Library. A copy is also owned by Sarah Bartlett.

37. Cheney, 96.

38. May Alcott to Alfred Whitman, Concord, 5 February 1860, Houghton Library.

39. For the benefit performances, see Louisa Alcott to Alfred Whitman, Boston, 17 April 1859, and Concord, 2 January 1864, Houghton Library; and Cheney, 155, 164–165, 198, 317.

40. All references to "Mrs. Jarley's Waxworks" are either from the MS copy made by Louisa Alcott for Alfred Whitman, Houghton Library, or from Louisa Alcott's arrangement, in MS at Orchard House. George Bartlett also arranged *Mrs. Jarley's Waxworks* (New York, n.d.).

41. The writer is grateful to Sarah R. Bartlett for the playbill of 8 July 1867. Another copy is at Orchard House. J. T. Trowbridge's *Coupon Bonds* (Boston, 1866) was dramatized for the occasion.

42. "Pauline's Passion and Punishment," *Frank Leslie's Illustrated Newspaper* 15, nos. 379 and 380 (3 and 10 January 1863), appeared anonymously, but is identified in a letter from E. G. Squier to Louisa M. Alcott, c. 18 December 1862, Orchard House; "V.V.; or, Plots and Counterplots," *The Flag of Our Union*, 20, nos. 5, 6, 7, and 8 (4, 11, 18, and 25 February 1865), appeared under the pseudonym of A. M. Barnard, and is identified by Leona Rostenberg, "Some Anonymous and Pseudonymous Thrillers of Louisa M. Alcott," reprinted in this collection; *Moods* (Boston, 1865); *The Mysterious Key, and What It Opened* (Boston, 1867); *The Skeleton in the Closet* (Boston, 1867).

43. See "The Sisters' Trial," *Saturday Evening Gazette*, no. 4 (26 January 1856); *Work: A Story of Experience* (Boston, 1873), 34–55; *Little Women* (Boston, 1920), 12–14, 24–28; *My Boys* (Boston, 1872), 15–16; *My Girls* (Boston, 1878), 17–19; *Eight Cousins* (Boston, 1920), 155 ff.; *Rose in Bloom* (Boston, 1920), 44; *Under the Lilacs* (Boston, 1920), 252 ff.; *Jo's Boys* (Boston, 1920), 237 ff.; and *Jack and Jill* (Boston, 1920), 118 ff.

44. For details, see Anna Pratt to Alfred Whitman, Concord, 18 June 1871, Houghton Library; and Cheney, 284, 330, 335.

Alcott's First Book

U nder the heading "Twenty-two Years Old" Louisa Alcott on 1 January 1855 opened her diary for the new year with a few paragraphs about her first book:

> The principal event of the winter is the appearance of my book "Flower Fables." An edition of sixteen hundred. It has sold very well, and people seem to like it. I feel quite proud that the little tales that I wrote for Ellen E. when I was sixteen should now bring money and fame.
>
> I will put in some of the notices as "varieties." Mothers are always foolish over their first-born.
>
> Miss Wealthy Stevens paid for the book, and I received $32.[1]

Until now those brief remarks have constituted substantially all that is known about the publication of Alcott's first book: the writing of the tales for Emerson's daughter Ellen when the author was sixteen, the appearance of the book, its underwriting, and the author's receipts. Now the story behind that terse recital can be told, and the cast of characters involved in the publication can be fleshed out.

About six months prior to her triumphant statement regarding the "principal event of the winter," Alcott had written to her older sister Anna: "I've shed my quart [of tears] . . . over the book not coming out, for that was a sad blow, and I waited so long it was dreadful when my castle in the air came tumbling about my ears. Pride made me laugh in public, but I wailed in private, and no one knew it."[2] The book for whose publication she had "waited so long" was obviously the book that would be entitled *Flower Fables*. Yet within six months—between the letter to Anna and the New Year's journal entry—that very book, according to the author, was bringing "money and fame." How had this personal fairy tale been effected?

The imprint of *Flower Fables* reads "Boston: George W. Briggs & Co., 1855." The firm of George W. Briggs appears to have escaped the recorded annals of midcentury publishers. Compared with the giants of the time in Boston—Little, Brown; Munroe & Company; Crosby, Nichols; Phillips, Sampson; Ticknor & Fields—Mr. Briggs was a very minor publisher indeed.

Born in Warwick, Rhode Island, in July 1816, the son of John and Sarah Briggs, George Washington Briggs moved to Boston and in 1842 began business as bookseller and binder at 405 Washington Street.[3] Briggs never strayed from that street of booksellers and publishers. In 1850 he was located at number 376, which was renumbered 456 in 1853. By 1850 he had acquired an associate, Avery D. Putnam, and the establishment was known as the Liberty Tree Bookstore. The block too was named in honor of the Liberty Tree that had once stood at the corner of Washington and Essex Streets.[4] By 1855 Briggs had become a "general book agent, stationer and dealer in . . . cosmetic products," and in November of the following year, at the age of forty, he died.[5]

Briggs's publishing credits, though far from extensive, suggest his interests. He apparently had a predilection for inspirational and religious works, as well as for literature in general and for children's literature in particular. Besides stocking "Colored Picture Cards, with Games for Children of all ages," he published *The Good Boys' and Girls' Picture Gallery* (1848), a reissue of Jane Austen's *Pride and Prejudice* (1849), a pseudonymous compilation entitled *Flowers That Never Fade* (1853), and in December 1854—the same month he issued *Flower Fables*—the poems of another young writer, the eighteen-year-old William Winter, future drama critic and historian.

Although after her husband's death the widow Anna or Anne Briggs, who held the copyright to *Flowers That Never Fade*, dealt in books briefly, the stand at 456 Washington Street was taken over by Avery D. Putnam and Avery's younger brother Austin G. Putnam. They operated as Putnam & Brother until Avery's departure, when Austin continued on his own for a time. Like Briggs, who hailed from Rhode Island, Avery Putnam was connected to Rhode Island through his wife, Ellen.

The Rhode Island connection suggests one reason that Briggs published *Flower Fables.*

Why did George W. Briggs & Co. publish Louisa Alcott's first book? Both Ralph Waldo Emerson and Bronson Alcott appear to have had a hand in his selection. Several of Briggs's imprints had been designed for children, and this of course made him suitable for seeing through the press the fairy tales that Louisa Alcott had concocted for other children, especially for nine-year-old Ellen Emerson. Ellen had shown the stories to her mother, Lidian Emerson, who subsequently had advised their publication.

By 1842, when George Briggs set out his shingle on Boston's Washington Street, Emerson was quite well acquainted with a more or less distinguished relative of the publisher, George Ware Briggs. George Ware Briggs also hailed from Rhode Island. He had taught in Providence, graduated from Harvard Divinity School, and served as associate pastor of the First Church in Plymouth, Massachusetts. Indeed, the Emersons had entertained George Ware Briggs in their home in Concord, and Emerson had heard the pastor deliver "an excellent abolition speech" in 1843.[6] There is little doubt that he had also heard that Briggs's namesake and relative was setting up as a bookseller on Boston's Washington Street.

By the end of 1854, Briggs had been in the business of books for twelve years, and although he had no great quantity of publications on his list, he did have—through his pastor relative, at least—Emersonian connections.[7] He was apparently also known to Alcott's father, for in November 1854 Bronson Alcott recorded in his journal that he had consulted with Briggs about the publication of *Flower Fables:* "Today see Briggs, the publisher, concerning Louisa's book of 'Flower Fables' which he is printing as a child's Christmas gift."[8] On 19 December 1854 it appeared before the public.[9]

The author had, as she recalled, written "the little tales . . . for Ellen E." when she was sixteen. In 1848 Louisa Alcott had opened a school in the Hillside barn in Concord, where the family lived—a school attended by her younger sisters and her younger neighbors, including

Ellen Emerson. Since Alcott was already becoming a teller of tales, the narration of stories was one of her principal pedagogical techniques.

Influenced in part by neighbor Thoreau, who had introduced young Alcott to the delights of the Concord woods, in part by her readings in such books as *The Story without an End,* and in part by her own imagination, she had woven her fairy tales for the delight of the children. The love of the tender Violet conquered the Frost King; Dr. Dewdrop, the Water Cure physician, ministered to the village elves; Thistledown was redeemed through his love of Lily-Bell. Since it was Ellen Emerson who seemed to take the most delight in Alcott's flower fables, the sixteen-year-old narrator presented the nine-year-old Ellen with the stories as she had written them down—"The Frost King" in a green notebook, "The Fairy Dell" between gray marbled covers tied with pink ribbons.[10]

Six years later, Alcott would make another, more formal presentation of *Flower Fables* to Ellen Emerson after George W. Briggs & Co. had seen the little volume through the press. By the end of 1848 the Alcotts had moved from Concord to Boston, where in 1852 they settled at 20 Pinckney Street and tried to extract a living from whatever availed in the way of sewing or teaching, domestic service or nursing. It was for a close neighbor who lived at 10 Pinckney Street that Louisa Alcott did a considerable amount of sewing. Miss Wealthy Stevens was not only a generous employer but a sympathetic listener. A relative, probably the sister, of William B. Stevens, who served for years as teller of Boston's Globe Bank and later as its president, Miss Stevens was in a position to pay for the publication of *Flower Fables.* Moved by the story of its recent rejection, convinced perhaps that the tales reflected considerable talent and imagination, she doubtless offered to subsidize the volume.

The part taken by the Stevens family in the production of Alcott's first book is indicated by the copyright notice that appears on the title verso: "Entered according to Act of Congress, in the year 1854, by W. B. Stevens, in the Clerk's Office of the District Court of the District of Massachusetts." The part taken by the Stevenses in Louisa Alcott's professional life has, until now, been less apparent.

The interests of William B. Stevens were not confined to the banking business. Early in life he was drama critic and financial editor of the *Boston Post* and author of a tragedy for the Tremont Theatre. Most interesting, for Louisa Alcott, is the fact that William B. Stevens had been named after his maternal uncle William Burdick, who in 1814 had founded the *Saturday Evening Gazette*. For five years, between November 1854 (shortly before *Flower Fables* was copyrighted) and 1859, the *Saturday Evening Gazette* would be a major medium for Alcott. Although proprietorship of the paper had been transferred to William Warland Clapp, there is little doubt that William Burdick Stevens and his sister had given the younger author entrée to the periodical that launched her earliest efforts.[11]

Just in time for Christmas 1854, *Flower Fables*, bound in blue, red, or brown cloth, its covers bearing a gilt oval cartouche, made its appearance. Since the book owed much to the Emersons, a quotation from Emerson's *Wood-Notes* adorned the title page. Printed by the well-known firm of stereotypers and printers Metcalf and Company of Cambridge, the little book was enriched with six wood engravings by an unknown illustrator. The physical entity of the volume acknowledges its origins. The dedication reads: "To / Ellen Emerson, / For Whom They Were Fancied, / These Flower Fables / Are Inscribed, / By Her Friend, / The Author. / Boston, Dec. 9, 1854."

Along with a copy of the book, Alcott sent a letter to the fifteen-year-old Ellen Emerson:

Hoping that age has not lessened your love for the *Fairy folk* I have ventured to place your name in my little book, for your interest in their sayings & doings, first called forth these "Flower Fables," most of which were fancied long ago in Concord woods & fields. The pictures are not what I hoped they would be & it is very evident that the designer is not as well acquainted with fairy forms & faces as you & I are, so we must each *imagine* to suit ourselves & I hope if the fairies tell me any more stories, they will let an Elfin artist *illustrate* them. So dear Ellen will you accept the accompanying book, with many wishes for a merry "Christmas, & a happy New Year," from your friend, Louisa M. Alcott.—[12]

Ellen Emerson's overwhelmed response is recorded in a letter she addressed to a friend on 21 December 1854:

A very dignified young woman addresses you, a girl who this morning received a book *dedicated to her*. Do you understand? I am anxious that you should feel a sufficient respect for me now that I have got a book dedicated to me. It is Louisa

Alcott's "Flower Fables." When the Alcotts lived here Louisa used to read her stories to me and I used to go wild about them, and made her write them for me. She says that 'twas I who made her publish them for I showed the written ones to Mother who liked them so much she advised Louisa to print a book. Then they were showed to some more and everyone was pleased with them. So this morning I saw a bundle on the entry table directed to me. I opened it and found the "Flower Fables" all bound and printed very nicely with pictures, but on turning it over I saw my name in large letters and discovered that 'twas dedicated to me! Of course, I fell down in a swoon since I could not express my emotion, there being nobody in the house, and read it and looked at it from every point of view.[13]

At about the same time that Alcott bestowed a copy of *Flower Fables* upon her young admirer, she presented one to her mother, along with a very poignant letter:

Into your Christmas stocking I have put my "first-born," knowing that you will accept it with all its faults (for grandmothers are always kind), and look upon it merely as an earnest of what I may yet do, for, with so much to cheer me on, I hope to pass in time from fairies and fables to men and realities.

Whatever beauty or poetry is to be found in my little book is owing to your interest in and encouragement of all my efforts from the first to the last, and if ever I do anything to be proud of, my greatest happiness will be that I can thank you for that, as I may do for all the good there is in me, and I shall be content to write if it gives you pleasure. . . .[14]

Flower Fables gave pleasure generally. On 19 December 1854 Briggs advertised it in the *Boston Evening Transcript* in the following euphoric terms:

Flower Fables. This day published by Geo. W. Briggs & Co. the *most beautiful* Fairy book that has appeared for a long time, written *when in her sixteenth year,* by Louisa May Alcott, a young lady of Boston. It will be the most popular juvenile issued this season.[15]

The following day the *Transcript's* page 1 carried a brief notice:

Messrs. George W. Briggs & Co. have published an illustrated work entitled *Flower Fables,* by Louisa May Alcott. It contains several agreeable sketches, in prose and verse, adapted to the capacity of intelligent young persons.

On 23 December the *Saturday Evening Gazette,* which had recently run Alcott's "The Rival Prima Donnas" under the pseudonym "Flora Fairfield," published an appropriately flowery review of her book (mistitled *Flower Tables*):

Very sweet are these little legends of faery land, which those of our young friends, who are so fond of tales of enchantment, will, we are sure, peruse with avidity. The interest which children take in fairy tales is well known, and the infant mind is more susceptible to truths under such a guise, than in the more direct tales of a moral character.[16]

Although the author was understandably pleased with the reception of *Flower Fables,* she was also troubled. In her 1854 "Notes and Memoranda," in which she listed her receipts from the book as thirty-five dollars rather than the thirty-two dollars in her 1855 journal, she also wrote: "I only got a very small sum for them owing to Mr Briggs' dishonesty."[17]

This opinion seems to stem rather from the self-delusion of a very young author than from any known facts. *Flower Fables* was priced, according to *Norton's Literary Gazette* of 1 January 1855, at sixty-two cents, and later, in the *Bibliotheca Americana,* at seventy-five cents. At sixty-two cents each, without discounts, 550 sold copies would have grossed $341, and if the author received ten percent of the sales price, her royalty would have amounted to $34.10. If sixteen hundred copies were printed, the sale of one third of the edition within a very short time of publication was certainly remarkable, since the author was completely unknown. Her compensation in the year 1855 was scarcely trifling, and seems to throw no suspicion upon George W. Briggs's honesty.

In any event, by 1856, George W. Briggs had departed not only Boston's Washington Street but the planet Earth. After a long illness, he died suddenly in his office in November.[18] His place was taken by Putnam & Brother, and the *Bibliotheca Americana* of 1855–1858, listing the price of *Flower Fables* as seventy-five cents, cites its publisher as A. G. Putnam. Neither *Flower Fables* nor the firm that had published it had reached an end. Indeed, their subsequent histories are remarkable, for each had a sequel, and the Putnam story includes the kind of sensational touch that intrigued the author of *Flower Fables* when she turned to writing her blood-and-thunders.

THE PUTNAM TRAGEDY

Between 1857 and 1859, Austin G. Putnam—without the "& Brother"—continued business at the Washington Street stand. By 1860 Degen & Co., Books and Stationery, took over the establishment—an interesting development since in 1865, at the end of the Civil War, Henry D. Degen and the well-known Dana Estes joined forces at 23 Cornhill, carrying on the Briggs tradition by specializing in children's books. Meanwhile Oliver L. Briggs, probably a relative of the original Briggs, occupied the old stand at 456 Washington Street as bookseller and stationer, abandoning the business some years later to deal in billiard tables and "walnut goods."[19]

Before that time, in 1859, Austin Putnam's brother Avery D. Putnam turned up in New York City, where he became a provisions merchant on Pearl Street.[20] On 26 April 1871, some months before the famous publishing firm of Estes and Lauriat was formed in Boston, and when the celebrated Louisa May Alcott was abroad on her grand tour, the former Briggs associate Avery D. Putnam took a ride on a New York horsecar that ended with his murder and introduced a gaudy bit of melodrama to the later history of *Flower Fables*' publisher.

By 1871, Austin Putnam's brother Avery was forty-four years old and had a family consisting of a wife, Ellen Louisa, and an eleven-year-old son. On Wednesday evening, 26 April of that year, he took a walk, dropped in to see a friend, Madame Duval, and agreed to accompany Madame and her daughter Jennie to their destination. Aboard the Broadway streetcar, the ladies were insulted by an off-duty car conductor, William Foster, who had been on a "protracted debauch."

Miss Duval, happening to look through the front window, Foster (standing on the front platform) pressed his face closely against the glass and made an insulting grimace. The ladies took no notice of him. He then opened the door. Mr. Putnam remonstrated with him, and Foster replied: "I'm going as far as you, and before you get out I'll give you hell."

Foster's oral abuse was followed by physical violence. He seized the car-hook from the conductor and fractured the victim's skull with it. Putnam died a few days later.

The "car-hook murder" struck the New York papers, and the tragedy evoked numerous editorials and letters from outraged citizens. Foster was promptly tried, convicted, and executed. As for Avery Putnam, his remains were removed aboard the steamer *Newport* to Providence, and buried in Mrs. Putnam's family vault at Swan Point Cemetery.[21]

Several accounts of the murder were subsequently published, including an illustrated pamphlet entitled *The "Car-Hook" Tragedy: The Life, Trial, Conviction and Execution of William Foster for the Murder of Avery D. Putnam*. There is no proof that these ever came to the attention of the author of *Flower Fables, Little Women*, and the more recently published *Little Men*. As "A.M. Barnard," author of the thrillers "Behind a Mask" and "A Marble Woman," Alcott, while deploring the tragedy, would assuredly have appreciated the reports of this brutal and unprovoked crime. She might even have incorporated details of the terrible deed into one of her anonymous or pseudonymous sensation stories, had she still been writing them.

Between 1871, when the Putnam murder occurred, and the last years of her life, Alcott was for the most part otherwise engaged, producing for her demanding public the domestic novels for young people that came to be almost universally known as the Little Women Series. Then a family and personal tragedy struck, eventually turning her mind back to the *Flower Fables* she had once imagined for Ellen Emerson.

A SEQUEL

In December 1879 Alcott's younger sister, the artist May Alcott Nieriker, died in Paris following the birth of her daughter. The child, named Louisa May, was sent to her aunt in 1880. That aunt was not only mother to little Lulu but storyteller too. As she had woven tales for neighbor Ellen Emerson when she was sixteen, Alcott now wove tales for Lulu, and as she had written the earlier stories in colored notebooks, she recorded the later stories in tiny volumes tied up in birch-bark covers. Eventually three volumes of what would be entitled *Lulu's Library* were published. For volume 2, *The Frost King*, the author chose to reuse and revise the stories in *Flower Fables*.

And so *Flower Fables* had its sequel. There was no problem now for the world-famous author to find a publisher. Thomas Niles of Roberts Brothers had supported and encouraged her creativity since he had published *Little Women* in 1868. On 13 July 1885, Alcott wrote to him:

I want to know if it is too late to do it and if it is worth doing; namely, to collect some of the little tales I tell Lulu and put them with (others) . . . and call it "Lulu's Library"? I have several tiny books written down for L.; and . . . it occurred to me that I might venture to copy these if it would do for a Christmas book for the younger set.[22]

As a "Christmas book for the younger set" had launched her career, another would herald its end. Volume 2 of *Lulu's Library* was published in October 1887 by Roberts Brothers. It contained six of the stories that had originally appeared in *Flower Fables,* now reworked with simpler, less fanciful, and more direct language, to suit the demands of a later generation.

Like *Flower Fables, The Frost King* was appropriately dedicated to Ellen Emerson. Repeating her action of more than thirty years before, the author sent a copy to the dedicatee with a letter:

I have ventured to dedicate this little book to you in memory of the happy old times when the stories were told to you & May & Lizzie & some other play mates.

We believed in fairies then, & I think we still do though our good & helpful spirits bear less fanciful names & shapes now.

The earlier tales you will remember in spite of some pruning of too plentiful adjectives; the later ones were told to Lulu who inherits her mother's love for pen & ink sketches of all kinds.

For the sake of mother & daughter I thought the little book might have some interest for one who never grows old or forgets those who love her. Among them is & always will be her friend *L. M. Alcott.*[23]

There was no mother now to whom Alcott could offer her latest born, and so in October 1887 she dispatched a copy to her aunt Louisa Bond with a letter:

I always gave Mother the first author's copy of a new book. As her representative on earth, may I send you, with my love, the little book to come out in November?

The tales were told at sixteen to May and her playmates; then are related to

May's daughter at five; and for the sake of these two you may care to have them for the little people.[24]

Alcott had come full circle. She could not have adapted the stories of *Flower Fables* and written her letters to Ellen Emerson and Aunt Louisa Bond without recalling the publication of the earlier tales and the parts played by the Stevenses, George W. Briggs, and the Putnam brothers.

Less than six months after publication of the second volume of *Lulu's Library*, Louisa May Alcott died. *Flower Fables*, now in the public domain, was not overlooked while the demand for books by America's best-loved author of juvenile stories persisted. An undated edition appeared, probably in the late 1880s, under the imprint of F. M. Lupton of New York. In 1898 Henry Altemus of Philadelphia issued a profusely illustrated reprint with a decorated cover in his Young People's Library—and that edition was reprinted as late as 1977. Mershon Company included *Flower Fables* in its Holly Library series in 1899. In 1900 W. B. Conkey of Chicago reprinted the book with a frontispiece portrait of the author. Six years later another reprint was published by Caldwell of Boston, and in 1909 the New York firm of McLoughlin Brothers issued an edition with decorations by Frances Bassett Comstock. McLoughlin specialized in games and books for children, recalling the specialty of Degen and Estes, who had replaced the Putnams on Washington Street. *Flower Fables* was obviously still a salable commodity.[25]

The innocent little book did not escape the revisionist attentions of Alcott's twentieth-century biographer Martha Saxton, who in her *Louisa May: A Modern Biography of Louisa May Alcott* analyzed *Flower Fables* in post-Freudian terms:

Louisa spelled out her nightmare, the enemies she battled, her fears of being isolated behind a wall of sins of her own making, and the terrifying nature of some of her impulses, which she had to shut away. In each fable the sinner repents and gains great love, and often a coveted journey home. She is received with great joy and warmth. The self-abasement produces a resolution and peace. Hard, patient, uncomplaining work always wins love, even from the Frost King. Each tale is a pathetically simple fulfillment of a wistful desire for love. This love always depends on goodness or repentance, charity, selflessness, and a lack of vanity. The tales are inept, with no well-developed drama or incident, but each one provides moral satisfaction. The relentlessly pointed endings were part of Louisa's practice drill to earn admission to her father's ideally just world.[26]

The "little legends of faery land" recounted by the sixteen-year-old Louisa Alcott to her young pupils and published as a Christmas book at the end of 1854 had come a very long way—from Thoreau, in effect, to Freud. Its price had also undergone a metamorphosis. Tagged at sixty-two cents when it appeared, *Flower Fables* fetched a hammer price of $2,250 at the January 1990 Bradley Martin sale. In the course of its long history it had involved many people and encapsulated many episodes: the generosity of its subsidizer, the work of its original publisher, the reactions of friends and public, even a murder on a New York horsecar.

Like so many of her stories and so much in her life, *Flower Fables* trailed enigmas and mysteries in its wake. The publishing history of Louisa Alcott's first book is a story that the author herself might have told, though she chose not to do so.

NOTES

The author's indebtedness to Victor A. Berch, Special Collections Librarian Emeritus of Brandeis University and incomparable literary detective, cannot be overstated. He followed clues with Sherlockian zeal and provided much of the information that enriches this history. I am grateful also to Dr. Laura V. Monti, of the Boston Public Library, and to my colleague Patterson Smith for information and materials they provided me.

1. *The Journals of Louisa May Alcott*, ed. Joel Myerson, Daniel Shealy, and Madeleine B. Stern (Boston: Little, Brown, 1989), 73.

2. *The Selected Letters of Louisa May Alcott*, ed. Joel Myerson, Daniel Shealy, and Madeleine B. Stern (Boston: Little, Brown, 1987), 9.

3. *Boston Evening Transcript* (10 November 1856).

4. Justin Winsor, *The Memorial History of Boston*, vol. 3 (Boston: Osgood, 1882), 159 n. 2. Victor A. Berch recently examined the corner and writes: "That very building still stands. It is on the edge of Boston's Chinatown district and the 'combat zone' (red-light district). In fact, there now stands one of those lurid establishments that specializes in 'girlie' shows, most likely at the very spot Briggs had his shop. The building, ancient as it is, still carries on its upper floors a relief of the Liberty Tree with the legend that this was where the original Liberty Tree stood." (Victor Berch to Madeleine B. Stern, 9 March 1990.)

5. I am grateful to the resources of the American Antiquarian Society and the

New-York Historical Society, as well as to Victor Berch, for Boston Directory information. See also Briggs advertisement in *Christian Freeman and Family Visitor* (6 July 1855).

6. *The Letters of Ralph Waldo Emerson,* vol. 2, ed. Ralph L. Rusk (New York: Columbia University Press, 1939), 299, 431; *Historical Catalogue of Brown University 1764–1904,* 142.

7. A remote but evident Emersonian connection is also apparent from a copy, seen by Victor Berch, of William Winter's *Poems* inscribed by William Ralph Emerson, Ralph Waldo's second cousin.

8. Extract from Bronson Alcott's diary for 17 November 1854, transcript for Franklin B. Sanborn (Houghton Library, Harvard University, bMS Am 1342); Madeleine B. Stern, *Louisa May Alcott* (Norman: University of Oklahoma Press, 1985), 72, 373.

9. *Bibliography of American Literature,* 142, and copyright give date of deposit as 18 December 1854. The original copyright refers to W. B. Stevens as "she," suggesting that Miss Stevens was the actual proprietor. Roorbach does not cite the work until the 1855–1858 *Supplement,* in which the publisher's name is A. G. Putnam.

10. Margaret M. Lothrop, *The Wayside: Home of Authors* (New York: American Book Co., 1940), 76; Stern, *Louisa May Alcott,* 57–58, 371.

11. For the Stevens connection see *Journals of LMA,* 73, 83 n. 27; Boston Directories, 1854–1857; *Boston Evening Transcript* (25 February 1892). This obituary of Stevens, giving the key to the *Saturday Evening Gazette* connection, was supplied by Victor Berch. For the *Saturday Evening Gazette,* see Frank Luther Mott, *A History of American Magazines 1850–1865,* vol. 2 (Cambridge: Belknap Press of Harvard University Press, 1957), 35 and 35 n. 41.

12. *Selected Letters of LMA,* 10–11.

13. *The Letters of Ellen Tucker Emerson Edited by Edith E. W. Gregg,* vol. 1 (Kent: Kent State University Press, 1982), 82.

14. *Selected Letters of LMA,* 11.

15. *Boston Daily Evening Transcript* (19 December 1854): 2.

16. Both reviews are reprinted in Madeleine B. Stern, ed., *Critical Essays on Louisa May Alcott* (Boston: G. K. Hall, 1984), 23.

17. *Journals of LMA,* 72.

18. *Boston Daily Atlas* (10 November 1856). Briggs is described as "an exemplary man in all the business and social relations of life." It is interesting that the Rev. Sylvanus Cobb was present at the time of Briggs's terminal attack. Cobb's son, Sylvanus Cobb, Jr., would become, with Louisa May Alcott, a major supplier of popular romances for the Boston publishers Elliott, Thomes and Talbot. See also *Trumpet and Universalist Magazine* (15 November 1856). Briggs died intestate. Probate Record 40725, Massachusetts Archives, Suffolk County.

19. The Degen firm consisted of the Rev. Henry V. Degen, publisher of the Methodist periodical *Guide to Holiness,* and his son Henry D. Degen. For Estes's association with Degen, see Raymond L. Kilgour, *Estes and Lauriat: A History*

1872–1898 (Ann Arbor: University of Michigan Press, 1957), 21; John Tebbel, *A History of Book Publishing in the United States,* vol. 2 (New York: Bowker, 1975), 395. According to Victor Berch, Oliver L. Briggs had at one time been an associate of Addison Richards.

20. New York City Directory, 1859.

21. For the murder, see *New York Times* (28 April–2 May and 8 May 1871); J. Edwards Remault, *The "Car-Hook" Tragedy* (Philadelphia: Barclay & Co., [1873]); Charles Sutton, *The New York Tombs* (Montclair, N.J.: Patterson Smith, 1973), 457–63; George W. Walling, *Recollections of a New York Chief of Police* (Montclair, N.J.: Patterson Smith, 1972), 154.

22. *Selected Letters of LMA,* 290.

23. Ibid., 320.

24. Ibid., 322.

25. For later editions of *Flower Fables* see Lucile Gulliver, *Louisa May Alcott: A Bibliography* (Boston: Little, Brown, 1932), [19]–20; National Union Catalogue; Judith C. Ullom, *Louisa May Alcott: A Centennial for Little Women, an Annotated Selected Bibliography,* nos. 3 and 4 (Washington: Library of Congress, 1969).

26. Martha Saxton, *Louisa May: A Modern Biography of Louisa May Alcott* (Boston: Houghton Mifflin, 1977), 199–200.

Louisa May Alcott and the Boston Saturday Evening Gazette

In the course of a long letter written to her older sister Anna in the spring of 1854, the twenty-one-year-old Louisa May Alcott mentioned: "I sent a little tale to the 'Gazette,' and Clapp asked H. W. [her cousin Hamilton Willis] if five dollars would be enough. Cousin H. said yes, and gave it to me, with kind words and a nice parcel of paper, saying in his funny way, 'Now, Lu, the door is open, go in and win.' "[1] Over the next five years, that "nice parcel of paper" would be consumed in the production of at least fourteen stories for the Boston *Saturday Evening Gazette*, a weekly newspaper that, along with the proprietor William Warland Clapp, Jr., would have much to do with opening the door to Louisa May Alcott's career as a professional writer.

That paper, like many American periodicals at midcentury, was the reflection if not the embodiment of its proprietor. Louisa Alcott had much in common with William Warland Clapp, Jr.[2] Both could trace their ancestry to seventeenth-century forebears in the old country; both were addicted to the theater; and both were involved with printer's ink. Clapp was just six years Alcott's senior, having been born in Boston in 1826, the son of that William Warland Clapp who founded the *Boston Advertiser* and later purchased the Boston *Saturday Evening Gazette*. After an education at Boston's "private schools," topped by "two years in France," Clapp with his brother Charles was placed in charge of the *Gazette*. Two years later, in 1849, William Warland Clapp, Jr., became sole proprietor. He was twenty-three years old, genial, jovial, wide-awake, intelligent, observing. He moved with a quick, firm step. His compact form was "well-proportioned," and a ruddy, healthful complexion bespoke energy and high spirits.

That exuberance and energy Clapp proceeded to apply to his weekly newspaper. The Boston *Saturday Evening Gazette* had been founded in 1814 by William Burdick, who happened to be the uncle of William Burdick Stevens and his sister Wealthy Stevens. By 1854, when Louisa May Alcott was seeking a publisher for her first book, *Flower Fables*, and was employed as a seamstress by her Boston neighbor, Wealthy Stevens, it was the Stevenses who copyrighted and subsidized *Flower Fables*, and doubtless also gave its author entrée to the newspaper founded by their uncle.[3]

By that time, William Warland Clapp, Jr., was in full command of the *Gazette* for which he also provided records of the Boston stage. Both he and William B. Stevens wrote plays, Clapp producing a "domestic comedietta," *My Husband's Mirror*, for Spencer's Boston Theatre. Louisa Alcott's devotion to the theater would express itself not only in original plays and adaptations but in acting and impersonations.[4] By 1857 the *Saturday Evening Gazette*, priced at three dollars a year, would be describing itself as "the best theatrical journal in the country."[5] It carried news, displaying a portrait of Puck with the motto: "I'll put a girdle round about the earth in forty minutes." It featured gossip of Boston life, humor, and especially narratives short or long that appealed to its readership. With associate editors Adam Wallace Thaxter and Benjamin Penhallow Shillaber, author of *Mrs. Partington Papers*, the Boston *Saturday Evening Gazette* developed during the 1850s into a popular family weekly—and a vehicle for the author of *Flower Fables*.

Alcott had entrée to the *Gazette* not only through her connection with the Stevenses but through her relationship to Hamilton Willis, who edited a financial gazetteer for the paper.[6] There is no doubt that she studied the *Gazette* carefully, assessing its style and interests, before she offered Clapp her stories. It would become her first association with a major magazine, an outlet that would eventually publish an important corpus of her stories both quantitatively and qualitatively. Moreover, several of those narratives, known previously only by title, have just recently been located; they not only expand Alcott's bibliography but enrich her literary history.[7]

So closely was Alcott at one time identified with the Boston *Saturday Evening Gazette* that the story behind her first published narrative was incorrectly attributed to that weekly. The story itself is simple. Alcott's young friend Llewellyn Willis carried the manuscript of an Alcott tale entitled "The Rival Painters. A Tale of Rome" to the office of the Boston *Olive Branch*, which, in return for five dollars, published the fiction in its issue of 8 May 1852. As far as is known, this was Alcott's first published story.[8] By 1875, after the author of the "The Rival Painters" had become the author of *Little Women, An Old-Fashioned Girl,* and *Little Men,* and was on her way to being categorized as America's best-loved author of juveniles, the *New York Graphic* ran the following entry under the heading "Boston Literary Matters":

[Louisa May Alcott] ventured one day to step into the editorial office of the Boston Saturday Evening Gazette with a small package neatly tied up. This package contained her first manuscript story. The editor read it, admired it, and published it, and the author received for its publication her first literary compensation.[9]

Alcott herself remembered the circumstances differently: "My first story . . . appeared in Ballou's Pictorial Museum [*sic*], and the five dollars paid for it was the most welcome money I ever earned. 'The Rival Prima Donnas' (sent to the Gazette some months later) fared still better, for it brought me ten dollars and a request for more."[10]

Alcott's memory, like the record in the *Graphic,* was faulty. Her first *Gazette* story was "The Rival Prima Donnas," and it *did* earn her a most welcome ten dollars, but it did not appear until 11 November 1854, when Clapp published it over the byline of "Flora Fairfield." The next month the *Gazette* reviewed the author's recently published *Flower Fables.*[11]

Her connection with the periodical had begun. In her journal Alcott wrote: "Decided to seek my fortune; so, with my little trunk of home-made clothes, $20 earned by stories sent to the 'Gazette,' and my MSS., I set forth with Mother's blessing one rainy day in the dullest month in the year."[12] She was just twenty-three years old. The family's poverty had never been more acute. The self-appointed breadwinner was determined to alleviate it by teaching, nursing, sewing, and especially by writing. Much of that writing would appear over the next few years in the pages of William Warland Clapp, Jr.'s *Saturday Evening Gazette*. "Flora Fairfield" was transformed into "L.M.A." for "A New Year's Blessing," published 5 January 1856, and "The Sisters' Trial," which appeared on 26 January. Indeed, the year 1856 saw publication of seven Alcott narratives, which brought her ten dollars apiece, money used to repair her wardrobe or provide her father with new shirts, her mother with a pair of boots.

For one of those stories, "Bertha," published in April, William Warland Clapp, Jr., issued an advertising poster that still exists. Years later, Alcott reminisced:

> One of the memorial moments of my life is that in which, as I trudged to school [as a teacher] on a wintry day, my eye fell upon a large yellow poster, with these delicious words: . . . "'Bertha,' a new tale by the author of 'The Rival Prima Donnas,' will appear in the *Saturday Evening Gazette*." I was late; it was bitter cold; people jostled me; I was mortally afraid I should be recognized, but there I stood feasting my eyes on the fascinating poster, and saying proudly to myself . . . "This, this is fame!" That day my pupils had an indulgent teacher; for while they struggled with their pothooks, I was writing immortal works; and, when they droned out the multiplication table, I was counting up the noble fortune my pen was to earn for me in the dim, delightful future. That afternoon my sisters made a pilgrimage to behold this famous placard, and, finding it torn by the wind, boldly stole it and came back to wave it like a triumphal banner in the bosom of the excited family. The tattered paper still exists, folded away with other relics of those early days.[13]

The "tattered paper" does indeed still exist, no longer tattered, since it has been restored. Alcott's recollection was imprecise, however, for the poster actually reads: "BOSTON / SATURDAY EVENING GAZETTE / FOR APRIL 19th, / will contain / BERTHA / an original tale, / By the Authoress of 'The Sisters' Trial,' 'The New Year's Blessing,' 'Little Genevieve,' etc." Louisa May Alcott's name has been inked in between the words *By* and *the Authoress* but appears nowhere in print on the placard.[14]

Despite the euphoria induced by the poster, Alcott was not entirely satisfied with her rewards from the *Gazette*. In September 1856, after "Bertha" had followed "Little Genevieve," and then "Mabel's May Day" had followed "Bertha" in the *Gazette*, she wrote to one Miss Seymour:

> Will you be so kind as to ask Mr Norris of the "Olive Branch" or Mrs Jennison of the "Ladies Enterprise," if they would take some stories from me. I am writing

for the "Gazette" & "Sunday News" but neither of them pay very well, & as money is the principle object of my life just now I want to add another string or two to my bow. . . . Mr Norris may remember a story I wrote for him some years ago, ["The Rival Painters. A Tale of Rome"] & may have seen some of my later ones in the Gazette which have been so kindly noticed & commented upon that I feel encouraged to offer my wares to any one who will lend a helping hand to a struggling fellow mortal who wishes to earn her living by her pen.[15]

On 4 October 1856, a provocative Alcott tale, "The Lady and the Woman," was published by the *Gazette*. On the ninth of the month the author felt emboldened to make a contractual proposition to William Warland Clapp, Jr.:

> I am anxious to know if the popularity of my contributions to the Gazette will warrant you to engage me for a story each month for the coming six at fifteen or twenty dollars each as the length or excellence may vary.
>
> I have had other offers in advance of this but am not sure of their reliability & prefer the Gazette as it circulates among a class of readers with whom I have other agreeable connexions than those of a literary character.
>
> Please let me hear from you at your earliest convenience, & shall be glad of the usual compensation for the last two stories.[16]

Clapp's response was prompt, for on 27 October Alcott wrote again to him: "I have recieved [*sic*] your letter containing $20 on Saturday, & thank you for your criticisms on my stories. I find it difficult to make them interesting & yet short enough to suit your paper. But hope to improve in both points."[17]

Despite the criticism, Clapp apparently acceded, at least in part, to his star author's request. In her journal for October 1856 Alcott's indefatigable pen recorded: "C[lapp] offers 10 dollars a month, and perhaps more,"[18] and on 2 November she wrote to her sister Anna: "Clapp will take a story a month which gives me ten dollars & nearly pays my board."[19] Years later she would recall: "The Evening Gazette used to pay me $10 for a story a month when I began."[20] Accordingly, from her attic room in Mrs. David Reed's Boston boarding house, she would, as she reported in her journal, "Fly round and take C[lapp] his stories."[21]

The stories spun in the Boston attic and carried to the *Gazette* office duly made their bows: "Ruth's Secret," appearing in December 1856, and a succession of newly located 1857 narratives were all carefully entered with their ten-dollar fees in the author's yearly memoranda of earnings. She did not always succeed in pleasing her editor. Clapp returned her "N Year's Tale" to her, writing: "My Dear Miss Alcott. I dont think the publication of this story would add to your literary reputation, & tho I dislike to say so I must tell you that I think it inferior to anything you have written. Pardon this freedom & believe me, Yrs Truly W. W. Clapp."[22]

The author of the well-advertised "Bertha" was, as she reported to her sister Anna,

> very much taken aback, not knowing that I had any "literary reputation" to sustain, & not caring much for his opinion for he didnt like "Lady & Woman" & [Theodore] Parker [the Unitarian minister whom Alcott admired] did, so though rather disturbed at seeing my $10 vanish I "possessed my soul in patience" & thought I'd send the story some where else & let Clapp ask for another before I sent it. I know he will for Ham[ilton Willis] says he likes my wares, & now he may wait for them.[23]

After the publication of her 1857 stories, "The Cross on the Church Tower," "Agatha's Confession," and "Little Sunbeam," there appears to be a gap in Alcott's *Gazette* appearances. As her father, Bronson Alcott, wrote in a letter to his daughter Anna, "I hope Louisa will better conditions by any change she may propose and carry out. Clapp is uncertain, but so are any others she may deal with in these times."[24] Not until March of 1859 did another story by Alcott appear in the *Gazette* columns—"Mark Field's Mistake," followed in April by its sequel, "Mark Field's Success." In September the newly discovered "Monk's Island" was run, followed five years later by "Mrs. Podgers' Teapot," and finally, in December 1867, by "What the Bells Saw and Said." For those last two narratives the author received twenty-five dollars apiece. Her professionalism had developed and was being recognized. She was gaining that "literary reputation" of which she had once been so uncertain.

It was not only the publication of Alcott's book *Hospital Sketches* in 1863 (records of her short career as army nurse in the Union Hotel Hospital during the Civil War) that increased her reputation and advanced her professionalism but the many stories that had been carried by the Boston *Saturday Evening Gazette* as well. The frequency with which they were published by that weekly between 1854 and 1859 is a clear indication of their popularity among subscribers. Her *Gazette* stories taught Alcott how to combine interest with brevity and how to interweave characterization with plot. In them she attempted at least four different genres of literary narrative: the sensational, the sentimental or romantic, the realistic, and the domestic; and on occasion she combined genres in a single story. In the columns of the *Gazette*, Alcott experimented with variety and began the literary development that culminated in professionalism. From a study of her narratives in the weekly, that development can be traced.[25]

Alcott's first *Gazette* story, "The Rival Prima Donnas," combined the romance of the opera stage—a background appealing to Clapp and to the author—with a sensational plot. Her triangle included the rival prima donnas Beatrice and Theresa, doubtless suggested by the great sopranos Jenny Lind and Henriette Sontag, whom the author had heard at Boston's Music Hall. The prima donnas were rivals not only on stage but in love, both enamored of the painter Claude, who is characterized by both a false smile and a false heart. The tale is one of deception on the part of Theresa and revenge on the part of Beatrice, who weaves a "rose-crown" for her rival that conceals among the roses a crown of iron.

"Look up, look up, Theresa, and receive the crown," cried a distant voice, that she well knew; and lifting her wondering eyes, the lovely singer shuddered as she met the dark glance that flashed upon her from the haggard face of the rival she had wronged, and in that glance each read the other's meaning; and while Theresa bowed her head in shame and fear, Beatrice, with a sudden smile, raised her white arms high above her head, and stood a moment gracefully holding a flower crown, while her eye sought out some distant object; then the garland *fell*, and high above the tumultuous applause, that shook the walls, roared the death-shriek of Theresa, and Beatrice, pointing to her as she lay amid the flowers, with the *iron* crown concealed among the roses on her blood-stained hair, cried in a voice that never ceased to echo on one guilty hearer's ear: "You bid me crown her, Claude; see, I have done it! better to 'die *crushed with flowers*,' than live to be what you have rendered me"; and with a wild, fearful laugh, she vanished from the sight of the horror-stricken crowd!

There the story—brief, vengeful, passionate—should have ended, but the author could not resist appending an epilogue:

Years passed away, and in a lonely convent lived and died a sad grey-haired man, worn and wasted with remorse, and in a quiet home for the insane, dwelt a beautiful, pale woman, who constantly wove garlands, and, like a swan, died singing mournfully—and these were BEATRICE and CLAUDE.

This early experiment with romantic sensationalism would be improved upon in the course of the next ten or fifteen years, but it laid the foundation for much of Alcott's later work in the genre. Moreover, the story was considered, not only by Alcott but doubtless also by Clapp, as worthy of dramatization. Having adapted it to the stage, the author offered her script to Thomas Barry of the Boston Theatre, who assured her that he himself would play Claude while Mrs. John Wood and Julia Barrow would be cast as the rivals. Although the plan fell through, Alcott did receive a pass to the Boston Theatre, and her manuscript dramatization was preserved.[26]

Still another *Gazette* tale pits two women against each other in their relationship to a man. The newly located "Agatha's Confession" stirs up a witch's brew whose ingredients include not only revenge and guilt but contagion, sleepwalking, and the horror of live burial. "Agatha's Confession" appeared in the five columns of page 3 usually allotted to Alcott's concoctions for the *Gazette,* and within that small space vividly characterized the poor and plain Agatha, the siren charmer Clara, and their beloved Philip. Clara, with evil intent, lures Philip from Agatha. Twice Agatha subdues the temptation of letting her rival perish, once by contagion, once by fire. Finally, however, she cannot resist a more horrendous temptation. Aware that Clara is not dead as she appears to be, since her forehead is damp, Agatha allows her rival to be buried alive. Subsequently, haunted by her crime, she reveals her secret in a fit of sleepwalking, and Agatha's confession adds to the Alcott canon a pre-Freudian case history. Violence, revenge, and a woman scorned would fascinate Alcott for years to come when she donned the gaudy cap of sensationalism. Indeed, as the dramatized version of "The Rival Prima Donnas" was preserved, so was the tale "Agatha's Confession." Ten years later Alcott would rework that narrative, without altering it radically, and serve it up again. This time it was offered, not to William Warland Clapp, Jr., but to Frank Leslie, publishing magnate of New York, founder of *Frank Leslie's Illustrated Newspaper* and a chain of periodicals. Clapp had paid her ten dollars for "Agatha's Confession" when he published it over her full name in 1857. Ten years later, when it ran anonymously as "Thrice Tempted" in *Frank Leslie's Chimney Corner*,[27] it earned her fifty dollars.

In 1859 Alcott was still experimenting with a combination of romance and sensationalism for the *Gazette*. On 3 September "The Monk's Island: A Legend of the Rhine. Written for the Evening Gazette. By Louisa M. Alcott" was emblazoned across page 1 of Clapp's weekly. Suggested by a Rhine legend described in Vaughan's *Hours with the Mystics*, the narrative is a highly imaginative pastiche. Its ingredients include a treasure chest, a dramatic conflict between passion and duty on the part of a German merchant betrothed to a German girl but enchanted by a Turkish maiden, a hero who flees temptation by becoming a monk, war and famine, a young man held captive for a heavy ransom, and the horror of leprosy. These sensational elements are welded together by the high-mindedness of almost all the characters, several of whom "flee temptation and walk upright in the path of duty." The effusion earned the author ten dollars, along with further experience in pitting virtue against passion and saintly characters against outrageous fortune.

Several Alcott stories that filled five columns in the *Gazette* were less sensational than sentimental. For their creation the author borrowed from Dickens, whom she idolized, and donned rose-colored glasses that saw virtue rewarded and error atoned. In January 1856, for example, the *Gazette* carried "A New Year's Blessing" in which Alice brings a benediction into the cheerless home of John Owen; in March readers could be uplifted by the tale of "Little Genevieve" who brings retribution to her erring parents. One of the most saccharinely sentimental of the Alcott *Gazette* narratives is a tale recently located, "Written for the Evening Gazette. By Louisa M. Alcott," and published in January 1857. Only a month before the author had noted in her journal: "Wrote a story, 'The Cross on the Church Tower,' suggested by the tower before my window."[28] The tale concerns the despairing, hopeless Walter, a poor rejected author on the verge of suicide, who is regenerated by the saintliness of "poor Jamie," a child with "withered limbs," and by "poor Jamie's" noble sister Nell. Both teach Walter what the Alcott parents had long striven to teach their often tempestuous daughter, "the beauty of self-denial and the blessedness of loving his neighbor better than himself." In the end, of course, Jamie dies, and Walter, learning that Nell's heart belongs to another, not only subdues his passion for her but generously bestows upon his beloved and her husband "the rich earnings of his pen." In the course of all this Dickensian moral sentiment—apparently devoured by a midcentury audience moved easily to tears—there is one most interesting and prophetic observation. The hero Walter, whose works have been rejected, writes a true story about Jamie and Nell, "weaving in few fancies of my own and leaving [the characters] . . . unchanged. . . . I painted no fictitious sorrows, what I had seen and keenly felt I could truly tell. . . . This book, unlike the others, was not rejected; for the simple truth told by an earnest pen, touched and interested." In *Little Women,* published a dozen years later, the author would include the following dialogue:

Jo March: What *can* there be in a simple little story . . . to make people praise it so?

Jo's father: There is truth in it, Jo, that's the secret; humor and pathos make it alive, and you have found your style at last.

Alcott had not found her style by 1856, when she wrote "The Cross on the Church Tower," but she already sensed that more realistic characterizations and more believable incidents would give verisimilitude to her narratives and perhaps increase their popularity. Her approaches to literary credibility can be discerned in some of her *Gazette* tales. Sentiment still plays a more pronounced role than realism in "Little Sunbeam," another newly located story. Nonetheless, the knowledgeable reader can hear faint echoes of reality in Meg's description of her domestic service, the sweeping and scrubbing that were part of Louisa Alcott's personal experience as a domestic in Dedham, Massachusetts, in the winter of 1851. Just so, Meg's illness was no doubt suggested by the illness of Louisa's sister Lizzie that persisted even while "Little Sunbeam" was written and published. Meg, unlike Lizzie, survives to bring sunshine into the lives of her benefactors—as well as the usual ten dollars into the coffers of Louisa M. Alcott. Meg's name would survive too, until, some twelve years later, it would be given to the oldest of the March girls, a character far more realistic and far more memorable.

It was in her *Gazette* story "The Lady and the Woman" that Alcott experimented successfully with realism and achieved a high degree of credibility in her characterizations and plot. Once again she produced a power struggle between two women rivals in love. But in this instance she painted a believable contrast—the languid belle Amelia Langdon, "fretful, useless, beautiful," against the straightforward, independent Kate Loring. These protagonists are true to life, and their rivalry for the love of Edward Windsor is entirely realistic. Kate's character especially is carefully drawn: "She had read and thought much on many subjects sadly unfashionable." She boasted a blunt sincerity, a quiet disregard for the false and foolish opinions of the world, and she harbored "peculiar" ideas on many topics. Kate is not only credible but likeable. She is a creature of flesh and blood, not a romantic imagining. The plot is simple, devoid of the fantastic sensationalism that often attracted Alcott. The reactions of the lady Amelia and woman Kate to a country flood help pinpoint their characters. And the end in which Amelia loses Edward Windsor to Kate is completely satisfying. The story is one of Alcott's early successes. It is also, in its characterization of Kate Loring, a foreshadowing of Jo March.

A foreshadowing of *Little Women* itself is clearly evident in another of Alcott's 1856 contributions to the *Gazette*, "The Sisters' Trial," in which the roots of her domestic novel are traceable. In that story are adumbrated the four sisters who would reappear as full-length portraits in Alcott's perennial classic. As the March sisters sit together contemplating Christmas when the curtain rises on *Little Women*, in "The Sisters' Trial," "Four sisters sat together round a cheerful fire on New Year's Eve." Poverty-stricken, they "must decide what work we will each choose by which to earn our bread," and so begins the self-analysis of each character. Agnes, capitalizing upon an ambition with which both Alcott and Clapp could sympathize, announces that she will be an actress. Ella will become a governess to "three little motherless girls," and so, like her creator, "will not be dependent on relatives rich in all but love to us." Amy—Alcott would retain even the name in *Little Women*—will go to Europe for a year "and pass my days in sketching, painting and taking care of" a lame friend. As for Nora, she will stay at home and write. When the sisters gather together a year later to report their experiences, Nora announces (much as Walter does in "The Cross on the Church Tower"): "My book was well received and made for me a place among those writers who have the power to please and touch the hearts of many."

Nora's remark was prophetic. When Alcott came to write *Little Women*, she infused into it many of the experiences of those four sisters who, as the March girls, would captivate readers for generations to come. She also made good use of the skills she had honed from her varied experiments for the Boston *Saturday Evening Gazette*. She made her last narrative contribution to the weekly—"What the Bells Saw and Said," for which she received twenty-five dollars—in December 1867. At the same time she had been engaged to edit another periodical, *Merry's Museum*, and had agreed to write the "girls book" with which she would forever be identified.

By then, the mentor who had demanded interest and brevity from his prolific author had transferred his proprietorship from the *Gazette* to the *Boston Journal*. During the Civil War, when the author of "The Lady and the Woman" and "The Sisters' Trial" was nursing in George-town, D.C., Clapp was earning the title of Colonel by serving as chairman of committees on recruiting and military affairs. At the war's end he associated himself with the *Boston Journal* and lost the services of his former star contributor. By that time she was producing a string of anonymous thrillers for Frank Leslie's expanding line of periodicals, including *Frank Leslie's Chimney Corner*. In the pages of that newspaper, where such sensational Alcott narratives as "A Nurse's Story," "La Jeune," and "Mrs. Vane's Charade" were carried, William Warland Clapp, Jr., was eulogized among "The Self-made Men of our Times." "Colonel Clapp," it was asserted, "is one of the best known men in Boston . . . a go-ahead chap from his very youth up." While Clapp still retained editorial interest in the *Gazette*, he was now associated with the management of the *Journal*, an association he would retain until his death in 1891.[29] Louisa Alcott had little connection with that paper, beyond sending to it in 1883 a letter published as "Louisa M. Alcott's Defence of Woman's Suffrage."[30] Five years later, the former mainstay of the *Gazette*, then universally known as America's best-loved author of juveniles, died.

As for the Boston *Saturday Evening Gazette*, the weekly was purchased at the end of the Civil War by the firm of Worthington, Flanders & Co., proprietors of the *Boston Daily Evening Traveler,* for the sum of twenty-five thousand dollars. At that time Clapp was succeeded in his managerial capacity by B. G. Goodsell and later by Col. Henry G. Parker. In 1906 the paper was merged with the *Boston Budget.*[31]

Louisa Alcott had learned much from her association with Clapp's weekly. It had served her as a vehicle during her apprentice years and had given her an opportunity to experiment with sensationalism and sentiment, realism and domesticity. The narratives she contributed to the *Gazette* reflect her passage from genre to genre, her ability to assess the demands of her readership, and her skill at shaping a story to fit a stipulated page of text.

Toward the end of her life Louisa May Alcott recalled her association with the *Gazette* and the stories she had contributed to it. Though not entirely accurate in detail, her recollections embody much of the truth:

A dozen [stories] a month were easily turned off, and well paid for, especially while a certain editor labored under the delusion that the writer was a man. The moment the truth was known the price was lowered; but the girl had learned the worth of her wares, and would not write for less, so continued to earn her fair wages in spite of sex. And here it may not be out of place to give another hint to some of the many story-loving girls who read the *Gazette,* and perhaps write for it. Now that women have made a place for themselves in journalism and literature, it is wise for them to cultivate, not only their intellectual faculties, but their practical ones also and understand the business details of their craft. The ignorance and helplessness of women writers is amazing, and only disastrous experience teaches them what they should have learned before. The brains that can earn money in this way can understand how to take care of it by a proper knowledge of contracts, copyrights, and the duties of publisher and author toward one another.[32]

The inference is clear. The Boston *Saturday Evening Gazette* had given to Louisa May Alcott not only an opportunity to essay varied genres of narrative, from the wild sensationalism of "Agatha's Confession" to the realism of "The Lady and the Woman," but had also apparently taught her the essentials of author-publisher relations. It was in large measure as a contributor to the *Gazette* that Alcott developed her literary professionalism. She served a productive apprenticeship in its columns, and when the door of the *Gazette* was opened to her, Alcott did indeed "go in and win."

LOUISA MAY ALCOTT'S CONTRIBUTIONS TO THE
BOSTON *SATURDAY EVENING GAZETTE*:
A CHRONOLOGICAL LISTING

1. "The Rival Prima Donnas," by Flora Fairfield (11 November 1854). Reprinted in Louisa May Alcott, *Selected Fiction*, ed. Daniel Shealy, Madeleine B. Stern, and Joel Myerson (Boston: Little, Brown, 1990).

2. "A New Year's Blessing" (5 January 1856).

3. "The Sisters' Trial" (26 January 1856). Reprinted in Alcott, *Selected Fiction*.

4. "Little Genevieve" (29 March 1856).

5. "Little Paul" (poem) (19 April 1856).

6. "Bertha" (19 and 26 April 1856).

7. "Mabel's May Day" (24 May 1856).

8. "Beach Bubbles" (poems) (21, 28 June; 12, 26 July; 2, 16, 23 August 1856).

9. "The Mother-Moon" (poem, one of the "Beach Bubbles") (23 August 1856). Reprinted in *The Little Pilgrim*, 1, no. 1 (January 1858).

10. "The Lady and the Woman" (4 October 1856). Reprinted in Alcott, *Selected Fiction*.

11. "Ruth's Secret" (6 December 1856).

12. "The Cross on the Church Tower" (24 January 1857).

13. "Agatha's Confession" (14 March 1857). Revised as "Thrice Tempted" and republished in *Frank Leslie's Chimney Corner* (20 July 1867). "Thrice Tempted" reprinted in Alcott, *Selected Fiction*.

14. "Little Sunbeam" (4 April 1857).

15. "Mark Field's Mistake" (12 March 1859).

16. "Mark Field's Success" (16 April 1859).

17. "The Monk's Island: A Legend of the Rhine" (3 September 1859).

18. "Mrs. Podgers' Teapot, a Christmas Story" (24 December 1864). Reprinted in Louisa M. Alcott, *Hospital Sketches and Camp and Fireside Stories* (Boston: Roberts Brothers, 1869).

19. "What the Bells Saw and Said" (21 December 1867). Reprinted in Louisa M. Alcott, *Proverb Stories* (Boston: Roberts Brothers, 1882).

20. "Woman's Part in the Concord Celebration" (8 May 1875). Reprinted from *The Woman's Journal* (1 May 1875).

1. *The Selected Letters of Louisa May Alcott,* ed. Joel Myerson, Daniel Shealy, and Madeleine B. Stern (Boston: Little, Brown, 1987), 9.

2. For Clapp, see *Boston Evening Transcript* (9 December 1891): 5; *Dictionary of American Biography* 4: 118; *Frank Leslie's Chimney Corner* (7 April 1866): 298; Frank Luther Mott, *A History of American Magazines 1850–1865* (Cambridge: Belknap Press of Harvard University Press, 1957), 35.

3. See "Alcott's First Book: Tales for Ellen E.," reprinted in this collection.

4. For biographical details of Alcott throughout, see Madeleine B. Stern, *Louisa May Alcott* (Norman: University of Oklahoma Press, 1985).

5. Mott, *A History of American Magazines 1850–1865,* 35, 198. For the *Gazette* see also *Frank Leslie's Chimney Corner* (7 April 1866): 298; Frederic Hudson, *Journalism in the United States from 1690 to 1872* (New York: Harper, n.d.), 396.

6. *Selected Letters of LMA,* 15 n. 3.

7. Tribute must be paid to Victor A. Berch, the extraordinary literary detective of Marlborough, Massachusetts, who found the previously unlocated Alcott stories in the Boston *Saturday Evening Gazette.* The writer is deeply indebted to him as well as to his unsurpassed research skills.

8. Stern, *Louisa May Alcott,* 67.

9. *New York Graphic* (25 September 1875); Kenneth Walter Cameron, *Concord Literary Renaissance* (Hartford: Transcendental Books, 1988), 47.

10. "Obituary. Death of Louisa M. Alcott," *Boston Journal* (7 March 1888); Cameron, *Concord Literary Renaissance,* 115.

11. Boston *Saturday Evening Gazette* (23 December 1854), [2]. Reprinted in Madeleine B. Stern, ed., *Critical Essays on Louisa May Alcott* (Boston: G. K. Hall, 1984), 23.

12. *The Journals of Louisa May Alcott,* ed. Joel Myerson, Daniel Shealy, and Madeleine B. Stern (Boston: Little, Brown, 1989), 75 [November 1855].

13. *Boston Journal* (7 March 1888); Cameron, *Concord Literary Renaissance,* 115.

14. The poster has been reproduced in *Journals of LMA,* following p. 164. The original is in the Orchard House, Concord, Mass.

15. *Selected Letters of LMA,* 16.

16. Ibid., 17.

17. Ibid., 18.

18. *Journals of LMA,* 79. Fees paid for stories are entered in the yearly "Notes and Memoranda" in the *Journals.* Occasionally there is a discrepancy, as in the case of the "The Sisters' Trial," for which the fee cited in "Notes and Memoranda" for 1856 is ten dollars, but only six dollars in the January 1856 journal where Alcott writes: "C[lapp] paid $6 for 'A Sister's Trial,' gave me more books to notice, and wants more tales." The later comment of LMA is: "[Should think he would at that price.]" See *Journals of LMA,* 78 and 82.

19. *Selected Letters of LMA,* 20.

20. Ibid., 233. LMA to Miss Churchill, 27 December [1878?].

21. *Journals of LMA*, 79.

22. *Selected Letters of LMA*, 27. The reference may be to "New Year's Gift," listed as earning five dollars in Alcott's "Notes and Memoranda" for 1857, but thus far unlocated. See *Journals of LMA*, 86.

23. *Selected Letters of LMA*, 27.

24. *The Letters of A. Bronson Alcott*, ed. Richard L. Hernstadt (Ames: Iowa State University Press, 1969), 264.

25. See also Daniel Shealy, "The Author-Publisher Relationships of Louisa May Alcott" (Ph.D. Diss., University of South Carolina, 1985), 5–7; Madeleine B. Stern, "Lousia M. Alcott in Periodicals," *Studies in the American Renaissance* 1977, 370–71.

26. Stern, *Louisa May Alcott*, 73, 76, 78, 79, 373. The manuscript of the dramatized version is in Orchard House, Concord, Mass.

27. "Thrice Tempted," *Frank Leslie's Chimney Corner* (20 July 1867). Reprinted in Louisa May Alcott, *Selected Fiction*, ed. Daniel Shealy, Madeleine B. Stern, and Joel Myerson (Boston: Little, Brown, 1990), 99–116.

28. *Journals of LMA*, 81.

29. For Clapp's later life, see *Boston Evening Transcript* (9 December 1891): 5; *Frank Leslie's Chimney Corner* (7 April 1866): 298.

30. *Boston Morning Journal* (8 March 1883). See *Selected Letters of LMA*, 269–70.

31. *Frank Leslie's Chimney Corner* (7 April 1866): 298; Mott, *A History of American Magazines 1850–1865*, 35 n. 41.

32. *The Critic* (17 March 1888); Cameron, *Concord Literary Renaissance*, 119. The prices for most of the *Gazette* stories listed by Alcott in her memoranda of earnings remain constant at ten dollars apiece. In a letter to publisher James Redpath (24 January 1864) she mentioned that her poems "Beach Bubbles," which appeared in the *Gazette* between 21 June and 23 August 1856, were "copy righted in my name by Mr Clapp" and "printed but never paid for." See *Selected Letters of LMA*, 101. This may have contributed to Alcott's recollection of publishers' injustice.

WORKS CITED

Cameron, Kenneth Walter. *Concord Literary Renaissance*. Hartford: Transcendental Books, 1988.

Herrnstadt, Richard L., ed. *The Letters of A. Bronson Alcott*. Ames: Iowa State University Press, 1969.

Hudson, Frederic. *Journalism in the United States from 1690 to 1872*. New York: Harper, n.d.

Mott, Frank Luther. *A History of American Magazines 1850–1865*. Cambridge: Belknap Press of Harvard University Press, 1957.

Myerson, Joel, Daniel Shealy, and Madeleine B. Stern, eds. *The Journals of Louisa May Alcott*. Boston: Little, Brown, 1989.

———. *The Selected Letters of Louisa May Alcott*. Boston: Little, Brown, 1987.

Shealy, Daniel. "The Author-Publisher Relationships of Louisa May Alcott."
Ph.D. diss., University of South Carolina, 1985.

Shealy, Daniel, Madeleine B. Stern, and Joel Myerson, eds. *Selected Fiction of Louisa May Alcott.* Boston: Little, Brown, 1990.

Stern, Madeleine B. "Louisa M. Alcott in Periodicals," *Studies in the American Renaissance* (1977): 370–71.

———. "Louisa May Alcott's 'Tales for Ellen E.'" *AB Bookman's Weekly* (12 November 1990): 1852.

———. *Louisa May Alcott.* Norman: University of Oklahoma Press, 1985.

Stern, Madeleine B., ed. *Critical Essays on Louisa May Alcott.* Boston: G. K. Hall, 1984.

An Early
Alcott
Sensation Story

recently discovered Alcott sensation story entitled "Marion Earle; or, Only an Actress!" made its debut in the *American Union* in 1858. The narrative is interesting on several counts, being one of Louisa May Alcott's early thrillers, very few of which have surfaced. Written in July 1858 when the author was twenty-five, it reflects, directly or obliquely, her reading, her life, and her convictions. In it she made use of Elizabeth Barrett Browning's *Aurora Leigh,* episodes in her own life, and especially her perennial addiction to the theater. She also set in it the pattern for her later sensation stories.

Browning's *Aurora Leigh* (published in 1857) presented, in the form of a versified novel or a novelized poem, sensational themes, social consciousness, and feminist leanings. It became an immediate success. Its cast of characters included not only Aurora and Romney Leigh but a stalwart and high-minded woman who leads a violent and melodramatic life, Marian Erle. Alcott's use of that name (in a variant spelling) is not the only point of similarity between the two tales. Alcott doubtless found in *Aurora Leigh* concepts and ideas that she enthusiastically supported, such as feminism in the form of sisterhood and the compassion due to unwed mothers. In both narratives there are also vivid descriptions of a sensational wedding scene.

In addition to traces from Browning's lengthy poem, episodes from Alcott's life are discernible in her "Marion Earle."[1] In March 1858 her younger sister Lizzie died from the effects of scarlet fever. Contagion, suggested by Lizzie's illness, would play a role in "Marion Earle; or, Only an Actress!" The engagement of Louisa's older sister Anna to

John Bridge Pratt the following month—"another sister is gone," as she put it in her journal[2]—would agitate Louisa sufficiently for her to sublimate her concern in an extraordinary wedding scene.

Above all, Alcott's lifelong addiction to the stage would play a major part in "Marion Earle." In June 1858 she wrote in her journal that, having seen the great actress Charlotte Cushman on the Boston stage, she had "had a stagestruck fit." The following month she "worked off [her] stage fever in writing a story."[3] At the end of the year when the young Thespian from Concord listed her earnings for 1858, they included six dollars for what she referred to as "Only An Actress."[4]

That story has now been found. Although "Marion Earle; or, Only an Actress!" earned Alcott only six dollars in 1858, as an encapsulation of her life at the time and as a foreshadowing of writings to come, it is invaluable.

Alcott's Marion Earle was "left an orphan, with a little sister [May] dependent on her." After vainly trying to support herself by the few occupations open to women, Marion has the courage to enter the profession "for which her talents fitted her," and becomes an actress. Meanwhile she has struggled through "poverty, injustice, and temptation," and been afflicted by the death of her young sister.

At this point in the narrative another woman protagonist is introduced: Agnes, a "motherless girl" who has been "robbed of the one treasure she possessed" by the elegant and wealthy Robert Leicester, to whom she has borne a son. Browning's Marian Earle, it will be remembered, has a child born after she has been drugged and raped. The unwed mother theme is threaded through both the Alcott and Browning stories, and both authors are deeply concerned with the plight of the unwed mother to whom compassion, though due, is denied. Alcott's Agnes pleads in vain with Robert Leicester's mother:

Let him keep the word he plighted to me, and give his little child a name! . . . I was an orphan, ignorant and young, . . . and he was very fond and tender for awhile—God forgive me—how I loved him! Worldly fears disturbed our peace; he left me, promising to come again. He never has. . . . By the love you bear your son, have compassion for mine.

Refused by Leicester's disdainful mother, Agnes next approaches the actress Marion Earle, who is compassion personified. "It is not for me to judge you or your error," Marion says, "but remembering my own weakness, to comfort and console as I in my sorrow would have been consoled." The actress promises the unwed mother a home, and tells her that she (Marion) is shortly to be married, though she fails to mention her bridegroom's name.

And so Alcott prepares the ground for the climax of her tale—the sensational wedding scene. A similar scene in the Browning narrative derives its drama from the bride's failure to appear for her marriage ceremony. In Alcott's version the sensational elements are wilder. Marion and her bridegroom, the reader is informed, had met abroad, journeyed together, and "from friends they glided into lovers, from lovers they were soon to pass into . . . closer union." At the wedding ceremony, which takes place in Mrs. Leicester's "spacious drawing-room," Agnes appears with her babe in her arms. She had not known the identity of Marion's future husband, nor had Marion known the name of Agnes' seducer. The shocking disclosure is made as the question is duly posed: "Robert Leicester, will you take this woman to be thy wedded wife?" At these words Agnes interrupts the proceedings: "*Will* you take this woman for your wife while I stand here with your child upon my breast?"

Now the absent bride of *Aurora Leigh* is converted into the substitute bride of the Alcott narrative. The actress Marion Earle is not only compassion but self-abnegation personified. She yields her place as bride to Agnes, and, despite protests, the unwed mother becomes Mrs. Robert Leicester. Was there perhaps some wishful thinking here on the part of Alcott, whose sister Anna—that other "sister . . . gone"—was pledged to marry John Pratt?

As soon as Agnes and Robert are married, the latter departs, Marion takes Agnes and the babe with her, and three years pass. The theme of feminist sisterhood now takes over. In a relationship not dissimilar to that between Browning's Aurora and Marian, the "two solitary women" of the Alcott narrative are "bound together by one sorrow and one love." The unwed mother has now been married, though in name only, and the two women live together as sisters, caring for each other and for Agnes' child.

Their quiet life is interrupted by the sudden reappearance of Robert Leicester, who has fallen upon evil days, lost his wealth, and caught the kind of contagious fever that had afflicted Alcott's younger sister Lizzie. Robert, however, survives, nursed back to health by a trio of women: Marion, Agnes, and a reformed Mrs. Leicester who is now not only gray-haired, wild-eyed, and poverty-stricken, but filled with remorse. Assuring herself that this once-divided family will at last be united, the saintly actress Marion Earle departs. Having contracted the contagion from Robert, she dies, leaving her now considerable fortune to Agnes' son.

And so the themes of feminism as sisterhood and compassion for unwed mothers, which had preoccupied Elizabeth Barrett Browning, are entwined with hints from Alcott's family life and her devotion to the theater to produce this early sensation story. In her vindication of actress-as-human-being the author converts the performer Marion Earle into a social benefactress. At the same time she provides what must have been a page-turner in 1858.

Some time between July 1858, when Alcott wrote the story, and 12 September of that year, "Marion Earle; or, Only an Actress!" by L. M. Alcott appeared in the pages of the *American Union*. Although it has for some time been suspected that that periodical was a medium for the author experimenting in the sensational genre, "Marion Earle" is the first of her stories that can be assigned to that paper. Ironically, it can be so assigned only because it was found reprinted in the *New York Atlas* of 12 September 1858, where it is described as "From the American Union." Its discoverer was Victor A. Berch, Librarian Emeritus of Brandeis University and literary detective par excellence. (The story of its discovery is perhaps as interesting as the story itself.)

By the 1860s Alcott was writing full steam, producing a steady flow of thrillers for the periodicals launched by two publishing houses—Frank Leslie's in New York and the firm of Elliott, Thomes and Talbot in Boston. On 7 January 1865 James R. Elliott of the Boston house wrote a business note to Alcott, offering terms for stories and mentioning en passant that his "rate will be fully equal to $16.00 for a first page story in the 'American Union' which paper I think you have contributed to while it was under the management of Messrs. Graves & Weston."[5]

The *American Union,* except for scattered issues preserved in libraries, has become a highly elusive nineteenth-century story paper. Hence Alcott's contributions, till recently, had never been found. With Victor Berch's discovery of "Marion Earle" by L. M. Alcott reprinted from the *American Union* in the *New York Atlas,* James R. Elliott's statement is corroborated and it can be assumed that the *American Union* was the principal vehicle in which Alcott aired her early experiments in sensationalism.

In her early memoranda of earnings Alcott kept account of the titles of her stories and the fees paid for them, and, as mentioned earlier, she listed "Only an Actress" at six dollars for 1858. The following year she listed in her journal several other delectable titles: "Ottilla's Oath," "Steel Bracelet," and "A Phantom Face," each of which earned her ten dollars.[6] Not one of those titles has been located, though in all likelihood they were published in the *American Union.* Indeed, in its 21 May 1859 issue that paper made the following announcement:

"The Steel Bracelet; or, *The Skeleton in the Closet!*" a deeply interesting Original Story, by L. M. Alcott, will occupy the first page of next week's paper. We call particular attention to it as an entertaining narrative of extraordinary merit.

Unfortunately no copy of that "next week's paper" appears to have survived. However, around 1867 the firm of Elliott, Thomes and Talbot, successors of Graves and Weston, issued in their series of Ten Cent Novelettes of Standard American Authors a fascinating thriller, *The Skeleton in the Closet* by L. M. Alcott.

The offices of Graves and Weston, publishers of the *American Union* during the 1850s, were located on Boston's Washington Street, not far from the Chauncy Street boardinghouse where Louisa Alcott was dashing out her tales. Priced at two dollars a year, the weekly accepted no advertisements and no continued stories, and used no illustrations. Each number was "complete in itself," and, boasting that it was the "best family newspaper," a "fireside" journal, it provided the future author of *Little Women* an outlet for her early sensation stories.[7]

Those stories set the pattern for much of Alcott's work that followed during the 1860s. The use of sources from her life and from literature in "Marion Earle" is discernible in her later thrillers. So too is the feminist theme, whether expressed in the strong, powerful, passionate heroine who frequently wins in the power struggle with men, or in the insistence upon sisterhood that appears in "Marion Earle." Especially Alcott's fascination with the theater is traceable in many later narratives where the heroine is an actress either on stage or in life. The gallery led by Marion Earle includes Virginie Varens of "V. V.," Jean Muir of "Behind a Mask," Clotilde of "A Double Tragedy," and Natalie of "La Jeune." While none of these later creations can vie in saintly self-denial with Marion Earle, they all represent phases of the theatrical life and reflect their author's devotion to the footlights.[8]

Long after Alcott had abandoned the sensational genre for the domestic and, following the success of *Little Women, An Old-Fashioned Girl,* and *Little Men,* had become the most popular American "youth's companion," an anonymous story appeared in *Demorest's Monthly Magazine* for April 1876 entitled "Only an Actress." For many years scholars, recalling that title as listed in her 1858 memoranda, assumed that the *Demorest* story was Alcott's. Now the record must be corrected. The anonymous "Only an Actress" in *Demorest's* in 1876 is an altogether different tale from "Marion Earle; or, Only an Actress!" and must be expunged from the Alcott canon. It is possible, however, that although she did not write the narrative, Alcott did read it, attracted by the title that doubtless reminded her of her own early experiment. Shortly after its publication in *Demorest's,* on 29 June 1876, Alcott wrote a letter to Lucy Stone in which she quoted the following lines:

> Earth's fanatics make
> Too often Heaven's saints.[9]

The quotation is from Elizabeth Barrett Browning's *Aurora Leigh.* Had a complex association of ideas carried Alcott back, via her own "Only an Actress," to the long Browning poem?

In any event, now that Alcott's "Marion Earle" has at last been discovered, there is no question that the author of *Little Women* began her forays into sensationalism early in her career, and that—like most writers aiming at professionalism—she mingled in them the products of a gaudy imagination, episodes from her life, and suggestions from her reading.

1. For details of Alcott's life, see Madeleine B. Stern, *Louisa May Alcott* (Norman: University of Oklahoma Press, 1985).

2. *The Journals of Louisa May Alcott*, ed. Joel Myerson, Daniel Shealy, and Madeleine B. Stern (Boston: Little, Brown, 1989), 89.

3. Ibid., 90.

4. Ibid., 92.

5. The original discoverer of Alcott's connection with Elliott, Thomes and Talbot, and of her pseudonymous thrillers, is Leona Rostenberg. She quotes Elliott's letter from the originals in the Houghton Library at Harvard University in her "Some Anonymous and Pseudonymous Thrillers of Louisa M. Alcott," reprinted in this collection.

6. *Journals of LMA*, 96.

7. For the *American Union*, see *American Union* (23 September 1854, 15 March 1856, 10 March 1861), copies in New-York Historical Society; Boston Directories, 1855–1862, whose listings indicate that Graves and Weston published the *American Union* through 1860, after which Elliott and Thomes became publishers; *Freaks of Genius: Unknown Thrillers of Louisa May Alcott*, ed. Daniel Shealy, Madeleine B. Stern, and Joel Myerson (Westport, Conn.: Greenwood Press, 1991), 2–3; Madeleine B. Stern, *Imprints on History: Book Publishers and American Frontiers* (Bloomington: Indiana University Press, 1956), 209 f. (The writer is most grateful to Mr. Charles W. Mann, Chief, Rare Books and Special Collections, Penn State University Libraries, for a photocopy of Alcott's "Marion Earle; or, Only an Actress!" from the *New York Atlas*.)

8. For these stories, see *Behind a Mask: The Unknown Thrillers of Louisa May Alcott*, ed. Madeleine B. Stern (New York: William Morrow, 1975); *A Double Life: Newly Discovered Thrillers of Louisa May Alcott*, ed. Madeleine B. Stern, Joel Myerson, and Daniel Shealy (Boston: Little, Brown, 1988); *Freaks of Genius: Unknown Thrillers of Louisa May Alcott*, ed. Daniel Shealy, Madeleine B. Stern, and Joel Myerson; and *Plots and Counterplots: More Unknown Thrillers of Louisa May Alcott*, ed. Madeleine B. Stern (New York: William Morrow, 1976).

9. *The Selected Letters of Louisa May Alcott*, ed. Joel Myerson, Daniel Shealy, and Madeleine B. Stern (Boston: Little, Brown, 1987), 217–18 and 218 n. 1. (The writer is indebted to Victor A. Berch for supplying a photocopy of the anonymous "Only an Actress" from *Demorest's Monthly Magazine*. Her gratitude to him is profound.)

Blood-and-Thunder

Some Anonymous and Pseudonymous Thrillers of Louisa M. Alcott

Leona Rostenberg

When Jo March, dressed in her best, entered the office of the *Weekly Volcano* she found herself confronted by three men "sitting with their heels rather higher than their hats" and smoking long black cigars. Jo had come to offer her latest thriller to the condescending Mr. Dashwood and his partners, the editors of the *Weekly Volcano*.

How exactly Louisa M. Alcott has revealed her experiences and tribulations as a writer of sensational fiction in *Little Women* cannot be determined. Nevertheless there is sufficient indication that in reality she had aspired as Jo, had known the counterparts of the critical Mr. Dashwood and his associates, and had seen the pages of an authentic *Weekly Volcano* emblazoned with her thrillers.

Although Alcott during the early years of her literary career contributed to the popular Boston *Saturday Evening Gazette* and the proud young *Atlantic Monthly,* she did not disdain publications of lesser repute. By 1862 she wrote regularly for *Frank Leslie's Illustrated Newspaper,* a small folio journal selling at ten cents a copy, replete with alluring pictures, New York gossip, murder trials, and ringside bouts. Leslie considered her tales "so dramatic, vivid and full of plot"[1] that he announced her anonymous story "Pauline's Passion and Punishment," appearing in January 1863, as a prize winner.[2] Her tale "Enigmas" was published in the May issues of 1864.[3] In Alcott's opinion this thriller was much liked by readers of "sensation rubbish, but having gotten my fifty dollars I was resigned."[4] By her own admission, however, Louisa Alcott enjoyed writing tales injected with the "lurid" not only because of the lucrative rewards, which she sorely needed, but because of "her passion for wild adventurous life and even melodramatic action."[5] The realization that the publication of her stories in Leslie's paper and others of such character would not enhance her reputation may have induced her "resignation." Despite this attitude, "Enigmas" was not to be her last tale of blood and thunder.

Shrouded in pseudonymity, Louisa Alcott's stories appeared during the sixties in the Boston penny dreadful *The Flag of Our Union*. Founded by Fred Gleason in 1842 and later sold to the enterprising Maturin Murray Ballou, this weekly in 1863 passed into the hands of James R. Elliott, William H. Thomes, and Newton Talbot, the first two of whom had worked with Leslie for Gleason's publications.[6] Of the three partners the best known is William H. Thomes, author of several successful adventure stories. Originally from Portland, he drifted to Boston and took to sea during the early forties. Back in Boston and ready for new adventure, he formed the Boston and California Joint Stock Mining Company, whose members were "to take their Bibles in one hand and their great New England civilization in the other and conquer all wickedness that stood in their path."[7] Thomes appears to have conquered neither wickedness nor the West, for he was back in Boston in 1857 to become a reporter for the *Herald* until 1860.[8] The following year he associated himself with James R. Elliott as co-publisher of the *American Union* with offices at 100 Washington Street.[9] Prior to his partnership with Thomes, Elliott had published *The True Flag* with W. U. Moulton and M. V. Lincoln.[10] It appears that with the transfer of *The Flag of Our Union* to Elliott and Thomes, Talbot, who had worked as cashier for the Ballou publications, decided to continue his connections and hence became the third partner in 1863.[11]

The firm, located first at 118 Washington Street and later at 63 Congress Street, issued not only *The Flag of Our Union* but other former cheap Ballou periodicals: the *Dollar Monthly*, the *Monthly Novelette*, and the *American Union*. Among their contributors were the popular Sylvanus Cobb, Jr., Francis Durivage, Rochester and Amanda Hale, whose stories bristled with tales of the South Seas, mulattos, banishment, love, and crime. *The Flag of Our Union*, which Gleason claimed enjoyed a circulation of one hundred thousand and brought its owner a yearly income of twenty-five thousand dollars, had increased from four to sixteen pages under Elliott's management.[12] Although it originally prided itself on containing no advertisements, it now brought to the public's attention the soothing properties of Redding's Russia Salve and Wistar's Balsam. Under the direction of Elliott, Thomes and Talbot the annual subscription rate had risen from two to four dollars. It was described by the editors as the "Best Literary Journal" with a corps of contributors embracing "The Best Writers in the Country."

Alcott's contributions to *The Flag*, tales of violence and revenge peopled with convicts and opium addicts, appeared anonymously, and pseudonymously as the products of A. M. Barnard. This name may have been suggested either by fancy or a chain of associations. The *A* may have been derived from any one of the family names, Amos, Abba, or Anna. The *M* more than likely represented her mother's maiden name, May, also Louisa Alcott's middle name. Her father claimed Henry Barnard, the Connecticut schoolmaster, as a close friend, and the suitability of this surname may have attracted his inspired daughter. Louisa Alcott's choice of a pseudonym for her stories in *The Flag* again betrays her own attitude toward the penny dreadfuls and her own thrillers. Although Elliott had written to her that *The Flag* was "a literary paper that none need to blush for, and a credit to contribute to its columns, rather than otherwise," Alcott was unwilling to risk a reputation already founded upon *Flower Fables* and *Hospital Sketches*.[13] Since she permitted poems to appear under her own name, it would seem that she did not altogether condemn the periodical but was loath to link her name with the sensational stories she had contributed. Elliott, however, did not fully share her attitude. He was eager for her stories to appear under her own name but consented to her pseudonym "A. M. Barnard, or 'any other man' " with which she wished "to father" her tales as long as she would contribute to his publications.[14]

The exact number of stories written by Louisa Alcott for *The Flag of Our Union* and their dates of appearance cannot be accurately determined at the present time. The most complete run of this periodical, owned by the Library of Congress, has now been stored away for safekeeping, with the result that a thorough investigation of the stories by A. M. Barnard is now impossible. The 1865 issues owned by the Boston Public Library and the few odd numbers at the Widener Library have contributed to the identification of three works and have corroborated Alcott's choice of the pseudonym A. M. Barnard.

In a letter of 5 January 1865 Elliott referred to the coming publication of Alcott's story "V. V.; or, Plots and Counterplots," which was to appear in *The Flag* "By a Well Known Author" in four installments during February 1865.[15] Elliott remarked that he intended to print it in *The Flag* "in place of publishing it as a novelette in cheap style." Had Alcott consented to the use of her own name the story would have brought her an additional twenty-five dollars.[16] It appears either that Elliott decided to return to his original plan of issuing "V. V." in novelette form or that the tale enjoyed considerable popularity, for the firm published it also as a ten-cent novelette in their series of Standard American Authors. Hence it appeared in octavo size, one hundred pages in length, and bound in blue wrappers bearing the caption "V. V. By A. M. Barnard complete" centered with a medallion on the front cover. According to the Union Catalogue there is only one copy of this publication in an American library, which is catalogued in the New York Public Library under the name of A. M. Barnard.[17]

That Elliott was satisfied with the suitability of "V. V." for *The Flag* is indicated in a letter of 7 January 1865, in which he begged for additional material. "I should be pleased to have you write me some stories for the Flag, of about 25 to 40 pages of such MS. as 'V. V.' " Again he entreated her to have the story appear under her own name. According to Elliott, the offer of sixteen dollars would equal the price paid for a first-page story by the *American Union* to which he believed Miss Alcott had formerly contributed.[18] In the same letter he requested a poem or two for *The Flag*. A postscript adds, "I will purchase another novelette of you at any time you may wish to dispose of one."[19] A letter addressed to Alcott two weeks later reiterates the same request. "You may send me anything in either the sketch or novelette line that you do not wish to 'father', or that you wish A. M. Barnard, or 'any other man' to be responsible for, & if they suit me I will purchase them." He now promised three dollars a column run inside length for sketches written under her own name.[20] Although Miss Alcott's published journal makes no reference to Elliott's repeated demands, she accepted his offer since her story, "A Marble Woman, or The Mysterious Model, A Novel of Absorbing Interest by A. M. Barnard, Author of V. V. or Plots and

Counterplots" appeared in *The Flag* in four installments from 20 May to 10 June 1865.[21] Elliott's proposal of "a poem or two" "under your own name" was also met, since her poems, "In the Garret" and "The Sanitary Fair," appeared in March and April 1865.[22]

Miss Alcott's facility in dashing off these saleable thrillers stimulated Elliott's desire for additional material. In a letter of June 1865 he asked for another sensation story of about 145 to 150 pages, "such MSS. as your last 'The Marble Woman' so that I can have it by the middle of July."[23] Intensely eager now for her stories, he had become less insistent about her identity and did not care about the use of "*any* particular name, if you prefer any other nome [*sic*] de plume . . . use it, as it is for one of my cheap novelettes."[24] Although he appeared to be indifferent to her choice of a pseudonym, there is some indication that he had boasted the author of "A Marble Woman" and Louisa M. Alcott to be one. In a somewhat apologetic tone to the irate author he regretted that she should have any feeling with regard to her nom de plume. "I am sure that I have not given currency to the idea that 'A. M. Barnard' & yourself were identical."[25]

There is no proof that Elliott had turned a journalistic Judas, but there is indication that his enthusiasm for Alcott's thrillers had not waned during her year's absence abroad. From July 1865 to July 1866 she traveled in Europe, strolling along the shores of Lake Leman, sailing at Vevey, where she met her golden-haired Laurie, quite unmindful of the weekly issues of *The Flag of Our Union*.

A diary entry written shortly after her return at the beginning of August 1866 refers for the first time to Elliott as "E."; "Found plenty to do as orders from E[lliott] and L[eslie] . . . waited for me."[26] She apparently set to work immediately and completed within a short time "Behind a Mask," which appeared in *The Flag* after 11 August 1866.[27] In Elliott's opinion this was a story of peculiar power. "[I] have no doubt but my readers will be quite as much fascinated with it as I was myself while reading the Ms."[28] He now offered the fairly popular author sixty-five dollars for this story and five dollars for each poem signed "by *Miss Alcott*," asking for another thriller to be ready by the twentieth of September.[29] His offer of sixty-five dollars was apparently rejected, since Alcott's journal for the period states that she received seventy-five dollars from E. for a story as well as five dollars for a poem.[30]

Elliott's demand for another story for 20 September was also met. Alcott writes, "E. . . . wanted a long story in 24 chapters and I wrote it in a fortnight 125 pages."[31] Apparently in her fervor she had not realized that even *The Flag of Our Union* had set certain limits to the sensational character of its contributions, for much to her own surprise she records in September 1866, "E. would not have it saying it was too long and too sensational."[32] But A. M. Barnard was not to be balked. She curbed her passion somewhat for the too bloody and the too thunderous and submitted another tale, "The Abbot's Ghost, or, Maurice Treherne's Temptation," the last installment of which is to be found in *The Flag of Our Union* of 26 January 1867.[33]

It cannot be determined at the present whether other of Louisa Alcott's stories appeared in later issues of *The Flag of Our Union*. With the publication of *Little Women* in October 1868, Alcott could have easily afforded to sever all association with A. M. Barnard. To Jo now was relegated the task of submitting her thrillers to the firm of Dashwood and Company. It was her progenitor who could now smile with some sympathy at her heroine's sallies into the domain of blood and thunder and who could recall, perhaps with some reluctance, the career of A. M. Barnard, successful contributor to penny dreadfuls.

FIVE LETTERS FROM JAMES R. ELLIOTT TO LOUISA M. ALCOTT

I

Journal Building, 118 Washington Street, Boston
Jan. 5. 1865

Louisa M. Alcott
Dear Madam,

I forward you this evening the 3 first copies of the "Flag" in its new form. I think it is now a literary paper that none need to blush for, and a credit to contribute to its columns, rather than otherwise.

Now I have a proposition to make you. I want to publish your story "V. V." in it, in place of publishing it as a novelette in cheap style, as I had intended, and will give you $25. more for the story provided I can publish it under your own name.

Please look the "Flag" over & let me know as early as Saturday & oblige

Very Truly Yours
J. R. Elliott
Editor

II

118 Washington Street, Jan. 7. 1865

Dear Miss Alcott,

I should be pleased to have you write me some stories for the Flag, of about 25 to 40 pages of such MS. as "V. V." I want them over your own name of course, & will give you $2.00 a column (short columns you will notice) for them. That rate will be fully equal to $16.00 for a first page story in the "American Union" which paper I think you contributed to while it was under the management of Messrs. Graves & Weston. Will you not contribute a poem or two for the "Flag" also? I do not know as that is in your line, if it is I shall be glad to recieve [*sic*] poems from your pen. I have entered your name on our *gratis* list & you will receive the "Flag" regularly.

Very Truly Yours
J. R. Elliott

P. S. I will purchase another novelette of you at any time you may wish to dispose of one. "V. V." will be commenced in No. 5 about two week[s]. What title would you suggest in place of "V. V.?" Or what for a second title? Please answer at your earliest convenience.　J. R. E.

III

Boston Jan. 21, 1865

Dear Miss Alcott

You may send me anything in either the sketch or novelette line that you do not wish to "father", or that you wish A. M. Barnard, or "any other man" to be responsible for, & if they suit me I will purchase them. I will pay for poems under your own name. Also I will give you $3.00 per column (run in inside length) for sketches under your own name. Let me hear from you.

Very Truly Yours
J. R. Elliott

IV

63 Congress Street, June 15, 1865

Dear Miss Alcott,

Have you written anything in the novel line you would like to have me publish "by A. M. Barnard, author of "V. V.", "The Marble Woman", & c. & c.? If not can you furnish me with a sensation story of about 145 to 150 pages such MSS. as your last "The Marble Woman" so that I can have it by the middle of July? I dont care about even *any* particular name, if you prefer any other nome de plume for that one story use it, as it is for one of my cheap novelettes.

I will give you $50. for such a story, & don't want it to exceed 150 pages of MSS. the size of "The Marble Woman,"—140 pages will answer, or 145 will be better. By the way my friends think the "Marble Woman" is just splendid; & *I* think no author of novels need be ashamed to own it for a bantling. I am sorry you should have had any feeling in regard to the nome de plume. I am sure that I have not given currency to the idea that "A. M. Barnard" & yourself were identical.

Please let me hear from you by return mail, if possible, in regard to the short novel.

Very Truly Yours
J. R. Elliott

V

63 Congress Street, Aug. 11, 1866

Dear Miss Alcott

The story entitled "Behind a Mask" is accepted. I think it a story of peculiar power, and have no doubt but my readers will be quite as much fascinated with it as I was myself while reading the Ms. I will give you $65. for it. That amounts awaits your order.

I should like another by the 20th of September. Can I have one? I sh'd be happy to pay you $5. each for two or three poems by *Miss Alcott.*

Very Truly Yours
J. R. Elliott

NOTES

1. Ednah D. Cheney, ed., *Louisa May Alcott: Her Life, Letters, and Journals* (Boston, 1920), 131. Hereinafter "Cheney."

2. A letter written by Leslie's editor, E. George Squier, is dated 18 December 1862: "My Dear Madame, Your tale 'Pauline' this morning was awarded the $100 prize for the best short tale for Mr. Leslie's newspaper, and you will hear from him in due course in reference to what you may regard as an essential part of the matter. I presume that it will be on hand for those little Christmas purchases. Allow me to congratulate you on your success and to recommend you to submit whatever you may hereafter have of the same sort for Mr. Leslie's acceptance. Truly yr. obdt. servant. E. G. Squier." MS in Orchard House, Concord. Alcott writes in April 1863: "Received $100 from F. L. for a tale which won the prize last January." Cheney, 151. "Pauline's Passion and Punishment" appeared in *Leslie's Illustrated Newspaper* 15, nos. 379 and 380 (3 and 10 January 1863).

3. *Frank Leslie's Illustrated Newspaper* 18, nos. 450 and 451 (14 and 21 May 1864).

4. Cheney, 158. The prize was really one hundred dollars, not fifty dollars.

5. Ibid., 63, 105.

6. Frank Luther Mott, *A History of American Magazines from 1741 to 1885*, vol. 2 (New York, 1930–38), 31, 35, 36, 64, 411.

7. For an account of Thomes's western adventures and literary activity, see George R. Stewart, *Take Your Bible in One Hand: The Life of William Henry Thomes* (San Francisco, 1939).

8. Boston Directories, 1858–60.

9. Ibid., 1861.

10. Ibid., 1858–60.

11. Ibid., 1858–62.

12. George W. Browne, "Pioneers of 'Popular Literature,' " *Granite State Magazine* 3, no. 2 (February 1907).

13. See Letter I, 5 January 1865. Letters from Louisa M. Alcott MSS, Box II, Houghton Library. Letters I–V are included at the end of this chapter.

14. Letter III, 21 January 1865.

15. *Flag of Our Union* 20, no. 5 (4 February 1865): 73–75; no. 6 (11 February 1865): 88–91; no. 7 (18 February 1865): 105–7; no. 8 (25 February 1865): 121–23.

16. Letter I.

17. "V. V." was copyrighted by Thomes & Talbot in 1865. *The Flag* had a special column under the heading of "Ten Cent Novelettes" advertising these cheap thrillers. To date, the announcement of "V. V." has not been traced. It is listed, however, as number 80 on the novelette cover. Two later thrillers by Alcott, appearing under her own name, were published in this series. *The Skeleton in the Closet*, included in Perley Parker's *The Foundling*, pp. 77–99, was issued in November 1867 as number 49, and *The Mysterious Key* followed as number 50 in December 1867. There is one copy of the former work in a private collection; of the latter there are three known copies, the deposit copy in the Library of Congress and two in private collections.

18. Letter II, 7 January 1865. *American Union*, a four-page periodical, had been purchased from Graves and Weston by Ballou, from whom Elliott and Thomes bought it in 1861.

19. Letter II.

20. Letter III.

21. *The Flag of Our Union* 20, no. 20 (20 May 1865): 313–15; no. 21 (27 May 1865): 329–30; no. 22 (3 June 1865): 345–47; no. 23 (10 June 1865): 361–64.

22. Both poems appeared under Alcott's own name in *The Flag of Our Union* 20, no. 11 (18 March 1865): 166, and no. 16 (22 April 1865): 254.

23. Letter IV, 15 June 1865.

24. Ibid.

25. Ibid.

26. August 1866, Cheney, 184.

27. Letter V, 11 August 1866.

28. Ibid.

29. Ibid.

30. August 1866: "One [tale] for E. for which he paid $75, also a bit of poetry for $5." Cheney, 184.

31. Ibid.

32. Ibid., 185.

33. "The Abbot's Ghost, or Maurice Treherne's Temptation. A Christmas Story by A. M. Barnard, Author of 'V. V.,' 'A Marble Woman,' 'Behind A Mask,' etc. etc." appeared in *The Flag* 27, no. 4 (26 January 1867).

Five Letters
That Changed
an Image

Leona Rostenberg and Madeleine B. Stern

PART ONE: LEONA ROSTENBERG

The story is not mine—it belongs to Madeleine Stern, who wrote such a capital biography of Louisa May Alcott. On one occasion, however, I enjoyed a small part of the research for that life and shared with Madeleine the excitement of the discovery of Louisa Alcott's thrillers. In pursuit of the material for her biography my partner left no source, no place, no related individual unmolested. She delved into archives and pursued collectors in the field.

Among the latter was the charming, urbane Carroll A. Wilson of Horatio Street, New York City, who invited Madeleine—with me in tow—to examine his Alcott manuscripts and books. And so we hied to Horatio Street, enjoying an evening of rich Alcottiana and the person of Carroll Wilson. Madeleine noted his many observations on this remarkable lady from Concord and listened most attentively to an indirect Alcott remark: "I think, Miss Stern, you should go ahead and get a Guggenheim Fellowship and finish your biography of Louisa Alcott." Later in the evening he turned to me: "Miss Rostenberg, I know you are deeply interested in the history of printing and publishing and its various facets. There are some indications that Louisa Alcott wrote some short thrillers either anonymously or pseudonymously. You go ahead and find them."

We both heeded Mr. Wilson's injunctions. Madeleine Stern received a Guggenheim fellowship, and during a spell of research on the life of Louisa I discovered a small cache of letters that would provide a bombshell for the American literary world and change for many the image of that excellent author of *Little Women*.

I had taken a brief leave of absence from my work in rare books to help Madeleine with her research on the Alcott family papers housed at Houghton Library, Harvard University. Madeleine had already done considerable research on the biography and I, fired by Carroll Wilson's remarks about the possibility of her thrillers, wondered whether any evidence of their existence would now emerge. We knew that his conjecture was quite possible. Had not Jo, Louisa's counterpart in *Little Women*, written for the *Weekly Volcano* and the *Blarneystone Banner?* Were there not allusions to several mysterious initials "L" and "E" in her journal? And did not the same source supply hints about sensational stories plied by her pen? Were "L" and "E" possibly publishers to whom she sent such stories? My head whirled with the possibility that the clues to publishers and stories lurked in the Alcott manuscript material at Houghton.

It was a bright April morning in 1943 when we sat next to each other within the quiet and academic hush of Houghton. Before us were stacked cartons of Alcottiana emitting the mustiness of the past, the redolence of another age. On the second day of our research I picked up a small packet of letters. Opening the first I read: "118 Washington Street, Boston, Jan. 5. 1865, Louisa M. Alcott, Dear Madam." The letter was signed "J. R. Elliott, Editor." My eyes swept the page. My mind immediately reverted to the letter *E* in the journal. Was I about to solve the mystery of L.M.A.'s thrillers? Was I to prove Carroll Wilson's surmise and attain the success of my mission?

I reread the letter. It contained three clues to an unknown thriller by Louisa Alcott: the name of the periodical, *The Flag of Our Union*, the identity of the publisher, and the title of the story.

The academic hush of Houghton Library was suddenly disturbed by a barbaric yawp. Madeleine looked up at my unseemly behavior, but, as she glanced at the letter I handed her, she was too dazed to emulate my raucous behavior. With fast-beating heart and a somewhat shaky hand, I picked up the second letter, dated 7 January 1865 from J. R. Elliott to "Dear Miss Alcott." I did not take time to show this letter to my partner. In a state of ebullience I began to read letter 3. Dated, "Boston January 21, 1865," it was addressed to "Dear Miss Alcott." I could scarcely believe what I had read. *L.M.A. is A. M. Barnard.* I nudged Madeleine. I had become a proven literary sleuth, my prize almost netted.

Upon reading letter 4 I noticed that J. R. Elliott had moved from Washington Street to 63 Congress Street. Had business so prospered now that he had "A. M. Barnard" in his stable? This lengthiest and most revealing letter to Louisa Alcott is dated 15 June 1865.

I sat back and mused. The author of *Little Women,* the "Children's Friend," had written "V. V.," "The Marble Woman," and in all likelihood other sensational stories. I rather limply took up the last letter in the batch.

I had indeed netted a very big catch. I had proved Carroll Wilson's conjecture beyond a doubt. Louisa Alcott had written sensational stories anonymously and pseudonymously. What other similar tales had she written—some the property of J. R. Elliott and other publishers of cheap periodicals? I reread the letters. I was the first person to meet A. M. Barnard, to become acquainted with a new Louisa who had abandoned the repose and propriety of Concord to seek another world peopled with villains, vengeful women, blood, and violence.

Unable to stand the quiet any longer and frantic to show Madeleine my copies of the letters, I suggested we have lunch. The biographer of Louisa Alcott read the material utterly transfixed. "Fantastic," she murmured, "you will have to write it up."

During our researches, the discovery of another letter had resulted in the identification of the mysterious "Mr. L" of Louisa's journal and of another periodical for which she had produced her thrillers. In 1862 the young woman from Concord had won a prize of one hundred dollars for a story, "Pauline's Passion and Punishment," which ran in *Leslie's Weekly.*

Louisa, apparently emboldened by her success, looked to wider fields and submitted the vivid stories of her fertile imagination to "E" of *The Flag.* The future author of *Little Women* then became the spinner of popular gothics for this Boston periodical.

And so that small batch of letters from James R. Elliott had disclosed a Louisa Alcott insisting upon anonymity or pseudonymity for her contributions to a Boston penny dreadful. Moreover, it had disclosed the pseudonym and titles of some of her stories that later research traced and identified. Following her effusion for Frank Leslie, between 1865 and 1867 the author had contributed to *The Flag of Our Union* or Elliott's series of Ten Cent Novelettes, these delectable titles: "V.V.; or, Plots and Counterplots By a Well Known Author"; "A Marble Woman; or, the Mysterious Model by A. M. Barnard"; "Behind a Mask; or, A Woman's Power by A. M. Barnard"; "The Abbot's Ghost; or, Maurice Treherne's Temptation by A. M. Barnard"; "The Skeleton in the Closet"; and "The Mysterious Key, and What It Opened."

Having thoroughly digested my Houghton find, I wrote an article, "Some Anonymous and Pseudonymous Thrillers of Louisa M. Alcott," which appeared in the *Papers of the Bibliographical Society of America* in October 1943. Carroll Wilson was pleased and the scholarly world raised its eyebrows. But the denouement of the find had not yet taken place. That part of the story was Madeleine Stern's.

PART TWO: MADELEINE B. STERN

During the next thirty years, Leona Rostenberg's startling revelation made in the *Papers of the Bibliographical Society of America* filtered through the scholarly community—filtered, but did not percolate. The disclosure did, as we shall see, make some difference in Alcott criticism, and hence altered to some extent the image of the creative artist Louisa May Alcott. But, although it was now proven that the "Children's Friend" had indeed written thrillers in her salad days, the precise nature of those thrillers could not be appreciated since the narratives themselves had never been reprinted. They still remained buried in the now crumbling folio sheets that had rolled from the garish presses of Frank Leslie and Elliott, Thomes and Talbot during the 1860s.

Then, one climactic morning in the 1970s, I awoke with a brainstorm. Practically the entire world of print had been subjected to the onslaught of the reprinters-but never those Alcott thrillers. I decided to ferret them out and make them public. And so, from the files of those nineteenth-century lurid story papers in the New York Public Library and the New-York Historical Society, Harvard's Houghton Library and the American Antiquarian Society, the Rare Book Division of the Library of Congress and the University of Virginia's Alderman Library, I gathered together nine of the tales imagined by an experimenting author from Concord, Massachusetts, before her emergence as the "Children's Friend." Four were published by William Morrow on 1 July 1975 under the title of *Behind a Mask: The Unknown Thrillers of Louisa May Alcott;* the remaining five were published precisely one year later by the same house under the title of *Plots and Counterplots: More Unknown Thrillers of Louisa May Alcott.*

Listen, briefly, to the opening lines of the first published thriller that can be assigned to Louisa Alcott. This is the one that won the prize of one hundred dollars from *Frank Leslie's Illustrated Newspaper* where it ran in two successive installments on 3 and 10 January 1863. Its title is "Pauline's Passion and Punishment," and it appeared anonymously:

> To and fro, like a wild creature in its cage, paced that handsome woman, with bent head, locked hands, and restless steps. Some mental storm, swift and sudden as a tempest of the tropics, had swept over her and left its marks behind. As if in anger at the beauty now proved powerless, all ornaments had been flung away, yet still it shone undimmed, and filled her with a passionate regret. A jewel glittered at her feet, leaving the lace rent to shreds on the indignant bosom that had worn it; the wreaths of hair that had crowned her with a woman's most womanly adornment fell disordered upon shoulders that gleamed the fairer for the scarlet of the pomegranate flowers clinging to the bright meshes that had imprisoned them an hour ago; and over the face, once so affluent in youthful bloom, a stern pallor had fallen like a blight, for pride was slowly conquering passion, and despair had murdered hope.

This, then, is Pauline of the "Passion and Punishment": a proud and passionate woman who has lost all—fortune, and, as a result of one man's perfidy, love. She is left—in the opening paragraph—with her fury and her desire for revenge, emotions that become the motivating forces in an ironic plot. Scorned by her lover, she arouses the devotion of the young southern romantic Manuel, who, attracted by her implicit sexuality, becomes not only her husband but her accomplice in the intended destruction of her lover. That destruction is not envisioned as murder but as some more subtle revenge: "There are fates more terrible than death, weapons more keen than poniards, more noiseless than pistols. . . . Leave Gilbert to remorse—and me." And so, on page 1 of her thriller, the already skillful author has sketched in her characters, spotlighted her heroine, set her tropical scene, and triggered her suspenseful plot.

What of the other stories that poured from the Alcott inkstand between 1863, when the first thriller appeared, and 1869, when part 2 of *Little Women* was published? There were "A Whisper in the Dark," an anonymous Leslie story revolving around mind control, and "V.V.; or, Plots and Counterplots," the devastating narrative of an evil, manipulating heroine, Virginie Varens, part sylph and femme fatale, part viper and Machiavelli, whose devices included poison inside an opal and drugged coffee. Her "plots and counterplots," over the byline of "A Well Known Author," were all unraveled for readers of *The Flag of Our Union*, where at the end, in an ultimate triumph, V.V. escapes from her punishment, standing forth as the most Mephistophelian of the Alcott heroines.

Other, similar heroines appeared in the oeuvre of the future "Children's Friend." In the best of the thrillers, "Behind a Mask; or, A Woman's Power," for which the author used the pseudonym of A. M. Barnard, heroine Jean Muir is, like V.V., many things—a woman bent upon revenge, a woman filled with feminist fury directed against the male lords of creation, an actress, a fascinating flirt, a woman with a mysterious past—in short, a psychological if not a Gothic witch, who, proud and passionate, mysterious and mocking, wields a subtle spell. Indeed, her story was in 1983 dramatized and performed to small but enthralled audiences off Broadway.

The roster of dark, delicious, delectable dramas continued during the 1860s with "A Marble Woman; or, The Mysterious Model," "The Abbot's Ghost; or, Maurice Treherne's Temptation," "The Skeleton in the Closet," "The Mysterious Key, and What It Opened," and, the last of the thrillers, the brief but startling shocker, "Perilous Play," which illuminated in the pages of Leslie's "Great Family Paper of America" the delights of that "Indian stuff which brings one fantastic visions"—hashish.

In all the Alcott thrillers the themes are shocking indeed to readers who know Louisa Alcott only as the "Children's Friend." To enumerate them briefly, we find in the sizzling pages of these narratives manipulative heroines and mind control, madness, child-brides and a hint at incest, hashish experimentation and opium addiction. Especially we find the manipulating heroine whose feminist fury is launched, usually with success, against an antifeminist world.

When the gruesome Alcott gothics were reprinted in the 1970s, they naturally raised eyebrows. The fact that the author of the Little Women series had once sat at her desk, an old green and red party wrap draped around her as a "glory cloak," dipped her pen into gall, and produced a succession of shockers that chilled the blood sat uneasily with many who remembered Louisa Alcott only as the mother of *Little Women.* Now, Louisa Alcott's own mask had been removed. Her motivations—partly economic, partly psychological—had been exposed. The riotous imagination, the dramatic instinct, the increasing narrative skill, and of course the indefatigable right hand had resulted in a corpus of suspenseful page-turners as surprising as they were, in a sense, revolutionary. For, once the mask had been removed, a new image began to emerge—the image of a many-sided human being, a multifaceted writer with a complex mind, an author as familiar with the macabre attractions of opium and hashish as she was with the wholesome pleasures of apples and ginger cookies.

In short, the reputation of the author of *Little Women* underwent a metamorphosis. She was becoming more than a writer of juveniles; she was emerging as an author of stature whose experimenting pen had delved into the varieties of the creative experience.

In *Critical Essays on Louisa M. Alcott*[1] the changing reputation and the increasing stature of Louisa May Alcott becomes clearly apparent. The altered, more complex image that she now presents to the world of scholarship and literary criticism is largely due to the discovery and belated reprinting of the Alcott thrillers. No longer can her work be dismissed as "agreeable sketches . . . adapted to the capacity of intelligent young persons," or, as part 1 of *Little Women* was described in 1868, as "an agreeable little story. . . . The girls depicted all belong to healthy types." Ah, no. Now the critical apparatus based upon the Alcott oeuvre includes such disquisitions as "Does *Little Women* Belittle Women?" by Stephanie Harrington; "Money, Job, Little Women: Female Realism" by Ellen Moers; "*Little Women:* Alcott's Civil War" by Judith Fetterley; "Beneath the Surface: Power and Passion in *Little Women*" by Madelon Bedell; "Subversive Miss Alcott" by Elizabeth Vincent; "When the Little Angels Revolted" by Mildred Adams.[2] Louisa Alcott has been compared with Jane Austen, Horatio Alger, and D. H. Lawrence. Her literary use of Henry David Thoreau has been investigated; Henry

James's comments upon her have been dissected. Her greatest character, Jo March, has been analyzed as male model and female person; her own persona has been almost clinically cross-sectioned in a study by Jane Van Buren entitled "Louisa May Alcott: A Study in Persona and Idealization," which perceives Alcott as suffering "an existential crisis of non-being" that imposed upon her the "total separation of the sentimental and the Gothic genres."

It is true that even before the reprinting of the thrillers Louisa Alcott had begun to be reassessed, but it should be remembered that that reassessment took place, for the most part, after Leona Rostenberg had proved the fact that the thrillers existed. Once they had been reprinted, the floodgate was opened and the new Alcott criticism assumed its torrential course.

In 1977, Martha Saxton published *Louisa May: A Modern Biography of Louisa May Alcott*,[3] in which Alcott is characterized as a "depressed and sullen . . . withdrawn, hostile introvert" whose childhood, such as it was, was followed by a "miserable and lonely girlhood." Saxton's Alcott is a woman who alternates between "resentment" and "self-inflicted spite," whose "sexual awakening went unnoticed" and whose "sexuality remained a mystery" to her, whose "devils of guilt" vied with her "deep fear of men." To the Freudian overtones in this biography were added *Behind a Mask* undertones, and, unfortunately, in the intention to shock, this modern biographer of Alcott seems to have omitted the life. Nonetheless, the Saxton biography evoked the following remarks from critic Ann Douglas. Writing under the heading of "Mysteries of Louisa May Alcott" in the *New York Review of Books* in September 1978, she stated: "Martha Saxton's recent biography . . . is a major step in the process of reassessment. Her book follows logically upon Madeleine Stern's critical . . . republication of Alcott's lost 'thrillers' written before *Little Women*. Saxton offers a psychological and cultural study of Alcott and her milieu, emphasizing the darker sides of her life and career. Although Alcott is diverse enough to provide material for books very different from Saxton's, Saxton has powerfully delineated what has too long been ignored: the compulsions and fears that both inspired and limited the 'children's friend.' "

And so the revisionists assembled on the bandwagon as the image presented by the "Children's Friend" underwent reconstruction. The creator of feminist heroines in the gothic thrillers was reappraised as creator of a matriarchal domain presided over by Jo March. In comparing *Little Women* with *Pride and Prejudice*, the critic Nina Auerbach in 1978 discovered in *Little Women* "the primacy of the female family, both as moral-emotional magnet and as work of art."[4] And, a year later, Judith Fetterley wrote in "*Little Women*: Alcott's Civil War" that it is "hard to reconcile the authorial image inherent in *Little Women* with the personality capable of the sensational 'Behind a Mask,'" adding: "The work of Stern in identifying and recovering Alcott's sensation fiction provides an important context for the reading of *Little Women* and for an understanding of the implications of its style. . . . Alcott's sensation fiction provides an important gloss on the sexual politics involved in Jo's renunciation of the writing of such fiction and on the sexual politics of Jo's relation with Professor Bhaer under whose influence she gives it up."[5] And, summing up recent revisionist criticism, Fetterley questions Elizabeth Janeway's description of Jo March as "the one young woman in nineteenth-century fiction who maintains her individual independence, who gives up no part of her autonomy as payment for being born a woman—and gets away with it." Rather, she accepts "Alcott's recognition that she must write not about the external world of male power embodied in the Civil War but about the internal world of Jo's struggle between resistance and capitulation to the doctrines of little womanhood"—a recognition that "indicates her understanding of Jo's exclusion from the real sources of power."

The critics are rewriting Louisa Alcott for the scholarly journals and the annual conferences of literary associations. While some of their reassessment is distortion, much of it is long overdue and perfectly valid. The paradoxes of a creative artist equally adept at the sensational and the sentimental, the gothic and the domestic, demanded study. A major gap in the new portrait, however, is a general failure to realize not only that Louisa May Alcott was a more complex human being and a more adventurous writer than had once been supposed, but that she was basically a professional and an experimenter in a wide range of literary genres that took her from fairy tales to realistic war sketches and from gothic shockers to the portrait of a family in *Little Women*.

It is to a great extent due to the discovery and the subsequent reprinting of the nine Alcott sensation tales that Louisa Alcott is being revised by posterity. Her entitlement to a high place in the hierarchy of American writers has at last become apparent. Louisa Alcott's mask has been removed, and from behind that mask she is emerging as a rich and varied writer whose works are becoming increasingly susceptible to productive critical analysis. Although Louisa Alcott was indeed the "Children's Friend," it is now perceived that she was far more. The multifaceted career of this experimenting author is being traced in all its fascinating phases, and the mastery to which it led is being recognized. All this is due, by and large, to the discovery of five short letters from a Boston publishing house to a struggling young author from Concord, Massachusetts, letters that opened up new perceptions and led the way to critical reassessment. Thanks to the notes penned by James R. Elliott around the end of the Civil War, the unmasked "Children's Friend" has become a fertile field for literary exploration. Those five letters may not have changed the world, but they assuredly altered the image, extended the reputation, and increased the stature of our best-loved author of juveniles.

NOTES

1. Madeleine B. Stern, ed., *Critical Essays on Louisa M. Alcott* (Boston: G. K. Hall, 1984).

2. All these essays appeared in ibid.

3. Martha Saxton, *Louisa May: A Modern Biography of Louisa May Alcott* (Boston: Houghton Mifflin, 1977).

4. Nina Auerbach, *Communities of Women: An Idea in Fiction* (Cambridge: Harvard University Press, 1978), reprinted in Stern, ed., *Critical Essays.*

5. Judith Fetterley, "*Little Women:* Alcott's Civil War," *Feminist Studies* (Summer 1979), reprinted in Stern, ed., *Critical Essays.*

Behind

a

Mask

B ehind a Mask: The Unknown Thrillers of Louisa May Alcott[1] has
been 115 years in the making. Its gaudy, gruesome Gothic narratives were written and published during one war, discovered
during another, and just recently republished. If the period of gestation
has anything to do with the quality of the product, then *Behind a Mask*
should be a very good book indeed.

Many of its stories were written against the background of the Civil
War, between Antietam and Appomattox. They were dashed off in
secret by a young woman in her thirties whose equipment included a
riotous imagination, a dramatic instinct, and an indefatigable right
hand. Seated at her desk, an old green and red party wrap draped around
her as a "glory cloak," she dipped her pen into gory ink and produced
shockers that were devoured in the 1860s—tales of jealousy and revenge,
murder and insanity, feminist anger, passion, and punishment.

By the end of that decade, with the publication of part 2 of *Little
Women,* the author of those thrillers would be known to most of the
literate world as the "Children's Friend." She was no children's friend
when she produced "Pauline's Passion and Punishment"; "A Whisper
in the Dark"; "A Marble Woman; or, The Mysterious Model"; "V.V.;
or, Plots and Counterplots"; "The Abbot's Ghost"; "Behind a Mask;
or, A Woman's Power." She was a compulsive writer, churning out
narratives anonymously or pseudonymously—sensational stories that
provided her with a psychological catharsis at the same time that they
filled an economic need. Because she was highly skilled even then, those
stories continue to chill the blood and raise the eyebrows today. Her

secret shockers of the 1860s are now suspenseful page-turners of the 1970s. But they are more than that: they are revelations of a complex mind, a many-sided human being, a multifaceted writer who happened upon fame as Louisa May Alcott.[2]

She was not Louisa May Alcott when she penned these tales. She was "a lady of Massachusetts" or "a Well Known Author" or "A. M. Barnard." When she depicted her proud and passionate heroines— those lush, exotic femmes fatales who manipulated the men they be- guiled—the creator sat incognito behind a mask. Blood-and-thunder tales, she wrote, "are easy to 'compoze' & are better paid than moral & elaborate works of Shakespeare."[3] Eventually she could command two dollars or three dollars a column, a rate that yielded her fifty or sixty- five dollars for a four-part serial.

The money was sorely needed by the Alcott family prior to their transformation into Marches. The four "little women" had grown up not only in the climate of love but in the climate of poverty, for Bronson Alcott had no gift for money-making and the cost of coal, the price of shoes, discussions of ways and means formed an obbligato to Louisa's early years. Later on she was often the only breadwinner in the family.

But it was not economic need alone that was responsible for her blood-and-thunder tales. In these flamboyant narratives Louisa Alcott could give vent to the passions and frustrations of thirty difficult years. In so doing she achieved an emotional catharsis for herself and, in an oblique manner, foreshadowed the angry feminism of a later century.

Her own anger had traceable autobiographical causes. Life in Con- cord, despite the proximity of such illustrissimi as Emerson, Thoreau, and Hawthorne, was far from a haven of sweetness and light. At mid- century the family poverty had never been more extreme, and the Al- cotts, considering that it was better to be earning a living in a city than to be starving in a country paradise, moved temporarily to Boston. There Mrs. Alcott opened an intelligence office at which an elderly gentleman, the Honorable James Richardson, attorney of Dedham, ap- peared one day to apply for a companion to his sister. He painted a roseate scene of his home, its books and flowers, its piano and fine society. The companion would be one of the family, required to help only in the lighter work. When Mrs. Alcott turned to her daughter, asking if she could suggest anyone for the situation, Louisa replied briefly, "Only myself." And so, in 1851, at the age of nineteen, Louisa Alcott went out to service.

Years later she wrote an account of her experience entitled simply "How I Went Out to Service." Had it not been bowdlerized, it would have been entitled "My Humiliation at Dedham." The Richardson home was unfortunately not as it had been represented. The light housework was heavy indeed. And as for the Honorable James Richardson, he plied the young domestic with so many maudlin attentions that Louisa finally delivered an ultimatum: she had come as companion to his sister, not to him. As a result of her strike for independence, all the household work was assigned to her, from digging paths through the snow to fetching water from the well, from splitting the kindling to sifting the ashes. The final degradation was the command to polish the master's boots with the blacking hose—at which Louisa balked. For her seven weeks of drudgery she received four dollars, which the outraged Alcott family promptly returned. There seems little doubt that the experience had lasting effects, that out of her humiliation an anger was born that would express itself both directly and indirectly when she wrote her clandestine stories. Her proud and passionate heroines, many of whom begin their careers as child-brides, are angry women raising fists at the male lords of creation. A goodly portion of the author's own anger was surely generated in Dedham.[4]

Many of A. M. Barnard's heroines entertain thoughts of suicide. A few years after her catastrophic taste of domestic service, Louisa Alcott herself entertained such thoughts. Frustrated in all her attempts to find work—teaching or sewing—she found that her courage had all but failed and as she looked at the waters of the Mill Dam she was tempted to find the solution of her problems in their oblivion. The temptation was evanescent, but it left her with a theme and an understanding. The Temptation at the Mill Dam, like the Humiliation at Dedham, was part of the psychological equipment of a writer of thrillers.

A third episode that provided grist for her mill was the illness Louisa Alcott suffered after she had served six weeks as a nurse during the Civil War. Her severe attack of what was called typhoid pneumonia was accompanied by sinister dreams from which she would awaken unrefreshed. She herself said of them: "The most vivid and enduring was the conviction that I had married a stout, handsome Spaniard,

dressed in black velvet, with very soft hands, and a voice that was con-
tinually saying, 'Lie still, my dear!' . . . the Spanish spouse . . . was
always coming after me, appearing out of closets, in at windows, or
threatening me dreadfully all night long. . . .

"A mob at Baltimore breaking down the door to get me, being hung
for a witch, burned, stoned, and otherwise maltreated, were some of my
fancies. Also being tempted to join Dr. W. and two of the nurses in
worshipping the Devil. Also tending millions of rich men who never
died or got well."[5]

Those dreams—that fevered delirium—would be interwoven into the
fabric of her blood-and-thunders, and so, though they may not be of
interest from a medical standpoint, they are of extreme interest as a
literary source.

Unlike these isolated incidents, there were several abiding strains in
Louisa Alcott that contributed to the pattern of her sensational tales.
One of these was her lifelong devotion to the theater. As a child she
had dreamed of the Ten Dramatic Passions. When she was ten she was
author-director of the Louy Alcott troupe. At fifteen, with her sister
Anna, she wrote and acted in melodramas produced for the neighbors
in the Hillside barn in Concord. Their love scenes and dramatic con-
frontations, their disguises, desertions, and suicides, their magic herbs,
love potions, and death phials could be introduced with subtle varia-
tions for an audience of subscribers to flamboyant weeklies. Much of
her skill in lively dialogue, suspenseful plotting, and broad-stroke character delineation may be traced to Louisa Alcott's persisting romance
with greasepaint. Her addiction to the theater provided both a source
and a training ground for her blood-and-thunders.

So too did her omnivorous reading, especially in the field of fiction.
There is little doubt that she dipped from time to time in the gore of
the Gothic novel, whose ruined abbeys and frowning castles provided
her with background touches, whose romantic language suggested a
phrase here and there, and whose unholy themes introduced her to
pacts with the devil and all sorts of supernatural agencies from ghouls
to ghosts.

By and large, this was the autobiographical background of the Alcott
excursions into nightmarish themes—the sources for the tales of her

imagining. This was the grist for the mill of one who even in the early 1860s was a compulsive writer.

She had been the mainstay of the *Saturday Evening Gazette,* author of *Flower Fables,* contributor to the *Atlantic Monthly.* Her *Hospital Sketches* was to appear in 1863. The woman who would take her pen as her bridegroom had already experimented with varied literary techniques when she commented that blood-and-thunder tales were "easy to 'compoze' & . . . better paid than moral & elaborate works of Shakespeare." For her they were especially easy to compose since, in addition to an abiding fascination for the theater, Louisa Alcott had what she called a "natural ambition . . . for the lurid style." Her father astutely detected in the "elements" of her "temperament" both Saxon and Spanish strains.[6] "I indulge in gorgeous fancies," she remarked in a revealing conversation later on in life, "and wish that I dared inscribe them upon my pages."[7]

At the age of thirty she did dare inscribe her gorgeous fancies in lurid style upon her pages. With "Pauline's Passion and Punishment" she let down her literary hair and enriched the roster of her intriguing blood-and-thunders.[8] She followed "Pauline" with a more or less gruesome thriller, "A Whisper in the Dark," a story of mind control, and some years later provided *Frank Leslie's Chimney Corner* with the last and perhaps the most hair-raising of her shockers, "Perilous Play," a brief narrative concerned entirely with drug experimentation.

Meanwhile, Louisa Alcott had formed a lucrative relationship with still another publishing house, Elliott, Thomes and Talbot of Boston.[9] For their *Flag of Our Union* Louisa concocted her pseudonym of A. M. Barnard as well as such titillating narratives as "V.V.; or, Plots and Counterplots"; "A Marble Woman; or, The Mysterious Model," "Behind a Mask; or, A Woman's Power," and "The Abbot's Ghost; or, Maurice Treherne's Temptation." For their line of Ten Cent Novelettes, advertised as the handsomest and largest ten-cent books ever published, she supplied *The Skeleton in the Closet* and *The Mysterious Key.* Unbeknownst to A. M. Barnard, the thriller "V.V.; or, Plots and Counterplots" was reprinted as a Ten Cent Novelette around 1870. And so, between the blue wrappers of number 80 in that series of dime novels, the most Mephistophelian of the Alcott heroines still weaves a malignant web—the evil temptress Virginie Varens upon whose wrist the initials "V.V." have been indelibly tattooed. That paperback is desirable indeed, for it tells a tale not only of a Spanish dancer but of a writer from New England.

By 1869, with the publication of part 2 of *Little Women*, that writer had found so comfortable and rewarding a niche that she seldom had the time or inclination to stray from it. For the most part, her forays into the domains of madness and mind manipulation, opium addiction and hashish experimentation, murder, suicide, and revenge had ended.

A WELL-KEPT SECRET

Her thrillers had been clandestinely written and, with one or two exceptions, anonymously or pseudonymously published. She had kept her secret well, for it would not be discovered until some eighty years had passed. Then—against the background of another war—Louisa Alcott's pseudonym was revealed, her sallies into the horrors of the mind exposed, her mask torn off.

She herself had left tantalizing hints of her lurid literary life. Strewn through the early years of her journal was an array of initials designating unidentified editors, along with veiled allusions to the stories sent them. When the entries about those stories are lifted from the Alcott diaries of the 1860s they leave a string of clues for the initiate:

Wrote two tales for L. I enjoy romancing to suit myself; and though my tales are silly, they are not bad; and my sinners always have a good spot somewhere. I hope it is good drill for fancy and language, for I can do it fast; and Mr. L says my tales are so "dramatic, vivid, and full of plot," they are just what he wants. . . . Rewrote the last story, and sent it to L., who wants more than I can send him. So . . . I reel off my "thrilling" tales, and mess up my work in a queer but interesting way. [1862]

Received $100 from F. L. for a tale which won the prize last January. [1863]

. . . fell back on rubbishy tales, for they pay best, and I can't afford to starve on praise, when sensation stories are written in half the time and keep the family cosey. . . . L. asked me to be a regular contributor to his new paper, and I agreed if he'd pay beforehand; he said he would, and bespoke two tales at once, $50 each, . . . So here's another source of income and Alcott brains seem in demand, whereat I sing "Hallyluyer" and fill up my inkstand. [1865]

Wrote two long tales for L. . . . One for E. for which he paid $75. [1866]¹⁰

In 1868, when she began writing *Little Women*, she left more obvious clues in that domestic narrative. Since she had patterned Jo March after herself, it followed that Jo March's literary adventures had been patterned after Louisa Alcott's. Is there any reader who does not remember the following:

Jo . . . began to feel herself a power in the house, for by the magic of a pen, her "rubbish" turned into comforts for them all. *The Duke's Daughter* paid the butcher's bill, *A Phantom Hand* put down a new carpet, and the *Curse of the Coventrys* proved the blessing of the Marches in the way of groceries and gowns.

Indeed, one of Jo March's tales won a prize from the *Blarneystone Banner.*

Like most young scribblers, she went abroad for her characters and scenery; and banditti, counts, gypsies, nuns, and duchesses appeared upon her stage . . . as thrills could not be produced except by harrowing up the souls of the readers, history and romance, land and sea, science and art, police records and lunatic asylums, had to be ransacked for the purpose. . . . Eager to find material for stories, and bent on making them original in plot, if not masterly in execution, she searched newspapers for accidents, incidents, and crimes; she excited the suspicions of public librarians by asking for works on poisons; she studied faces in the street, and characters, good, bad, and indifferent, all about her; she delved in the dust of ancient times for facts or fictions . . . and introduced herself to folly, sin, and misery.

She introduced herself also—we all recall—to the publishers of the *Weekly Volcano:*

[Jo] told no one, but concocted a "thrilling tale," and boldly carried it . . . to . . . [the] editor. . . . she dressed herself in her best, and . . . bravely climbed two pairs of dark and dirty stairs to find herself in a disorderly room, a cloud of cigar smoke, and the presence of three gentlemen, sitting with their heels rather higher than their hats.

She had a steady market, "for in those dark ages, even all-perfect America read rubbish." And so, Jo March "rashly took a plunge into the frothy sea of sensational literature."¹¹

To destroy any doubt that Louisa Alcott's sensation stories had been the prototype for Jo March's, the author at one time listed the "facts in the stories that are true, though often changed as to time and place." Her list of course included "Jo's literary . . . experiences."[12]

But where did all these tantalizing clues lead? Merely to a confirmation of the feeling that Louisa Alcott, like her literary namesake, had taken "a plunge into the frothy sea of sensational literature" and that editors who had initials but no names had published her effusions in some *Blarneystone Banner* or *Weekly Volcano.* Even if that delightful letter of confession written in June 1862 to her young friend Alf Whitman was dredged up, it would not carry the researcher any further in the quest for facts, for there Louisa had simply remarked: "I intend to illuminate the Ledger with a blood & thunder tale as they are easy to 'compoze' & are better paid than moral & elaborate works of Shakespeare so dont be shocked if I send you a paper containing a picture of Indians, pirates, wolves, bears & distressed damsels in a grand tableau over a title like this 'The Maniac Bride' or The Bath of Blood A Thrilling Tale of Passion."[13]

What were the actual titles of Louisa Alcott's "Maniac Bride" or "Bath of Blood"? What periodicals had been the inspiration for Jo March's *Blarneystone Banner* and *Weekly Volcano?* With what pseudonym had she masked her gaudy endeavors? Finally, what sort of stories had she produced? Were they rubbish or superb rubbish or no rubbish at all? Would they reveal any undisclosed, undreamed-of facets of her nature? Between the 1860s, when the stories were written, and the 1940s, when the stories were identified, the questions remained unanswered.

LOUISA MAY ALCOTT UNMASKED

Then, in a later century, while the country was engaged in another conflict, World War II, Louisa May Alcott was unmasked by Leona Rostenberg, who in 1943 announced her extraordinary discovery in an article entitled "Some Anonymous and Pseudonymous Thrillers of Louisa M. Alcott," published in *The Papers of the Bibliographical Society of America.*[14] And there—for thirty more years—the matter rested.

During those busy years Leona Rostenberg and I established a rare book business, and, in addition, we both consumed quantities of paper writing and publishing books—among them my biography of Louisa May Alcott, in which reference was made to the clandestine thrillers.

Then, one bright morning in the early spring of 1974, I decided to trace those shockers and reprint them. And it must be obvious to anyone who reads them that there are compensations for the long delay. The impact of *Behind a Mask* is surely far stronger in 1975 or 1976 than it would have been ten or twenty years earlier, when its oblique feminist implications would scarcely have been appreciated.

Assembling the stories for *Behind a Mask* was no easy assignment. The problems of reproducing by Xerox, photostat, or even photograph from crumbling nineteenth-century weeklies or rare and fragile nineteenth-century dime novels need not be emphasized. After many long-distance telephone calls to librarian-friends, after some disappointments and thwarted hopes, copies of the thrillers finally reached me.[15] From them a selection was made, based upon type of narrative, number of words, and authorship—a variety of anonymous, pseudonymous, and bylined stories was desired. An introduction was written, not merely to re-announce the discovery, but to indicate that the four thrillers chosen were per se worth reading. Their value was twofold: in themselves they were skillful and suspenseful tales, cliff-hangers in which the astute author had been well served by the serial technique, page-turners that lured the reader on. Secondly, they were new windows upon the inner world of a complex writer. Reading them attentively, a critic could penetrate the facade of the "Children's Friend." The stories in *Behind a Mask* reflect a different Alcott indeed—not the weary provider of moral pap for the young, but a multifaceted writer who delved in darkness.

Once minor textual problems had been solved—the decision was to adhere to the original regardless of A. M. Barnard's aberrations in grammar or spelling—the text was ready. The title of the collection was a superb editorial inspiration. Illustrations consisted of a frontispiece portrait of the author, reproductions of two of the letters from James R. Elliott to Alcott and four cuts from *Frank Leslie's Illustrated Newspaper* depicting melodramatic stages in the course of "Pauline's Passion and Punishment." The volume, as a physical entity, was ready for its publication date, 1 July 1975.

The hoopla attendant upon rumors that Louisa Alcott had led a double literary life immediately began. As surviving agent of A. M. Barnard, I was interviewed by a variety of editors and journalists.[16] "Never again will you have *quite* the same image of this particular 'little woman,' " was the forecast in *Publishers Weekly.*[17] The *New York Times* jumped the gun and reviewed *Behind a Mask* one month before publication in the Summer Reading Issue of June 1.[18] Other reviews followed swiftly, widely, and for the most part gratifyingly. Some critics have found in *Behind a Mask* a feminist manifesto, which, in indirect terms, it is. Nearly all have found the blood-and-thunders fascinating reading, which, in very direct terms, they are.

What now of the remaining thrillers for which room could not be found in *Behind a Mask?* To my great pleasure, I can report that a second volume is to follow; *Plots and Counterplots: More Unknown Thrillers of Louisa May Alcott* will present the delectable delights of "A Whisper in the Dark"; "V.V.; or, Plots and Counterplots"; "A Marble Woman; or, The Mysterious Model"; *The Skeleton in the Closet;* and—the last of Jo March's necessity stories—"Perilous Play." The volume will form a companion piece to *Behind a Mask* as far as book design, illustrations, and format are concerned. It will reflect an even wilder side of the author of *Little Women,* for the five flamboyant tales encompass violence and madness, child-brides and manipulative Mephistophelian heroines, mind control and drug experimentation. It will prove, if proof is still needed, that the "Children's Friend" knew as much about macabre attractions as she did about the wholesome pleasures of domestic life.

These stories, like those in *Behind a Mask,* were written out of economic and psychological need by a skillful young writer from New England experimenting with various literary techniques during the 1860s. Their secret was unearthed by two sleuthing researchers in the 1940s. Now, at long last, after more than a century has passed, they make their bow between sturdy boards. With the publication of *Behind a Mask* and *Plots and Counterplots* the Concord Scheherazade emerges full-face from behind her mask.

NOTES

1. *Behind a Mask: The Unknown Thrillers of Louisa May Alcott,* ed. Madeleine Stern (New York: William Morrow, 1975).

2. For biographical details throughout, see Madeleine B. Stern, *Louisa May Alcott* (Norman: University of Oklahoma Press, 1971).

3. Louisa May Alcott to Alf Whitman, Concord, 22 June [1862] (Houghton Library, Harvard University).

4. Louisa May Alcott, "How I Went Out to Service," *The Independent* 26, no. 1331 (4 June 1874). James Richardson was identified with the help of the late Mr. Frank W. Kimball and Dr. Arthur M. Worthington, both of Dedham, Mass.

5. Ednah D. Cheney, ed., *Louisa May Alcott: Her Life, Letters, and Journals* (Boston, 1889), 146–47. Hereinafter "Cheney."

6. Bronson Alcott to Louisa Alcott, Concord, 17 December 1865, in Richard L. Herrnstadt, ed., *The Letters of A. Bronson Alcott* (Ames: Iowa State University Press, 1969), 379.

7. L. C. Pickett, *Across My Path: Memories of People I Have Known* (New York, 1916), 107–8; Madeleine B. Stern, "Louisa M. Alcott's Self-Criticism," *More Books: The Bulletin of the Boston Public Library* 20, no. 8 (October 1945): 341.

8. Stern, *Louisa May Alcott*, 128.

9. For Elliott, Thomes and Talbot, see Stern, *Imprints on History* (Bloomington: Indiana University Press, 1956), 206–20, 445–48.

10. Cheney, 131–32, 151, 165, 184.

11. Louisa May Alcott, *Little Women* (New York and London, 1975), 302, 382–83, 385–86.

12. Cheney, 193.

13. Louisa May Alcott to Alf Whitman, Concord, 22 June [1862] (Houghton Library, Harvard University).

14. Leona Rostenberg, "Some Anonymous and Pseudonymous Thrillers of Louisa M. Alcott," reprinted in this collection.

15. The cooperation of the following librarians is gratefully acknowledged: Dr. Julius P. Barclay and Joan Crane, Alderman Library, University of Virginia (for *The Mysterious Key* and *The Skeleton in the Closet*); Maud Cole, Rare Book Division, New York Public Library (for "V.V.; or, Plots and Counterplots"); Dr. James J. Heslin, New-York Historical Society (for portions of "Pauline's Passion and Punishment"); Carolyn Jakeman, Houghton Library, Harvard University (for "A Marble Woman; or, The Mysterious Model"); William Matheson, Rare Book Division, Library of Congress (for "The Abbot's Ghost; or, Maurice Treherne's Temptation"); Dr. Marcus A. McCorison, American Antiquarian Society (for "Behind a Mask; or, A Woman's Power").

16. Interviewers included Barbara Bannon, *Publishers Weekly;* Casper Citron, WQXR; David McCullough, *Book-of-the-Month Club News;* Joy Stilley, Associated Press: Barbara Walters, *Today* show.

17. *Publishers Weekly* (5 May 1975): 89.

18. *New York Times Book Review* (1 June 1975): 4–5, 30–31. The reviewer was Jane O'Reilly.

Developing Professionalism

Louisa's Wonder Book

L ouisa May Alcott died in 1888. In addition to her letters and journals, several biographies of her have appeared, and an Alcott bibliography has been printed. It is strange to think, at this late date, after the author has been analyzed and anatomized and unveiled so often, that in attics where children's books are tossed away, on the juvenile shelves of many a secondhand bookstore, and perhaps in libraries throughout the country, there is yet another book by Louisa May Alcott that has gone unclaimed through the years, unnoticed and unknown. The book is entitled *Will's Wonder Book*. It appeared anonymously in 1870, when Horace B. Fuller of Boston published it as the second volume of his Dirigo Series. The author herself was probably unaware of its existence as a printed book. Yet, at long last, its authorship can be established and, in addition, the volume may tentatively be linked with a lost Alcott manuscript whose history was as strange as it was eventful.

In August of 1864 Louisa May Alcott, aged twenty-eight and known to a limited public as the author of *Flower Fables* and *Hospital Sketches*, confided to her journal that she had written "another fairy tale, 'Jamie's Wonder Book,' and sent the 'Christmas Stories' to W. & W., with some lovely illustrations by Miss Greene. They liked the book very much, and said they would consult about publishing it, though their hands were full."[1] Nothing further was ever heard of "Jamie's Wonder Book." The publishers, "W. & W."—Walker, Wise & Company of Boston—had made a name for themselves through their Unitarian imprints as well as their charming juveniles, their Children's Library, and their Silver Penny Series, but by 1864 the firm was shortly to undergo a change of title with the admission of Horace B. Fuller to partnership, and apparently the hands of Walker, Wise were indeed too full to add "Jamie's Wonder Book" to their list. The author, invincible in the face of rejections, turned to writing potboilers for *The Flag of Our Union* and a novel, *Moods,* for Aaron K. Loring of Boston. Then, abandoning printer's ink to serve as companion to a young lady in delicate health, she went abroad.

After her return home, she received the following letter from Howard M. Ticknor of the Boston publishing firm Ticknor & Fields: "Will you kindly 'overhaul the catechism,' & see if you have anywhere a letter from me or from F[ields] proposing terms for the unlucky juvenile the MS. of [which] is playing hide and seek so aggravatingly with us? I think such a letter was written. If you have it, or if you remember the terms, will you please write me what the details were? I wish to effect a sort of settlement,—prospectively, for I am sure that that material will turn up. Also let me know how much you paid Miss Greene for drawings."[2]

In the same month of June 1867 the Springfield *Daily Republican* carried a short notice clarifying somewhat the fate of the unnamed "unlucky juvenile": "Miss Laura [*sic*] M. Alcott, who has been abroad for some time on a health-seeking mission, has returned, somewhat invigorated. Some little time ago she sent the manuscript of a novel [*sic*] to a publishing firm here, who, in some unaccountable manner, lost it. They sent her a check for $200, which may or may not be adequate compensation for the lost book."[3] Two weeks later the *American Literary Gazette* picked up the news, along with the error in the author's name, and added: "A check was sent her by way of remuneration, but this can hardly afford consolation for the irrecoverable possibilities of fame."[4]

What had happened seems all too clear. After Walker, Wise & Company rejected "Jamie's Wonder Book," the undaunted author in all probability had sent it on to other publishers, among them Ticknor & Fields, who, "in some unaccountable manner" lost the manuscript. Still undaunted, Alcott rewrote the story, as a later letter of hers to another member of the firm will indicate.[5] She had, however, several irons in the literary fire, in addition to the recreation of "Jamie's Wonder Book." *Little Women,* which would make the "possibilities of fame" far from "irrecoverable," was on its way. Moreover, in 1867, Horace B. Fuller, who had some time before joined the firm of Walker, Wise, where he had, incidentally, taken the place of Louisa Alcott's relative, Henry May Bond, and now, after an interval with Walker, Fuller & Company was on his own as publisher, announced that he had purchased the well-known juvenile magazine *Merry's Museum,* and engaged as editor Louisa M. Alcott, "the brilliant author of 'Hospital Sketches,'—who has hardly an equal, and who has no superior as a writer for youth in the country."[6] The cover, incidentally, was designed by the recurrent E. B. Greene.

As editor of *Merry's,* Alcott not only selected stories but contributed them as well, and in April 1868 a serial was begun under her own name, running for eight monthly installments through November of that year.[7] It was entitled in a style reminiscent of "Jamie's Wonder Book"— "Will's Wonder-Book." Young subscribers leafing the pages read what Grandma told Will and Polly about a variety of denizens of the animal world: of the bees and how they make cells; of ants and their nurseries; of spiders and how they spin; of crickets and moths and butterflies; of squirrels and moles and snails and seals; and finally of cats and dogs. By the end of the serial, the editor's "Dear Merrys" understood why "Will shot no more songbirds, never stoned frogs, drowned cats, or whipped his pony" and why Polly "neither screamed at spiders, nor ran away from toads . . . and was learning the sweetest charity toward whatever was ugly, weak, or friendless."

The author, not wanting her serial to remain embalmed in the pages of a monthly magazine, apparently sent it once again to Ticknor & Fields—later Fields, Osgood & Company—who, in an even more "unaccountable" way than before, seem to have lost the manuscript a second time! For subsequently, on 28 January, probably of 1874, Alcott, whose fame by then had proven definitely not "irrecoverable," wrote the following revealing letter to James Osgood regarding her old "unlucky juvenile":[8]

Mr. Niles [of Robert Brothers] tells me that my long lost Ms. has been found. As the tales have most of them been published singly the book is no longer of much value I fancy & I should be glad to put it in the fire.

The facts of the case are these. Eight or nine years ago H. Ticknor accepted the

Ms. & was to bring it out as a Christmas book I think. But it did not appear & on my return from Europe I was told that the Ms. was lost. So I rewrote it & waited a year or two longer, when . . . the doomed Ms. again vanished illustrations & all. I paid E. B. Greene for the pictures $30, & in the course of time the blocks were found & sent to me. I did not try the book again but at intervals sent several of the tales to various magazines & papers, for I considered them mine as Mr Fields gave me $150 for my loss of time & trouble & the matter was considered ended with him.

Even in my day of small things I fancy $150 would not be considered sufficient remuneration for a book, & not an unduly large compensation for the labor, loss & disappointment of the affair.

I should like to reclaim the Ms. which does not seem to have been of much value to any one but its author. Will you kindly let me know the rights of the case.

Louisa Alcott was apparently unaware that, though she considered the manuscript hers, another publisher had also claimed proprietary rights to it. Horace B. Fuller, who had engaged her to edit *Merry's Museum* and had published her serial "Will's Wonder-Book" in the pages of his magazine, had seized the opportunity in November 1870, when her popularity was at its zenith,[9] to publish the story in book form. His Dirigo Series consists of four volumes: *The Loggers, Will's Wonder Book, Mink Curtiss,* and *Famous Dogs.*[10] Each appeared anonymously in book form, and each had been published serially in *Merry's Museum.*[11] Issued in green cloth with green and gilt lettering, and announced as encased in a "neat box," the series sold at one dollar per volume.[12] The four books in the series are uniform in every particular. All have identical copyright entries on the verso of the title page, and each volume, measuring about five by seven inches, boasts a frontispiece with tissue protector, a small title vignette, a listing of the four works in the series, and a table of contents. The volumes have from four to six illustrations and run between seventy-four and seventy-eight pages. The publisher chose the name *Dirigo* for his series doubtless because *Dirigo,* "I direct," is the motto of the State of Maine, and the first volume, *The Loggers,* is subtitled *Six Months in the Forests of Maine.*

The second volume in the series, *Will's Wonder Book,* consists of seventy-four pages and includes, besides the serial as it had originally appeared in eight installments in *Merry's,* a ninth chapter, "Curious Birds and Beasts," which had previously been printed in *Merry's* as Louisa M.

Alcott's "My May Day among Curious Birds and Beasts"; a tenth chapter devoted to a monkey named Jacko; and a separate story entitled "Jimmy Jumper," outlining the career of an opossum from Tasmania.[13] In addition to the frontispiece, there are five illustrations, all of which had first appeared in *Merry's Museum*. Viewed as a single book or as one of a series, the volume forms a charming juvenile whose interest is now considerably enhanced since its authorship has been established.

Both "Jamie's Wonder Book," originally submitted to Walker, Wise but never again mentioned, and the lost but unnamed book submitted to Ticknor & Fields were described by the author as "Christmas" stories. Both had been illustrated by E. B. Greene.[14] Without too much conjecture, it seems possible to identify the two manuscripts as one, and that may in turn be identified with the similarly titled and newly discovered *Will's Wonder Book*, which appeared at first serially in *Merry's Museum* in 1868 and two years later as a Christmas book along with other stories.

If the manuscript of Louisa's "unlucky juvenile" has not turned up, it seems quite likely that the printed version has. It is entirely possible that Louisa Alcott never knew that her forays into the field of animal stories for children had been enshrined by Horace B. Fuller in book form. The wily publisher had issued her work in November 1870 and registered it for copyright on 27 December 1870, during which time the unknowing author was in Rome.[15] Yet *Will's Wonder Book*, bound in green cloth and sold for a dollar a copy, sent forth anonymously as a tale to lure children from play, can now be definitely assigned to her pen. What is more, the book was sufficiently popular to be reprinted. In 1876 and 1877, for example, the New York publisher James Miller, who had years before been associated with Horace B. Fuller's firm of Walker, Fuller as selling agents for the American Unitarian Association,[16] reprinted the four volumes of Fuller's Dirigo Series in one volume.[17] And there, sandwiched between *Mink Curtiss; or, Life in the Backwoods* and *The Loggers; or, Six Months in the Forests of Maine*, may be found the anonymous *Will's Wonder Book*. It need be anonymous no longer. After so many years, these animal stories may be returned to their rightful author. "Jamie's Wonder Book," first sent to Walker & Wise in 1864, rejected and lost, rewritten and lost again, has at last been found under the title of *Will's Wonder Book*. If its history is more interesting than its contents, it is still a not unworthy successor to *Flower Fables. Will's Wonder Book,* having suffered so many strange darts of destiny, may be restored to its niche as yet another Alcott juvenile. If *Little Women* proved to the world that the author's claim to fame was far from "irrecoverable," *Will's Wonder Book* is entitled to its small place in literary history. As Louisa's Wonder Book, it may surely claim a fame all its own.

NOTES

1. Ednah D. Cheney, ed., *Louisa May Alcott: Her Life, Letters, and Journals* (Boston, 1889), 159.

2. Howard M. Ticknor to Louisa May Alcott, Boston, 5 June 1867, Houghton Library, Harvard University, Box 1 MS Am 800.23. Courtesy Mr. William A. Jackson.

3. "From Boston," Springfield *Daily Republican* (15 June 1867): 1. Courtesy Margaret Rose, City Library Association, Springfield, Mass., and Mrs. Dorothea E. Spear, American Antiquarian Society.

4. *American Literary Gazette and Publishers' Circular* 9, no. 137 (1 July 1867).

5. See E.L.A., "Louisa Alcott's Doomed Manuscript," *More Books: The Bulletin of the Boston Public Library* 17 (May 1942): 221–22, and L. M. Alcott to James Osgood, Boston, 18 January [1874?] (Boston Public Library, courtesy Mr. Zoltán Haraszti).

6. *Merry's Museum* 54, no. 2 (December 1867).

7. Louisa M. Alcott, "Will's Wonder-Book," *Merry's Museum* n.s. 1, nos. 4–11 (April–November 1868). The quoted portion appears in the issue of November 1868, p. 461, and on p. 54 of the book version.

8. L. M. Alcott to James Osgood, Boston, 28 January [1874?] (Boston Public Library, courtesy Mr. Zoltán Haraszti). See also *More Books: The Bulletin of the Boston Public Library* 17 (May 1942): 221–22.

9. The Boston publisher A. K. Loring grasped a similar opportunity in 1870 by issuing a new edition of Louisa M. Alcott's *Moods,* but Fuller, though he published her work, refrained from publishing it under her name. Yet, despite its anonymity, *Will's Wonder Book* does bear the author's name at the end of the first chapter, on p. 14, corresponding with p. 152 of *Merry's Museum* 1, no. 4 (April 1868), where, with the conclusion of the first installment, the name of L. M. Alcott also appears. This name does not appear in the reprints mentioned in n. 17.

10. See *American Catalogue 1866–71,* p. 107. The four volumes of the series have been located in the Juvenile Collection of the Library of Congress Rare Books Division, and were examined through the courtesy of Mr. Frederick R. Goff, Chief, Rare Books Division, Library of Congress.

11. *The Loggers; or, Six Months in the Forests of Maine* had appeared in *Merry's Museum* 1, nos. 1–7 (January–July 1868).

Mink Curtiss; or, Life in the Backwoods had appeared in *Merry's Musuem* 1, nos. 6–7, 9–12 (June–July 1868 and September–December 1868), as "By an Old Hunter." The supposed author is Emerson Bennett. Bound with *Mink Curtiss* in the book version is "Under the Ice; or, The Lost Ibex Hunter," which had appeared in *Merry's Museum* 1, no. 11 (November 1868), as "From the German."

Famous Dogs had appeared, under the author's name, M. G. Sleeper, in *Merry's Museum* 2, nos. 1–4, 11 (January–April 1869 and November 1869). The chapter "Tig," which forms the fifth chapter of *Famous Dogs* in the book version, had appeared by M. G. Sleeper in *Merry's* 2, no. 5 (May 1869). The sixth chapter, "The Pet Eagle," had appeared by M. G. Sleeper in *Merry's* 2, no. 6 (June 1869). The eighth chapter, "The Black Swans," and the ninth chapter, "The Ride For Life," had appeared as sections of M. G. Sleeper's "Pets and Sports in Tasmania," in *Merry's Museum* 1, nos. 10–11 (October–November 1868).

12. See announcement of the series in *The American Booksellers' Guide* 2 (1 November 1870): 545, and listing of the series as a November publication (1 December 1870): 578.

13. For the periodical appearance of *Will's Wonder Book,* see n. 7. "My May Day among Curious Birds and Beasts" by L. M. Alcott had appeared in *Merry's* 1, no. 3 (March 1868). It was reprinted in *Aunt Jo's Scrap-Bag* 1. "Jacko" by "Cousin Alice" appeared in *Merry's* 1, no. 11 (November 1868). "Jimmy Jumper," a section of M. G. Sleeper's "Pets and Sports in Tasmania," appeared in *Merry's Museum* 1, no. 9 (September 1868).

14. E. B. Greene drew illustrations for *Merry's* also, but only the engraver's name appears on the reprinted cuts.

15. Copyright information courtesy Mr. Frederick R. Goff, Chief, Rare Books Division, Library of Congress.

16. See "Sketches of the Publishers. Walker, Fuller & Co., Boston," *Round Table* 3 (31 March 1866): 202, and *American Literary Gazette and Publishers' Circular* 6 (15 February 1866): 223. James Miller of New York and Walker, Fuller of Boston were joint publishers of the *Christian Examiner* in 1866.

17. This collected volume appears anonymously as *Mink Curtiss; or, Life in the Backwoods* (New York: James Miller, 1876 [and 1877]). The omnibus volume was later reprinted by Thomas R. Knox & Co. of New York, successors to James Miller [1885?].

Louisa M. Alcott's Literary Development, 1848–1868

The Witch's Cauldron
to the
Family Hearth

When Louisa Alcott first began to write in the Hillside attic, she dipped her pen into the romantic, melodramatic ink that has ever been the property of sixteen-year-old authors. Wandering through a stormy world where noblemen unsheathed their daggers and stamped their boots, Louisa and her sister Anna produced a series of "lurid" plays aptly termed by the latter *Comic Tragedies*.[1]

A Shakespearean twist was given to the plot now and then, when Rodolpho hired Hugo to murder Louis,[2] or when Ione was disguised as her own living statue.[3] Occasionally the playwright took a suggestion from Milton, making Ion exclaim, "Thou mayst chain my limbs, thou canst *not* bind my freeborn soul!"[4] Even childhood fairy tales were grist for a mill that could grind out any number of counts and lords with appropriate destinies and costumes for each.

For the benefit of her neighbor, young Ellen Emerson, Louisa left the dark domain of melodrama to spin her *Flower Fables*[5] in a sweeter though no less marvelous fairyland. Substituting Guido and Madeleine for her flower heroes, Louisa Alcott continued in this fairy-tale vein, receiving five dollars from the Reverend Mr. Thomas F. Norris of the *Olive Branch* for her first published story, "The Rival Painters. A Tale of Rome."

All was for the best even when the author turned her attention to the more possible though no less marvelous world that delighted Mr. W. W. Clapp, Jr., editor of the *Saturday Evening Gazette*. Though Louisa Alcott abandoned her fairies for human beings, she clung to the realm of cloying sweetness and cloudless light in order to increase her worldly stores by six or ten dollars. Having decided to make her fortune, "L. M. A." donned rose-colored glasses and followed the example of the Dickens of *Dombey and Son* and *The Old Curiosity Shop*[6] to see the benign influence that little children can exert upon an unyielding grandfather or upon an actress and her perfidious lover.[7] In the course of the year 1856, while Louisa Alcott sewed cambric neckties and pillowcases, she planned her stories and scribbled them down on Sundays, with the result that one tale after another covered the first page of the *Gazette*. If she viewed the world of reality at all, it was through a roseate haze that cloaked each story with a happy ending. To embellish the trappings of her imagination, she needed merely to draw down a copy of Emerson's Shakespeare or a volume of Dickens and borrow a touch here and there.

Louisa Alcott, however, needed money, and she enjoyed the "lurid," melodramatic plays that had turned the Hillside barn into a haunt of witches. The penny dreadfuls would pay as much as two or three dollars a column for a sensation story. What was simpler, then, than to turn the dark-browed villains and the unloved wives to work and earn a carpet for the floor or a few new gowns to fit up the girls? In 1862, little more than a year before Louisa was rewriting a fairy tale about the reformation of three little roses[8] for James Redpath, she was scribbling away at top speed on a "lurid" sensation story for *Frank Leslie's Illustrated Newspaper*.

Her blood-and-thunder narratives for Leslie and for the Boston firm of Elliott, Thomes and Talbot appeared anonymously or pseudonymously over the name of A. M. Barnard during the 1860s. In them she vented her feminist convictions while earning money for the Alcott Sinking Fund. Also, on occasion, she intertwined sensationalism with more realistic themes in a genre she soon mastered.

An astute observer who had read Alcott's first contribution to the *Atlantic Monthly*, in 1860, might have seen in "Love and Self-Love"[9] many of the elements that appeared in later sensational stories. The relations between Little Effie and Basil Ventnor, the elderly gentleman who marries the child to provide her with a home, happen to be knit together with a respectable and happy ending, but the themes of incompatibility and attempted suicide were to appear subsequently in pseudonymous works that might bring perhaps better payment, but, if their authorship were recognized, a less savory reputation.

Just so, the ingenious Louisa Alcott could with impunity interpolate a sensational story into so respectable a narrative as *Work*.[10] The chapter "Companion" differs not at all from the tales that were flung across the pages of the penny dreadfuls. Insanity, suicide, and thwarted love provide the destinies that pursue such characters as "a mad Carrol" and a lad who frequents the "gambling-tables and the hells where souls like his are lost." It is the companion herself, the sympathetic observer, who integrates the chapter with the rest of the book and contrives to make of it a fairly respectable interlude. Louisa Alcott had not been long in discovering that the narrative powers she was gaining from scribbling her tales of horror could be combined with other themes and put to good use against other backgrounds.

The sensation stories carried by the penny dreadfuls, with their vitriolic burden of murder and vengeance, might be even more enticing to the public if they were timely. The Civil War was bearing in its wake the great tide of long-oppressed slaves, the flotsam and jetsam of a weakening South, humanity turned fugitive, "contraband." Here was a theme at hand, so malleable that it could be integrated with a sensation plot and a reader would scarcely know when he had escaped from the real world of the Rebellion to the nightmarish domain of melodrama. Even before the Civil War, the South could provide the mulatto, a type becoming more and more familiar to the North, as a character for a tale. The slave owners would brand his hand with mysterious initials that might lead to a weird and sinister plot. The technique of the sensation yarn would suggest a white woman to love the mulatto, and Louisa Alcott could dispatch to a prospective publisher "M. L.,"[11] a story that was at once antislavery and melodramatic.

Even the ambitious *Atlantic* would not refuse a tale in which the tempestuous story of a stolen wife and a vengeful plan for murder was carefully worked round such characters as the contraband Bob and his white brother Ned, a wounded Reb. By placing the brothers in the same hospital room and introducing a nurse who could evoke from Bob the sad story of his past, Alcott created a plot with its roots in abolition and its branches in the realms of blood-and-thunder. Forgetting the latter, no doubt, and concentrating on the virtues of the former, Fields paid fifty dollars for "My Contraband"[12] and published it in November 1863 for his Brahmin public.

The technique was simple, the rewards tempting. Louisa Alcott, recalling possibly the life of Fanny Kemble on her husband's plantation, wove another yarn about an island where the slaves plotted a sanguinary escape for liberty, and Gabriel, the righteous convictions of the North within him, freed them all, wrenched away "the rattle of fetters," baptized them with his own repentant tears. For "An Hour,"[13] compounded thus of the abolitionist doctrine and the stormy passions of a Dismal Swamp, Louisa Alcott reached the readers of *The Commonwealth* and received thirty-five dollars to pay the family debts.

Such stories could be manufactured easily once the pattern had been established. A little variety might be introduced by a slight change of character so that, for example, a Reb would lie next to a Northerner in a hospital ward. Poison could take the place of attempted strangulation. The result would be "The Blue and the Gray"[14] instead of "My Contraband." The elements of the story were violence, jealousy, and the will to murder—elements that Louisa Alcott had offered, and was still offering, to the editors of the penny dreadfuls, but they were stirred now in a new crucible in which contrabands and mulattoes were heroes and abolition the loud, staunch war cry. And so Louisa Alcott could serve the Union cause while she fulfilled her longings for the "lurid" and the sensational. The rewards of such patriotism were twofold, for the author could reach a more respectable public and still place a fifty-dollar bill into the ever-gaping family coffers.

The step from stories in which the Civil War theme was combined with a sensational plot to stories from which melodrama was eliminated and simple scenes of the Rebellion delineated in a straight and forthright manner was one of the most significant in Louisa Alcott's career. She herself perhaps did not realize how important to her future was the laying aside of murder, poison, and jealousy for the depiction of "A Hospital Christmas,"[15] in which a meager dinner, the arrival of a holiday box, the news of a child's birth, and the death (from natural causes) of a patient formed the sole elements of a simple, moving narrative. Surely the day Louisa Alcott thus turned to a realistic portrayal of an everyday war scene was as significant for her as the day, some four years later, when she sat down to write a girls' story for Thomas Niles. For, having once discarded the wild, tumultuous impossibilities that had peopled her imagination, she was left with little or no plot, and hence with the necessity of expanding her characters. This change from the alloy to the simple, from the "lurid" to the true, carrying with it an emphasis upon character instead of narrative, may—if one can mark any climacteric in a writer's life—be called the turning point of Louisa Alcott's career. She was developing now as the literary world was developing, from the strange to the natural, from the romantic to the realistic. She was paving the way for her future triumphs. She was beginning at last to write stories of a more lasting nature.

It would, no doubt, be convenient if Louisa Alcott had in every instance followed her sensational war stories with the more realistic variety. Dates, however, are not so important as themes. Even if the two types had appeared simultaneously, the flow of truthful and simple war scenes from her pen would have marked her growth and indicated that she was approaching maturity. As it is, a few months did intervene between "My Contraband" and "A Hospital Christmas," months during which Louisa Alcott had been able to pay for May's drawing lessons, had turned assiduously to her Dickens, and had realized, no doubt, that if the public could enjoy his more realistic characterizations it might also be ready for "straight" war stories without benefit of terror, mad passion, and strangulation.

The whining grumbler on the hospital cot, the kind attendant,[16] the mental courage of a wounded man awaiting death,[17] the heroism of two loyal brothers,[18] the embittered Massachusetts volunteer too early old[19]—these enlisted her attention now, and though "A Hospital Christmas," for example, brought only eighteen dollars from *The Commonwealth* in contrast to the fifty dollars Louisa Alcott had received for "My Contraband," she gained more than she lost by this turn from the heavy-booted villains of old to the living men who moved about her. Now, if she wished, she could turn the key on her murderous counts and scarred mulattoes, and open the door through which a host of human beings, simple, kindly, and real, would walk as they did in life.

She herself had seen them—the willing nurse with her bandages and lint, her brown soap and sponge; the withered old Irishman on a cot, "overpowered by the honor of having a lady wash him"; the tall New

Hampshire man with his memories of his fallen mate; the doctor who regarded a dilapidated body as a damaged garment and set to work on it "with the enthusiasm of an accomplished surgical seamstress." At the Union Hotel Hospital in Georgetown, during six long weeks, Louisa Alcott had received enough impressions of human beings to carry her through a lifetime of story writing without the necessity of manufacturing such heroes as were never seen on land or sea. After she returned home, she brushed up her *Hospital Sketches*,[20] taking the details from the letters she had written to Concord, and laid the foundations of an art that would lead her to fame and fortune. Once again she washed feverish faces and smoothed tumbled beds, went the rounds with the doctors, observed the watchman's crooked legs and the tears of a twelve-year-old drummer boy, heard again the direful stories of Fredericksburg, and wrote what she had witnessed. No need now to invent a clash of arms between a dark–robed scoundrel and a noble lord. These men had met on the battlefield and had come to her for succor. War was as much a story of basins and lint, bandages and spoons, as of daggers and shields and gunpowder. All this she had experienced and put on paper. Romance was evicted and in its stead a crowd of living people thronged the page. Louisa Alcott had risen from her dreams and gazed on Truth, the never-failing source for storytellers.

The source might have risen in a Georgetown hospital, but the author would not be long in discovering that there was a fountainhead of Truth bubbling freely in her home at Concord. Even before the Civil War she had begun to sip of it, evolving in Mark Field[21] a realistic character who finds himself after struggle and sacrifice and arrives at success through humanitarianism and humility. Closer to home there had been the lives of four sisters compelled to earn their living in the ways best suited to their talents. Without romanticizing too much, Louisa Alcott had been able to sketch in "The Sisters' Trial"[22] one year in the careers of the actress Agnes, the writer Nora, the artist Amy, and the governness Ella. Four "little women" had found their way into print long before they had made the author's fortune. When Anna Alcott fell in love with John Pratt, her sister had once again found grist for her mill, seeing in their wholesome romance ample foundation for "A Modern Cinderella."[23] A pundit might very well declare that the early date of this significant story, 1860, sets askew any attempt to trace Louisa Alcott's penchant for domestic life as an outgrowth of her work on realistic war scenes. Here again, therefore, let it be stated that the seeds of a writer's interests may be planted early, but they germinate slowly. Needless to say, the bulk of the stories that eventually grew about the Alcott family hearth *followed* the author's sojourn in Georgetown and finally accorded to her a niche in literary history. The inference is that once the author discovered the saleability of truthful war scenes, she returned to Concord ready to find in the actual figures of her daily life characters for her stories. If realism were an interesting and even profitable technique to apply to the soldiers of the Civil War, surely it could be extended to the Concord neighbors, to her sisters, to herself. Louisa Alcott was back where she had started—in the Hillside barn—but she had begun to search the minds of the youthful actors instead of the black-robed villains, to see in the easily gratified audience as wide a scope for stories as in the ghouls and spirits with which she had tried to enchant them.

In its way, "A Modern Cinderella" is as significant in Louisa Alcott's development as *Hospital Sketches,* for the story is, even more markedly than "The Sisters' Trial," a skeleton of *Little Women.* She began, as she confessed, "with Nan for the heroine and John for the hero,"[24] but it was impossible to write a story about Anna's romance without introducing both her sister May and herself. The emphasis may be upon the simple, wholehearted love of Anna and her John, but realism demanded that the writer incorporate into the picture a sister who looked picturesque before her easel and another who could lose herself in the delights of *Wilhelm Meister* but hardly knew a needle from a crowbar. Laura is clearly a preliminary sketch of Amy; Nan needs only a touch here and there to emerge as the capable eldest sister, Meg; and Di, putting her mind through "a course of sprouts . . . from Sue to Swedenborg," corking her inkstand to plunge "at housework as if it were a five-barred gate," drowning "her idle fancies in her washtub," but determined one day to "make herself one great blot"[25] when the divine afflatus chose to descend upon her—surely Di is a Jo March in miniature. The course of Nan's love, despite the proverb, did run smooth, and Louisa Alcott was forced once again to resort to expanding her characters since her "plot" consisted of nothing more involved than a hardware clerk's wooing of her own sister.

In her own way, Louisa Alcott also traveled widely in Concord, finding in her neighbors and her family the groundwork for her tales. Gradually she began to inject into her simple stories of domestic life the humor that played about the corners of her mind. Her experience in acting in the "tavern" comedies[26] of the day was useful, teaching her to heighten an amusing situation or introduce a bit of homely and humorous dialogue.

As she had seen the wounded men of Georgetown, she had observed the tyro-gymnasts who made up "in starch and studs what they lost in color"; the old ladies who "tossed beanbags till their caps were awry";[27] the masquerades where little Bo-Peep was more interesting than the best-draped villain of the theater, for her scarlet overdress concealed a being of flesh and blood. "The King of Clubs," worked out of such details as these, has more than a passing interest, for just as Di is Jo March in outline, so August Bopp, the new leader of the class in gymnastics, may well have been an adumbration of Professor Bhaer. Like his successor, Mr. Bopp was a German who had come to America to earn a home for himself and his dependent. His "eminent nose," blond beard, and crop of "bonnie brown hair" were to appear later adorning the face of Professor Bhaer, and his gentle strength, his patient courage, would shine once again reflected in the life of the better known professor of Plumfield.

The little white village of Concord harbored many such characters, gave material for many such tales. Simple, wholesome Debby, "the young crusader against established absurdities," lived not too far from the Lexington Road, and her affected Aunt Pen, who lost a set of teeth in the water, could not dwell much farther than Boston.[28] Surely Mrs. Podgers lived and moved and had her being in one of the neighboring farms; surely her teapot graced a tidy table of actuality, and the generosity of Mr. Jerusalem Turner was not untraceable.[29] Nelly's little hospital for the spiders and mice of the fields, modeled after that of the United States Sanitary Commission, might well have been planned by one of the Concord children.[30]

If the neighbors suggested so many lively character sketches, Louisa Alcott could find in her own life the material for a long and truthful story. Her travels both in America and Europe were already providing the source for many an amusing sketch.[31] Finally, in *Work,* on which she scribbled on and off for several years, she produced the sort of autobiographical novel with which most young authors today begin their careers. With her, however, it was not a beginning but an end, for after many forays into the dark forest of dreams the author had at last returned to the family hearth that was to brighten her days forever. Here she could sketch her own experiences in private theatricals, glorify somewhat her career in domestic service, enlarge upon her trials as a seamstress and a nurse, add to the humdrum lot of a girl who sought a living, a touch of romance, and unearth among the episodes of her life her own character, strong and unflinching before the world. The actual technique embarked upon in *Work* was to become a mannerism, a stereotype later on. Louisa Alcott would never forget that she had been apprenticed as a writer of short stories. Her full-length novels consist almost always of a series of episodes more or less related, a scrap-bag of stories tied together with the knot of character. From *Work* to *Little Women* the bridge is short. Louisa Alcott needed only to reduce the tragedies of mature life to the more sentimental tears of youth; her form of humor, inducing a chuckle with a homely phrase, would stand her in good stead when she wrote for children. If *Work* had centered upon her own trials and tribulations abroad in the world, she must simply return for a second look at her place in the family circle before taking up her pen to write the story for girls that was to establish her fame.

There is always one exception that proves the rule. Before she undertook *Little Women,* there was another novel in which Louisa Alcott took a fling at the world of dark if not "lurid" passion. In the early edition of *Moods*[32] Sylvia discovers a solution to her romantic problems only in death, that ever-convenient ending for melodramatic heroines who find themselves at odds with convention. Death, sleepwalking, shipwreck— the details of plot remind one of the violent deeds in *Comic Tragedies.* The author had matured, however, for she took space to interweave among the glaring threads of Sylvia's turbulent loves many a verbose remark on goodness and godliness, books and nature, dreams and visions, marriage and death. These deviations mark her growth. Passion and violence were not so all-sufficing that they could not be interrupted by a little essay on wisdom or a rambling account of intellectual love. *Moods,* meager enough in worth, is yet better knit together than most of the episodic novels that were to follow. And within the account of stormy passion and death is imbedded a chapter that recalls the substance of "A Modern Cinderella" and points forward to *Little Women*. The golden wedding,[33] where Sylvia, Adam, and Geoffrey find themselves as uninvited guests, is an episode in which the melodramatic is forgotten and the simple delights of country songs and dances, hearty goodwill, and honest generosity take the stage. And so the exception does actually prove the rule. The stormy Moods were to be exorcised and in their place would come the songs and dances of Concord, for Louisa Alcott was once again back at the family hearth from which no bearded villains or witches' wands would lure her away for long.

Though *Moods* sold rapidly at first, it would be but a short time before the author discovered that stories from her own roof-tree would sell far more rapidly. The fantastic would be buried, the realistic resurrected. Healthful romance would displace exotic passion; hygienic clothing would be recommended to the exclusion of flowing draperies and tight-fitting boots; mischievous boys and grouchy aunts would take a stage deserted by Spanish nobles; and all such themes would be exalted on the altar of domesticity.[34] When Thomas Niles asked her for a girls' story,[35] Louisa Alcott would know to which girls she must turn for her characters and would be ready to draw from the circle at home enough tales to satisfy her admirers. The fire in the family hearth was to send out a glow that would warm and comfort the author to the end of her days.

NOTES

1. *Comic Tragedies*, written by "Jo" and "Meg" and acted by the "Little Women" (Boston: Roberts, 1893). The plays were written and acted at Hillside principally in 1848.

Louisa Alcott did not lose her interest in melodramatic plays. Years later, she dramatized her own story "The Rival Prima Donnas," issued under the pseudonym of Flora Fairfield in the *Saturday Evening Gazette* (11 November 1854). The dramatized version, the MS of which is in Orchard House, was never produced.

2. "Norna, or the Witch's Curse," *Comic Tragedies*, 34 ff. Cf. *Macbeth*.

3. "The Greek Slave," *Comic Tragedies*.

4. "Ion," *Comic Tragedies*, 229.

5. Louisa May Alcott, *Flower Fables* (Boston: George W. Briggs, 1855). It brought the author thirty-two dollars. Though the book was not published until 1855, it was written "for Ellen E.[merson] when I was sixteen." See Ednah D.

Cheney, ed., *Louisa May Alcott: Her Life, Letters, and Journals* (Boston: Roberts, 1889), 79. Hereinafter "Cheney."

6. For the more specific influence of *Dombey and Son* upon Louisa Alcott, see "Little Paul," *Saturday Evening Gazette* 16 (19 April 1856), a poem patterned by Louisa upon the life of Paul Dombey. One of the author's favorite roles in private theatricals was that of Mrs. Jarley, of *The Old Curiosity Shop*. In her childhood Louisa had organized "The Pickwick Club" with her sisters and produced "The Olive Leaf," scattered copies of which are extant.

7. See "A New Year's Blessing," *Saturday Evening Gazette* 1 (5 January 1856), and "Little Genevieve," ibid. 13 (29 March 1856).

8. *The Rose Family. A Fairy Tale* (Boston: James Redpath, 1864). In a diary entry for December 1863, Louisa Alcott writes: "Rewrote the fairy tales, one of which was published; but . . . it was late for the holidays, . . . so the poor 'Rose Family' fared badly." Cheney, 155. The story was reprinted in *Morning-Glories, and Other Stories*.

9. "Love and Self-Love," *Atlantic Monthly* 5, no. 29 (March 1860). The story appeared anonymously but is identified by a letter from A. B. Alcott to Sister Betsey, Concord, 5 June 1860, MS in *Family Letters* V, Concord Public Library. Reference to this letter is made through the courtesy of Mr. F. W. Pratt of Concord, Mass.

10. *Work: A Story of Experience* (Boston: Roberts, 1873). The story was begun as "Success" in 1862. See Cheney, 129.

11. "M. L.," though written before February 1860 (see Cheney, 120), was not published until 1863. It appeared originally in *The Commonwealth* 1, nos. 21, 22, 23, 24, 25 (24 and 31 January, 7, 14, and 22 February 1863). It was reprinted in *Journal of Negro History* 14, no. 4 (October 1929).

12. "My Contraband; or, The Brothers," first appearing as "The Brothers" in the *Atlantic Monthly* 12, no. 73 (November 1863), was written in August 1863 and brought fifty dollars. It was reprinted in *Hospital Sketches and Camp and Fireside Stories* (Boston: Roberts, 1869).

13. "An Hour" was apparently rejected by *Our Young Folks* and sent in November 1864 to *The Commonwealth* 3, nos. 13 and 14 (26 November and 3 December 1864). Alcott received thirty-five dollars for it. The story was reprinted in *Camp and Fireside Stories*.

14. "The Blue and the Gray, A Hospital Sketch" first appeared in *Putnam's Magazine* 1, no. 6 (June 1868) and was reprinted in *Camp and Fireside Stories*.

15. "A Hospital Christmas" first appeared in *The Commonwealth* 2, nos. 19 and 20 (8 and 15 January 1864). It brought eighteen dollars and was reprinted in *Camp and Fireside Stories*.

16. The characters appear in "A Hospital Christmas."

17. See "The Hospital Lamp," *Daily Morning Drum-Beat* 3 and 4 (24 and 25 February 1864). The story reappears as an episode in "The Romance of a Summer Day."

18. See "Love and Loyalty," begun in April 1864 and first published in *The*

United States Service Magazine 2, nos. 1, 2, 3, 5, 6 (July, August, September, November, December 1864). Charles B. Richardson promised one hundred dollars for the story. It was reprinted in *Camp and Fireside Stories*.

19. See "On Picket Duty," in *On Picket Duty, and Other Tales* (Boston: James Redpath, 1864).

20. *Hospital Sketches* (Boston: James Redpath, 1863). The sketches appeared originally in *The Commonwealth* 1, nos. 38, 39, 41, 43 (22 and 29 May, 12 and 26 June 1863). "Night Scene in a Hospital," taken from *Sketches*, was published in *Daily Morning Drum-Beat* Extra Number (11 March 1864). Louisa Alcott's interest in the soldiers was not confined to her attendance upon them in the hospital. See L.M.A., "Colored Soldiers' Letters," *The Commonwealth* 2, no. 44 (1 July 1864).

21. "Mark Field's Mistake" and its sequel, "Mark Field's Success," were published in the *Saturday Evening Gazette* 45, nos. 11 and 16 (12 March and 16 April 1859).

22. "The Sisters' Trial" appeared in the *Saturday Evening Gazette* 4 (26 January 1856).

23. "A Modern Cinderella: or, The Little Old Shoe" written in March 1860, first appeared in the *Atlantic Monthly* 6, no. 36 (October 1860), bringing seventy-five dollars. It was reprinted in *Camp and Fireside Stories*.

24. Cheney, 120.

25. The quotations are from "A Modern Cinderella," in *Camp and Fireside Stories*, 274, 286, 287, and 262 respectively.

26. Many of the plays in which Louisa Alcott acted were set in taverns. "The Crooked Billet," a roadside inn, is the scene of *The Jacobite* by J. R. Planché, for example, in which Louisa Alcott played Widow Pottle in July 1855 and on 11 September 1855.

27. The quotations are from "The King of Clubs," in *Camp and Fireside Stories*, 99–100. "The King of Clubs and the Queen of Hearts" was written in April 1862 and brought thirty dollars when it was first published in *The Monitor* (Concord, Mass.) 1, nos. 1, 2, 3, 4, 5, 6, 7 (19 and 26 April, 3, 10, 17, and 24 May, and 7 June 1862). It was reprinted in *On Picket Duty*. It is interesting to note that the character of August Bopp was, in all probability, suggested by a Concord boy, Seymour Severance. See Louisa Alcott to Alfred Whitman, Concord, 25 January 1860 (MS in Houghton Library, Harvard University).

28. See "Debby's Début," *Atlantic Monthly* 12, no. 70 (August 1863). The story is reminiscent of "The Lady and the Woman," *Saturday Evening Gazette* 40 (4 October 1856), in which strong-minded Kate Loring fights against fashionable absurdities and is rewarded with the love of Mr. Windsor.

29. See "Mrs. Podgers' Teapot, A Christmas Story," written in November 1864, first published in the *Saturday Evening Gazette* 50, no. 52 (24 December 1864), and reprinted in *Camp and Fireside Stories*.

30. See "Nelly's Hospital," *Our Young Folks* 1, no. 4 (April 1865), reprinted in Washington by the United States Sanitary Commission, 1868.

31. See "Letters from the Mountains," *The Commonwealth* 1, nos. 47, 48, 49, 51 (24 and 31 July, 7 and 21 August 1863), "Up the Rhine," *The Independent* 19, no. 972 (18 July 1867), and "Life in a Pension," *The Independent* 19, no. 988 (7 November 1867).

32. *Moods* was first published in Boston by Loring, 1865. The story was revised, with the ending changed, and published in Boston by Roberts in 1882. In the preface to the later edition the author comments on her changes resulting in "a wiser if less romantic fate" for the heroine than in the former edition.

33. See also "A Golden Wedding: and What Came of it," *The Commonwealth* 2, nos. 35 and 36 (29 April and 6 May 1864).

34. See *Kitty's Class Day* (Boston: Loring, 1868); *Aunt Kipp* (Boston: Loring 1868); and *Psyche's Art* (Boston: Loring, 1868).

35. *Little Women* was not the first manuscript submitted in response to a request. Louisa Alcott had had experience in writing to order. See, for example, "Happy Women," *New York Ledger* 24, no. 7 (11 April 1868). She had also had experience in writing for specific occasions. See, for example, the Christmas story "What the Bells Saw and Said," *Saturday Evening Gazette* 53, no. 51 (21 December 1867), reprinted in *Proverb Stories*.

The First Appearance
of a *Little Women*
Incident

The November 1867 issue of *Merry's Museum*, an unpretentious juvenile monthly that had just fallen into the hands of a new owner, Horace B. Fuller, carried a prospectus for 1868, announcing, among the "pleasant improvements," a new editor, described as "an experienced and competent person." This newcomer was identified a month later as "Louisa M. Alcott, the brilliant author of 'Hospital Sketches,'—who has hardly an equal, and who has no superior as a writer for youth, in the country. . . ."

Fuller's description of Alcott bore traces of publishing if not poetic license, for she was at that time known to the juvenile public only through her *Flower Fables* (1855) and *Morning-Glories* (1867). For the *Saturday Evening Gazette* she had, it is true, written several saccharine tales, and the penny dreadfuls *The Flag of Our Union* and *Frank Leslie's Illustrated Newspaper* had been emblazoned with her sensational contributions.[1] Such reputation as she could honestly claim was based upon *Hospital Sketches,* not her juvenilia. The new publisher, however, should be credited with considerable foresight, since *Little Women* was under way when Fuller offered Alcott five hundred dollars a year for the editorship of the *Museum.*[2]

In order to fulfill her employer's promises Alcott had supplied the January 1868 issue of the "rejuvenated" monthly with a story and two poems, had garnered two serials and a number of tales, and had maintained the various popular departments. She herself, moreover, was responsible for filling the section known as "Merry's Monthly Chat with His Friends." The policy of publishing the letters of young readers was altered somewhat in order to include what Louisa Alcott called her "editorial." As Cousin Tribulation—carried over from the Tribulation Periwinkle letters in *Hospital Sketches*—she wrote for "Dear Merrys" various incidents, principally autobiographical, that could be twisted to offer a lesson in virtue and good works.

The episode chosen for the January 1868 "Chat" was one that would be reprinted, with slight changes, in *Little Women*. Since it was not until July that she finished the first part of the classic, and not until the end of August that she received the proofs, this early appearance of a section of the story gives to that issue of *Merry's Museum* a bibliographical significance it would otherwise lack. The episode selected relates the manner in which the March girls gave up their breakfast to a poor family on Christmas morning, and a comparison between the *Merry's* version and that which was to appear later in chapter 2 of *Little Women* may be fruitful.

The most interesting variation within the two forms is the fact that the *Merry's* version is the more autobiographical. The writer uses the first person, gives truer names to the sisters—Nan, Lu, Beth, and May, instead of Meg, Jo, Beth, and Amy—and her characterization of herself is, if harsher, more realistic. Lu's first thought upon hearing her mother's suggestion that the girls give their breakfast as a Christmas present to their poor neighbors is, in the *Merry's* version, "I wish we'd eaten it up." It is Nan who exclaims, "I'm so glad you come [*sic*] before we began." In the *Little Women* version it is the impetuous Jo who takes those words from her sister's mouth and thus appears more generous than hungry. The poor family is the same in both versions, with the exception that they bear the name of Hummel in *Little Women* and go nameless in *Merry's*. Louisa Alcott had already, in an anonymous story, "Living in an Omnibus," which appeared in the October 1867 issue of *Merry's Museum*, used the Hummel family as her protagonists.

She published no further *Little Women* incidents as "editorials" in *Merry's*. Perhaps Thomas Niles objected to this manner of preprinting the story. Perhaps the editor, "finding that a good deal of disappointment is felt by some of our readers at the discontinuance of the correspondence,"[3] decided to give less space to Cousin Tribulation and more to the W—e's and A. W.'s who deluged the office with stories and poetry.[4] At any rate, although Cousin Tribulation did continue "moral" episodes as part of her "Chat," she also found space to insert an account of Van Amburgh's Menagerie or the new "Potatoe [*sic*] Pantomime."

To be sure, this is only one of the many narratives that Louisa Alcott wrote originally for a periodical and afterward incorporated into a book of some kind. Her tales in the *Youth's Companion, The Independent,* and *St. Nicholas* saw later publication in the various volumes of children's stories issued by Roberts Brothers. She was, indeed, more than the "competent" juvenilist whom Mr. Fuller had so heartily introduced in his prospectus—she was a shrewd Yankee who liked her bread buttered on both sides.

NOTES

1. Leona Rostenberg, "Some Anonymous and Pseudonymous Thrillers of Louisa M. Alcott," reprinted in this collection.

2. Ednah D. Cheney, ed., *Louisa May Alcott: Her Life, Letters, and Journals* (Boston, 1889), 186.

3. "Merry's Monthly Chat with His Friends," *Merry's Museum* (April 1868): 164.

4. Ibid. (May 1868): 208, and (October 1868): 420.

Louisa M. Alcott in Periodicals

"My first story was printed, and $5 paid for it. It was written in Concord when I was sixteen. Great rubbish! Read it aloud to sisters, and when they praised it, not knowing the author, I proudly announced her name."[1]

As it turned out, this statement, written by Louisa May Alcott in her 1852 journal, was portentous. At the age of nineteen, writing in a house on Boston's High Street where her mother had opened an intelligence office, or employment agency, to increase the meager family income,[2] Louisa was referring to "The Rival Painters. A Tale of Rome."[3] This was the story of Guido, a Florentine artist who fell in love with Madeline, and of his rival, Count Ferdinand. Madeline's father announced he would give his daughter to one who "hath painted a picture the most perfect in grace, and beauty of form, design and coloring." In his lesser love the count painted Madeline, but Guido sketched a portrait of his mother that won the prize. And on 8 May 1852 Louisa Alcott won the satisfaction of seeing her story, if not her name, in the *Olive Branch*. During the next fifteen years she would try her hand at a variety of occupations from sewing to washing, from domestic service to teaching. The family was poor, the cost of coal and the price of shoes high, and Bronson Alcott's lofty discourses on universal love did little to augment the family treasury. For the most part, however, Louisa Alcott wrote for her living and took her pen for her bridegroom.

Between 1852, when her first prose story was published, and 1888, when she died, she would produce about 210 poems and sketches, stories and serials that would be published in some forty different periodicals. Thus the bulk of Louisa Alcott's writings appeared in the periodical literature of the day. Though some of those writings were reprinted in book form (as well as in other periodicals) many of them had solo magazine appearances and still await the research of the literary detective. Even the stories and serials that were reprinted as books—and these include several of her major works as well as most of the short-story collections—first appeared in periodicals, and so those periodicals are invested with great bibliographic and bibliophilic interest. Since most Alcott bibliographers have restricted themselves to her book publications, this vast area of periodical publications forms an unexplored mine both for the bibliographer who can trace her books to their beginnings much as the philologist traces the derivation of words, and for the biographer who can gain from these periodical appearances all sorts of insights, from dates of composition to dealings with editors. As for the writings that were never reprinted, they include revealing autobiographical narratives, propagandist articles, and sensational tales. They employ so many varied techniques—sweetness and light, blood-and-thunder, naturalism and realism—that this great body of unread material demands rediscovery.

To the literary critic this study must prove as fruitful as to the bibliographer and the biographer. Louisa Alcott owed much to her periodical appearances. From the exigencies of serialization she learned to apply the cliff-hanger technique to stories that were well paced and suspenseful, and for a variety of magazine audiences she learned to supply the demands of varied tastes. Her writings in periodicals reflect far more comprehensively and incisively than her *Little Women* series her development as a writer; Louisa Alcott was a far more complex writer than the appellation of "Children's Friend" has suggested. Her methods and her stories were aired in the periodicals of her day, and to them the bibliographer-biographer-critic must turn for a fuller comprehension of a fascinating literary figure who earned a place in many niches.

Alcott's first association with a major magazine was with the *Saturday Evening Gazette*. To it, beginning in 1854, she made fifteen contributions, one or two under the pseudonym Flora Fairfield. Most of the stories were indeed fair and flowery in the sweetness-and-light school, sentimental and silver-lined, although the first—"The Rival Prima Donnas"[4]—veered into violence and vengeance when one singer crushed her competitor to death by means of an iron ring placed upon her head. This effusion filled three columns of the 11 November 1854 issue, where it appeared over the name Flora Fairfield. Bringing five to ten dollars apiece, the narratives authored by Alcott were published during the next few years in the *Gazette.*

It was for the "F.L." of her journal that Louisa doffed the rose-colored glasses she had worn for readers of the *Saturday Evening Gazette* and turned to the unmitigated joys of sensationalism. *Frank Leslie's Illustrated Newspaper* ran the first major sensational story by Louisa Alcott and so began what might well be called a career within a career. For *The Flag of Our Union* Louisa M. Alcott, under the pseudonym of A. M. Barnard, produced her bloodiest and most thunderous thrillers. Letting down her literary tresses, Alcott might have become the American Mrs. Radcliffe had she not at length been diverted from her gory, gruesome, and fascinating course.

Intrigued by sensationalism throughout her life, Alcott was a realist when it came to living and a professional when it came to writing. When the opportunity arose for her not only to contribute to but to edit a magazine for young people, she discarded her gothic horrors for simplicity and propriety. The versatile author was thus sent on her way from "the witch's cauldron to the family hearth."

In September 1867 Louisa Alcott wrote in her diary a significant notation: "Niles, partner of Roberts, asked me to write a girls' book. Said I'd try.

"F. asked me to be the editor of 'Merry's Museum.' Said I'd try.

"Began at once on both new jobs."[5]

Merry's Museum had recently been acquired by Horace B. Fuller of Boston, who had long been interested in children's literature.[6] He had served an apprenticeship with the most extensive schoolbook house in New England, Hickling, Swan and Brown, before joining Walker, Wise & Company, a Unitarian publishing house that upheld the dignity and the rights not only of blacks and of women but of children. The firm included in its list several juvenile series and standard books for the young. Walker, Wise was for a short time metamorphosed into Walker, Fuller & Company until finally Horace B. Fuller set out on his own.

His primary interest was still in juvenile literature, and in October 1867 he announced his purchase of *Merry's Museum*. "Several important changes," he declared, "are contemplated in the management of Merry's Museum." It would be "clearly printed, on fine white paper . . . prepared expressly for our own use." It would be "beautifully illustrated with original designs." Its contributors would include "some of the best and most popular writers for the young," while its editor had "hardly an equal, and . . . no superior as a writer for youth in the country."

That editor certainly had an indefatigable right hand, keeping up her journal while she plunged into her new task. "Agreed with F.," she noted, "to be editor for $500 a year. Read manuscripts, write one story each month and an editorial. On the strength of this engagement went to Boston, took a room—No. 6 Hayward Place—furnished it, and set up housekeeping for myself."[7]

In the course of her editorship of *Merry's*, Louisa Alcott would not only edit stories and serials but provide the magazine with nearly thirty of her own contributions. One section of *Merry's Museum* was entitled "Merry's Monthly Chat with His Friends," and here Louisa May Alcott occupied the editorial armchair. The first number of the "new" *Merry's* testified to the editor's industry, including two of her poems and two of her stories along with installments of the serials "Little Pearl" and "The Loggers; or, Six Months in the Forests of Maine," adventures and articles illustrated by Elizabeth B. Greene, bits of educational information, acrostics, and rebuses. As an example of Louisa Alcott's writings before and during the composition of *Little Women*, all the 1868 issues of *Merry's Museum* are particularly interesting. The serial that ran between April and November of that year was a charming collection of animal stories for children—"Will's Wonder-Book."[8] Two years later *Will's Wonder Book* was also published in book form by the wily Horace B. Fuller without the author's knowledge or consent. More recently it was reprinted as the first of Clarke Historical Library's Juvenile Monographs.[9]

"Will's Wonder-Book" was perfectly adapted to the editor's Dear Merrys. Her contributions to other, quite different periodicals indicate both her versatility and her ability to gauge the varieties of public taste. Despite an early and devastating rebuke from the publisher James T. Fields, who advised, "Stick to your teaching, Miss Alcott. You can't write," Louisa Alcott persisted and in 1860, with "Love and Self-Love,"[10] made her bow in his already prestigious magazine, the *Atlantic Monthly*. The same year she supplied the *Atlantic* with a story that is actually a skeleton of *Little Women*. Even more markedly than "The Sisters' Trial" (which had appeared in the *Saturday Evening Gazette*), "A Modern Cinderella"[11] foreshadows the book.

Despite, or perhaps because of, the time she spent in nursing and the illness that resulted, the Civil War years were productive for Louisa Alcott. Although she offered to "write 'great guns'" for an *Atlantic Monthly* turned warlike, the principal medium she used for her war stories was *The Commonwealth*, an emancipation weekly begun by Moncure Daniel Conway and edited by her Concord friend Frank Sanborn. There her "Hospital Sketches"[12] had their trial run, along with other stories woven about the blue and the gray—and the black. In the columns of *The Commonwealth* appeared scenes Louisa Alcott had witnessed as a nurse in the Union Hotel Hospital, soldiers she had watched, the wounded she had tended. Her rewards were more than the forty-dollar payment for the series. Among those who applauded her efforts was Henry James, Sr., who found in "Hospital Sketches" an exquisite humanity.

There was humanity in her war stories, and there was truth in them. There was humor, along with perceptive observation, in the travel sketches she wrote for *The Independent*, a long-lived New York religious weekly edited by Theodore Tilton.[13] By 1868 Louisa Alcott had indeed attempted a wide variety of literary techniques, serving periodicals with divergent tastes. From sweetness and light to blood-and-thunder, from juvenilia to realistic war narratives she had explored a broad range of literary themes. When, on 14 February 1868, Robert Bonner of the *New York Ledger* appeared at 6 Hayward Place offering Miss Alcott one hundred dollars for a column of advice to young ladies, she produced a piece entitled "Happy Women,"[14] where working spinsters received the limelight. To sketches of home missionary, physician, and music teacher she added a sketch of herself—a happy writer who was finding a market for her wares.

In 1868 the first part of *Little Women* was published, in 1869 the second. The merchants of Boston, the families of New England, and in time the American public itself laughed and cried over a story destined to become a perennial best-seller. The author, who had dispatched her tales to William Warland Clapp, Jr., and Frank Leslie, to James R. Elliott and Frank Sanborn, to all the C.'s and L.'s and initialed editors of her journal, had found not only a market but a style. Henceforth, while her market would widen, her themes would narrow. With *Little Women* Louisa May Alcott walked into a niche where, except for a few literary adventures, she would comfortably remain for the next twenty years.

In the spring of 1872, after her grand tour, she noted in her journal: "Wrote another sketch for the 'Independent,' . . . and the events of my travels paid my winter's expenses. All is fish that comes to the literary net. Goethe puts his joys and sorrows into poems; I turn my adventures into bread and butter."[15] In large measure it was thanks to the abundant and varied periodical literature of the time that Louisa Alcott was able to do so. The bread and butter it provided became increasingly substantial—"$3,000 for a short serial in 1876"[16]—after the slimmer earnings of earlier years.

Her diary entry referring to Goethe was written in 1872, the year that *Merry's Museum* was absorbed by an older juvenile periodical, the *Youth's Companion*.[17] Founded in 1827 by Nathaniel Parker Willis, that monthly forty years later was controlled by Daniel Sharp Ford, who invented the name "Perry Mason" for his firm and proceeded to resemble that imaginary publisher—"a benevolent old gentleman with mutton-chop whiskers." The *Youth's Companion*, with its emphasis upon lists of premiums or prizes, was more of a family paper than *Merry's Museum*, although its serials had a strong appeal to the young. Ford, who tabooed crime and immorality, demanded of his fiction writers "liveliness, action, humor, and convincing youthful characters"—demands easily met by the author of *Little Women*. For thirty-five dollars apiece she could provide little tales written at odd moments, sometimes at the rate of two a day, while a six-part serial like her temperance story "Silver Pitchers"[18] brought seven hundred dollars. In time her contributions to the *Youth's Companion* outnumbered her contributions to any other periodical. The popular stories of Ford's star author appealed as widely to his family audience as the chemical cabinets and magic lanterns he offered as premiums. Alcott narratives that warned against transgression and enticed to virtue were easy to manufacture. Autobiographical tales, such as "A Happy Birthday,"[19] recounting her mother's seventy-third birthday celebration, or "Reminiscences"[20] of the illustrious Concord neighbor Ralph Waldo Emerson, appealed to and enlightened Daniel Ford's avid subscribers. Some of Alcott's *Companion* stories were reprinted by Roberts Brothers in collections—*Aunt Jo's Scrap-Bag* or *Lulu's Library*. Many, however, have never been reprinted. Yet they are well worth assembling as a "new" collection of stories by Louisa May Alcott.

Second only to the *Youth's Companion* as a periodical market for Alcott was the extremely popular magazine for children begun in 1873 by Roswell Smith and named after the saint associated with Christmas. The editor of *St. Nicholas* was Mary Mapes Dodge, whose tenets regarding a children's magazine were shared by her friend Louisa Alcott.[21] There should be no sermonizing, no wearisome recital of facts, no rattling of dry bones. It must not "be a milk-and-water variety of the periodical for adults. . . . it needs to be stronger, truer, bolder, more uncompromising than the other; . . . it must mean freshness and heartiness, life and joy. . . . A child's magazine is its playground." Such beliefs sat well with the former editor of *Merry's* and the author of *Little Women*. Besides, *St. Nicholas* was a handsome periodical, finely printed by the DeVinne press and profusely illustrated by distinguished artists and engravers. Although at first she refused Dodge's request for a serial, Louisa Alcott in March of 1874 made her first appearance in *St. Nicholas* with a story, "Roses and Forget-Me-Nots,"[22] which urged kindness to the lame and the poor and which would eventually be reprinted in one of *Aunt Jo's Scrap-Bags*. "Roses and Forget-Me-Nots" was the first of a long line of contributions including short stories and serials. In 1875 "Eight Cousins"[23] ran almost concurrently in *Good Things: A Picturesque Magazine for the Young of All Ages* and in *St. Nicholas*. Here Louisa Alcott crusaded without sermonizing for sound minds in sound bodies, exalting the three great remedies of sun, air, and water. In the course of her crusade she joined the health reformers who castigated medicine and tobacco, strong coffee and hot biscuits. The serial was so successful that it was followed by another, "Under the Lilacs,"[24] which in turn was followed by "Jack and Jill"[25] written at the rate of one chapter a day—all of them illuminating the pages of *St. Nicholas* before their transformation into book form.

Besides these full-length narratives, Louisa Alcott supplied the periodical with numerous short stories. No one who had seen the operetta could fail to respond to "Jimmy's Cruise in the 'Pinafore,'"[26] where, in spite of all temptations to belong to other nations, the hero remained an "Amer-i-can," and where the author could unite the moral of industry with the pleasures of amateur theatricals. Before its reprint appearance in a *Scrap-Bag,* "'Pinafore'" earned its indefatigable author one hundred dollars. Indeed, Alcott found it easier to supply Dodge with stories and serials than with a photograph of herself. "A pleasant one does not exist," she wrote to her editor, "& the picture of the forbidding woman photographers make me will carry disappointment & woe to the bosoms of the innocents who hope to see 'Jo young & lovely with hair in two tails down her back.'"[27]

The last serial Alcott supplied to *St. Nicholas* was a collection of old-time tales with a thread running through all from the spinning wheel introduced in the first—tales based upon Concord's revolutionary relics or her father's early days, stories into which a moral was tucked as one might hide pills in jelly. The Alcott pills were devoured eagerly by her young readers, and in 1884 the tales that would be reprinted as *Spinning-Wheel Stories* made their monthly bow in *St. Nicholas.*[28]

Several of Louisa Alcott's major works appeared as serials in periodicals before they were issued between boards: *An Old-Fashioned Girl*[29] in *Merry's Museum;* the autobiographical *Work*[30] in the *Christian Union;* as well as *Eight Cousins, Under the Lilacs,* and *Jack and Jill* in *St. Nicholas*—indications that the author knew how to butter her bread and spread it with jam to boot.

With *Harper's Young People*—a weekly begun in 1879—*St. Nicholas,* and the *Youth's Companion* alone accounted for some seventy stories and serials produced for the young and the young in heart by Louisa May Alcott.

The complex Alcott, however, had a word or two to say to those who were riper in years also, and for that purpose she made use of still another periodical whose columns were always open to her propaganda. "Yours for reforms of all kinds," she signed herself in one of her letters to the *Woman's Journal,* a Boston paper conducted by Lucy Stone and her husband, Henry B. Blackwell. Although the organ of no association, it was "thoroughly identified with the interests . . . of the American Woman Suffrage Association"[31] and its columns were receptive to Alcott's clarion calls for woman's rights and privileges. "Woman's Part in the Concord Celebration,"[32] letters reporting local suffrage or temperance activities, a town meeting, even an account of her disappointing mind-cure treatment, were welcomed by the *Woman's Journal,* where they clearly reflected the feminism that had been an oblique and indirect ingredient of Louisa Alcott's early thrillers for the blood-and-thunder periodicals.

She had come a long way since she had concocted the brew in her witch's cauldron. She had turned not only her adventures but her observations, her thoughts, herself into bread and butter, finding a periodical market suited to her varied themes. Some of those periodicals survived her. Two months after her death in 1888, the *Youth's Companion* ran an article that brought her life full circle. "Recollections of My Childhood"[33] appeared in the 24 May issue and was reprinted two days later in the *Woman's Journal.* In it her audience—both youthful and mature, indeed every member of the family circle—could read how Louy Alcott had fallen into the Frog Pond, gone barnstorming in Concord, and shaken a fist at fate. Indeed, in periodicals, over a period of thirty-five years, her life may be reconstructed. She had had many names and undergone many metamorphoses. She had been called A. M. Barnard in *The Flag of Our Union,* Cousin Tribulation in *Merry's Museum,* and Louisa May Alcott in a host of periodicals. One needs only the clues provided by the bibliographer, the insights of the biographer, and of course the periodicals themselves. We brush the dust from those weeklies and monthlies and we reanimate the past, for their pages are still alive with the stories she imagined and the stories that she lived.

Summary of Alcott in Periodicals, 1851–1888

The following list includes only first appearances; magazine reprints are not cited. In one instance only, the publication of "Eight Cousins" almost simultaneously in *Good Things* and *St. Nicholas* (Stern No. 154), is the entry included twice. Thus the total number of contributions is reduced from 212 to 211.

Stern Numbers refer to numbered items in the bibliography appended to *Louisa's Wonder Book: An Unknown Alcott Juvenile*, ed. Madeleine B. Stern (Mt. Pleasant, Mich.: Central Michigan University and Clarke Historical Library, 1975). A single asterisk indicates a poem; a double asterisk indicates a prose contribution run serially in two or more numbers.

Periodical	Number of Contributions	Years of Publications by Alcott	Stern Numbers
Peterson's Magazine	1*	1851	1
Olive Branch	1	1852	2
Dodge's Literary Museum	1	1852	3
Saturday Evening Gazette	11 + 3* + 1**	1854, 1856, 1859, 1864, 1867	4, 8–17, 20–21, 45, 63
The Little Pilgrim	2*	1858	18–19
The Liberator	1*	1860	22
Atlantic Monthly	4 + 1*	1860, 1863	23–24, 32–34
The Monitor	1**	1862	26
Frank Leslie's Illustrated Newspaper	3**	1863–64	27, 30, 41
The Commonwealth	2 + 6**	1863–64, 1867	28–29, 31, 36, 40, 42, 44, 57
Daily Morning Drum-Beat	1 + 1**	1864	38–39
The United States Service Magazine	1**	1864	43
The Flag of Our Union	4* + 4**	1865–67	47–48, 50–55
Our Young Folks	1	1865	49
The Independent	12 + 1**	1867–68, 1872–75, 1878, 1881	56, 59, 65, 84, 123–24, 137, 139, 148, 162, 165, 187, 201

(continued)

Periodical	Number of Contributions	Years of Publications by Alcott	Stern Numbers
Merry's Museum	20, 6* + 3**	1867–70	58, 62, 67–76, 79, 88–90, 92–93, 95–96, 98, 100–101, 103–4, 106–7, 111, 114
Boston Daily Advertiser	1	1867	61
The New York Ledger	1	1868	77
Putnam's Magazine	2	1868–69	82, 102
Frank Leslie's Chimney Corner	1 + 1**	1868–69	83, 94
National Anti-Slavery Standard	1	1868	86
Youth's Companion	30 + 3**	1868–70, 1872–77, 1882, 1888	87, 99, 108, 110, 112, 127, 129–32, 134–36, 142, 144, 146–47, 149–50, 155, 157, 159, 161, 163–64, 169, 171–72, 177, 181, 205, 209, 265
The New World	1	1869	91
The Christian Register	2	1870, 1872	113, 118
Boston Daily Evening Transcript	2	1871, 1873	115, 138

Periodical	Number of Contributions	Years of Publications by Alcott	Stern Numbers
Hearth and Home	3●●	1872, 1874	119, 122, 145
Christian Union	2●●	1872–73	120, 128
Young Folks' Journal	1●●	1874	141
St. Nicholas	24 + 6●●	1874–88	143, 151, 154, 167–68, 184, 188–89, 195, 199, 212, 217–18, 220, 222–25, 228–33, 235, 241, 249, 256, 258, 264
Woman's Journal	15 + 3●	1874–76, 1878–80, 1882–87	152, 156, 160, 173, 185, 190, 196, 204, 214–15, 226, 236–39, 243, 247, 253
Good Things: A Picturesque Magazine for the Young of All Ages	1●●	1874–75	154
Demorest's Monthly Magazine	1 + 1●●	1881–82	198, 207
Our Union	1	1877	182
Harper's Young People	6 + 2●●	1880, 1882, 1884–87	197, 213, 219, 240, 244, 251, 259–60
The Sword and Pen	1●●	1881	200

(continued)

Periodical	Number of Contributions	Years of Publications by Alcott	Stern Numbers
Concord Freeman	1	1882	206
The Union Signal	1	1883	216
The Brooklyn Magazine	2	1886	245–46
The Book Buyer	1	1886	250
The Young Crusader	1	1887	252
The Voice	1	1887	254
Ladies' Home Journal	1	1887	255
TOTALS 42	149 + 21* + 42** (212)		

NOTES

1. Ednah D. Cheney, ed., *Louisa May Alcott: Her Life, Letters, and Journals* (Boston: Roberts, 1889), 68. Hereinafter "Cheney."

2. For all biographical references, see Madeleine B. Stern, *Louisa May Alcott* (Norman: University of Oklahoma Press, 1950), passim.

3. Stern No. 2. These Stern Numbers refer to the Alcott bibliography appended to *Louisa's Wonder Book: An Unknown Alcott Juvenile*, ed. Madeleine B. Stern (Mt. Pleasant, Mich.: Central Michigan University and Clarke Historical Library, 1975). See also "Summary of Alcott in Periodicals," above.

4. Stern No. 4.

5. Cheney, 186.

6. For Fuller's life and career, see Madeleine B. Stern, *Imprints on History: Book Publishers and American Frontiers* (Bloomington: Indiana University Press, 1956), 45–59, 401–5.

7. Cheney, 186.

8. Stern No. 79.

9. This volume, *Louisa's Wonder Book,* contains a reprint of *Will's Wonder Book,* a detailed introduction, and an extensive Alcott bibliography by Madeleine B. Stern.

10. Stern No. 23.

11. Stern No. 24.

12. Stern No. 29.

13. It was *The Independent* that published (4 June 1874) the autobiographical "How I Went Out to Service" (Stern No. 148).

14. Stern No. 77.

15. Cheney, 262.

16. Ibid., 103.

17. For the *Youth's Companion*, see Frank Luther Mott, *A History of American Magazines 1850–1865* (Cambridge: Harvard University Press, 1957), 262–74.

18. Stern No. 161.

19. Stern No. 142.

20. Stern No. 205.

21. For *St. Nicholas*, see Mott, *A History of American Magazines 1865–1885* (Cambridge: Harvard University Press, 1957), 500–505. Dodge's tenets are quoted on p. 501.

22. Stern No. 143.

23. Stern No. 154.

24. Stern No. 184.

25. Stern No. 195.

26. Stern No. 189.

27. Louisa May Alcott to Mary Mapes Dodge, 17 August, n.y., quoted in Stern, *Louisa May Alcott*, 280.

28. See Stern Nos. 220, 222–25, 228–33, 235.

29. Stern No. 103.

30. Stern No. 128.

31. Mott, *A History of American Magazines 1865–1885,* 94.

32. Stern No. 160.

33. Stern No. 265.

Louisa Alcott's Feminist Letters

In July 1975 *Behind a Mask: The Unknown Thrillers of Louisa May Alcott* was published, followed a year later by *Plots and Counterplots: More Unknown Thrillers of Louisa May Alcott.*[1] Those collections of nine blood-and-thunder narratives written during the 1860s before the appearance of *Little Women* and never before assembled reflected a totally different image of the Louisa Alcott who achieved fame as the "Children's Friend." In those stories, most of them pseudonymous or anonymous, the author had wielded a lurid pen, invented plots of violence and revenge, and created heroines who were not only proud and passionate but filled with feminist anger. The manipulations of those obliquely feminist heroines of Louisa Alcott's salad days prompted many readers to view the author as a militant feminist herself, a previously unacclaimed leader in the cause of women.

It is time therefore to examine closely the nature and extent of Louisa Alcott's feminism. A study of the vengeful deeds of her heroines is less productive for this purpose than a study of her nonfictional writings on the subject. The small collection of what might be called her feminist letters has now been brought together for the first time. From their lucid and direct evidence, Louisa Alcott emerges as a feminist indeed, but by no means a militant feminist. She was a feminist because she was a humanist; she embraced the cause of woman because she embraced the causes of humanity.

Support of those causes was part of her inheritance. Her parents endorsed most of the reforms of the day from temperance to health food, from homeopathy to antislavery, but according to Bronson Alcott, the "reform of reforms" was woman suffrage. As for his wife, Abba May Alcott, she held with Margaret Fuller that the opening to women of "a great variety of employments" could have none but salutary effects, that woman's rights as "wife, mother, daughter, and owner of property" must be protected, and that "extension to woman of all civil rights" would contribute to "the welfare and progress of the State."[2] As city missionary and later as manager of an intelligence office in Boston Abba May Alcott was keenly aware of the needs and capabilities of women.

In 1853 a convention was called in Boston for revision of the Massachusetts constitution. Twelve preliminary petitions signed by more than two thousand individuals were presented, urging a constitutional amendment recognizing woman's right to the ballot. One of them, published in November 1853, was entitled *Petition of Abby May Alcott and Others to the Citizens of Massachusetts on Equal Political Rights of Woman*. The "and others" included such luminaries as Thomas Wentworth Higginson and Wendell Phillips, Theodore Parker and William Lloyd Garrison, Samuel E. Sewall and Samuel May, Jr.—and the petitioner's husband, A. Bronson Alcott. The Abba Alcott appeal pressing extension of civil rights to woman on the grounds of no taxation without representation was unsuccessful. As the historians of woman suffrage would comment, "the Massachusetts Convention did not deign to notice the prayer of 2000 women."[3]

Bronson Alcott, who had signed not only his wife's petition but the earlier call to the First National Woman's Rights Convention of 1850, was a consistent supporter of the cause. In 1856, at the Seventh National Woman's Rights Convention held in New York, Massachusetts was represented by speeches and letters from many adherents including A. Bronson Alcott. In 1881, when he was eighty-two, "the white-haired and venerable philosopher . . . paid a glowing tribute to the intellectual worth of woman" at the Boston May Anniversary of the National Association. Woman, he declared, had been the "inspiration font from which his own philosophical ideas had been drawn. Not until the women of our nation have been granted every privilege would the liberty of our republic be assured."[4]

Throughout his long life he had supported woman's rights in general and woman suffrage in particular. Answering an appeal from Lucy Stone, he wrote in 1867: "I have not been able to see Mr. Emerson till yesterday since receiving your note. He declined giving his signature to your Appeal, saying he would write his objections. . . . Having none myself, I gladly sign it, assured that woman is soon to have her place in the State with every right of the citizen. What Ideal Republics have fabled, ours is to be. Nor need we fear the boldest experiments which the moral sense of the best women conceive and advocate."[5]

Bronson Alcott upheld those "boldest experiments." To Lucy Stone, on 11 April 1874, he addressed a lengthy and enthusiastic approbation of woman suffrage, which he characterized as "this reform of reforms." With citations from Euripides, Plato, and Sophocles he recommended not merely enfranchisement for women but their active participation in government: "Does any reasonable man question if there be not as many women having public gifts as there are men? Are not the proofs multiplying wherever women have opportunities opened for proving their fitness under conditions as favorable as those given to men? The womanly gifts and graces are as necessary in the conduct and complementing public duties and affairs, as in private household concerns. Where women—the best women, lead is it unsafe for any to follow?" Alcott sensed the inevitability of women's "taking their places abreast of man," asking, "Does any observing man fail to perceive the signs of the time; discern what is in the air, the crisis approaching: who is the leader? Is it woman?"[6]

Bronson Alcott's letter to Lucy Stone concluded with the sentence "Mrs. Alcott and Louisa join in hearty hopes for your success." By 1874 Louisa Alcott's hopes for the success of woman suffrage were indeed hearty, though her participation in the cause was not yet as active as it would become. The year before, in answer to an apparent request that she attend the second session of the convention at Brooklyn's Plymouth Church, Louisa Alcott had replied she would be there in spirit but not in body, for she was "so busy just now proving 'woman's right to labor,' that I have no time to help prove 'woman's right to vote.'" During the 1870s, however, despite the fact that she was grinding out stories for the *Youth's Companion* and *St. Nicholas*, articles for *The Independent*, and full-length narratives including *Eight Cousins* and *Rose in Bloom*,[7] Louisa Alcott did take time to help prove woman's right to vote. She did this largely by writing letters advancing woman suffrage and expressing her growing impatience with the apathy of Concord, Massachusetts, toward that reform.

Louisa Alcott's feminist letters appeared in the *Woman's Journal*,[8] the only woman's suffrage paper published in Massachusetts. A Boston weekly, it had been set up by the New England Woman Suffrage Association in 1869, incorporated in 1870, owned by a joint stock company, and edited by Lucy Stone and her husband, Henry B. Blackwell. Its first issue appeared on 8 January 1870, but it was not until 14 November 1874 that Louisa Alcott's first contribution was published there. Between that year and 1887 she would contribute to that weekly newspaper "devoted to the interests of Woman" eighteen letters, articles, stories, and poems.[9] The nine feminist letters here assembled for the first time reflect both the paper's attitude and her own, an affirmation of woman's "educational, industrial, legal and political Equality and especially . . . her right of Suffrage." After 1879 the name of Louisa M. Alcott was listed in the masthead among occasional contributors, the 11 January issue of that year stating: "Among other features of new interest in the Woman's Journal, for the coming year, we are able to announce as occasional correspondents Louisa M. Alcott, Frances D. Gage and Mrs. Tracy Cutler."[10] The year before her death, the paper offered as a premium to new subscribers *Jo's Boys, and How They Turned Out* and carried among its endorsements the words of Louisa M. Alcott: "It is the only paper I take, and I find it invaluable to me."[11]

The tenor of Louisa Alcott's letters in the *Woman's Journal* is less lofty than that of her father's epistles to Lucy Stone, but perhaps for that very reason it is more markedly clear. One of the most notable— "Woman's Part in the Concord Celebration"—is filled with mocking but good-humored scorn for the mecca of the mind that honored the centennial of American Independence but dishonored its women citizens. For all the humor, Louisa Alcott ends on a trumpet note: "By and by there will come a day of reckoning, and then the tax-paying women of Concord will not be forgotten . . . *then* . . . following in the footsteps of their forefathers, [women] will utter another protest that shall be 'heard round the world.' " Her own protests at Concord's apathy were heard round the office of the *Woman's Journal* as the years passed. In 1882 Louisa Alcott's letter castigated the town that "takes no active part in any of the great reforms of the day, but seems to be content with the reflected glory of dead forefathers and imported geniuses," the town that she believed was "degenerating into a museum for revolutionary relics, or a happy hunting-ground for celebrity-seekers." Against the apathy of Concord's women, too, Louisa Alcott fired her shots, reminding them that for the sake of the ballot they might "leave the dishes till they get home, as they do when in a hurry to go to the sewing-society, Bible-class, or picnic. A hasty meal once a year will not harm the digestion of the lords of creation." For the most part, Louisa Alcott's letters to the *Woman's Journal* affirmed her belief in woman suffrage as a right to which women were entitled but also as a privilege for which they must make an active effort.

She herself, without militancy, had begun to make such an effort. In October 1875 Louisa Alcott attended the Woman's Congress in Syracuse, New York,[12] and because of her presence there that Congress honored not only women in general but one woman in particular. Maria Mitchell had opened the meeting; talks on art culture, science in the kitchen, and the aesthetics of dress had followed; Julia Ward Howe had given her much-repeated recitation of *The Battle Hymn of the Republic.* Finally, Mary Livermore had introduced Louisa May Alcott to the Congress. The author had received an ovation along with the honor of membership in the National Congress of the Women of the United States. A report of her attendance at that Congress was sent by Mary Livermore to the *Woman's Journal* and appeared in the 23 October 1875 issue:

> The author of "Little Women," who is a member of the Congress, was in attendance throughout the sessions. As soon as the papers announced her presence, a great commotion began among the young people. They must see her. A note was sent by them to the President, begging her to invite Miss Alcott to sit on the platform. . . . But their idol could not be coaxed to put herself on exhibition, and so their desire had to be compassed in another way. . . . At first it was the inevitable autograph album that brought the . . . damsels to the rear of the stage, crowding its wings—they wanted autographs. While these were being written, they used the Yankee privilege of asking questions, and their eyes, sometimes assisted by lorgnettes, gave in keeping to their memory, the lineaments of one who has long held them in thrall with her pen.[13]

When she came to write "My Girls" for the fourth volume of *Aunt Jo's Scrap-Bag,* Louisa Alcott recalled her attendance at the Woman's Congress:

On the stage was a whole array of successful women . . . discussing all the questions which should interest and educate their sex. . . .

Down below were grown people, many women, and a few men; but up in the gallery, like a garland of flowers, a circle of girlish faces . . . listening. . . . It was close and crowded down below, dusty and dark; but up in the gallery the fresh October air blew in. . . . There they were, the future Mary Livermores, Ednah Cheneys, Julia Howes, Maria Mitchells, Lucy Stones.[14]

By 1879 Louisa Alcott had the opportunity not merely of supporting the concept of woman suffrage but of exercising her right to the ballot. To be sure, it was a limited opportunity but Louisa Alcott was quick to grasp it and to urge it upon all the taxpaying women of Concord. On 16 April 1879 the Act to Give Women the Right to Vote for Members of School Committees was approved in Massachusetts.[15] In July Louisa Alcott recorded in her journal: "Was the first woman to register my name as a voter"; and the next month: "Sixteen callers to-day. Trying to stir up the women about suffrage; so timid and slow."[16] The *Woman's Journal* of 23 August reported with satisfaction in an otherwise inaccurate note that "Miss Alcott had been the first woman to register in the old town of Concord. Since that time several meetings have been held, and other names added. But it seemed right that that of Miss Alcott should lead all the rest."

Actually, "the old town of Concord" was as apathetic as ever. Of the "several meetings" mentioned in the *Woman's Journal,* three were held at the Alcott house. In September Alcott "drove about and drummed up women to my suffrage meeting"[17] and by October she reported the results in a straightforward letter to the *Woman's Journal:* "I am ashamed to say that out of a hundred women who pay taxes on property in Concord, only seven have as yet registered. . . . A very poor record for a town which ought to lead if it really possesses all the intelligence claimed for it."

The momentous event took place on 29 March 1880, when for the first time women were permitted to attend a Concord town meeting and cast their votes for school committee. Louisa Alcott's journal entry was brief: "Town meeting. Twenty women there, and voted first, thanks to Father. Polls closed,—in joke, we thought, as Judge Hoar proposed it; proved to be in earnest, and *we* elected a good school committee. Quiet time; no fuss."[18] Her report to the *Woman's Journal* was more detailed: "No bolt fell on our audacious heads, no earthquake shook the town, but a pleasing surprise created a general outbreak of laughter and applause, for, scarcely were we [the women] seated [after having voted] when Judge Hoar rose and proposed that the polls be closed. The motion was carried before the laugh subsided, and the polls were closed without a man's voting; a perfectly fair proceeding we thought since we were allowed no voice on any other question." For the first time in Concord's history, twenty women had voted at town meeting. As Louisa Alcott put it, "The ice is broken, and I predict that next year our ranks will be fuller."

During the next few years she continued to exercise the very limited privilege accorded her as a woman. In September 1880 she noted in her journal: "Paid my first *poll*-tax. As my *head* is my most valuable piece of property, I thought $2 a cheap tax on it. Saw my townswomen about voting, etc. Hard work to stir them up; cake and servants are more interesting."[19] In March 1881 she recorded, "Voted for school committee,"[20] and her April 1883 entry echoed her earlier comments: "Town meeting. Seven women vote. I am one of them, and A. [Anna Alcott Pratt] another. A poor show for a town that prides itself on its culture and independence."[21]

Louisa Alcott's championship of feminist causes was not confined to exercising her own limited right of suffrage. Her library apparently included both Mary Wollstonecraft and Margaret Fuller,[22] and in 1881 she herself urged publication of still another feminist writer. Although she declined writing a preface for Harriet H. Robinson's *Massachusetts in the Woman Suffrage Movement*, she pressed for its publication, interceding with the less than eager Thomas Niles of Roberts Brothers. Suggesting a small edition, she begged her publisher to examine the manuscript, reminding him that "we are going to win in time, and the friend of literary ladies ought to be also the friend of women generally."[23] A week later, after Niles had agreed to read the manuscript, Louisa Alcott thanked him and offered additional help. She recalled the days when antislavery was "in just the same state that Suffrage is now, and take more pride in the very small help we Alcotts could give than in all the books I ever wrote or ever shall write." It was time, she considered, to record the early stages in woman suffrage.[24] *Massachusetts in the Woman Suffrage Movement* was published by Roberts Brothers in

1881, and in an introduction its author acknowledged her special gratitude to "Louisa M. Alcott and Wendell Phillips for their encouragement, and sympathy with my work."[25]

Louisa Alcott advanced woman suffrage not only with literary but with financial support. Lucy Stone recalled her appearance one morning at the office of the *Woman's Journal* with a check for one hundred dollars. "'I made this before breakfast by my writing,' she said, 'and I know of no better place to invest it than in this cause.'"[26] In 1884, when a fund was voted to organize local suffrage associations throughout the state, Louisa Alcott subscribed one hundred dollars immediately.[27] One of her last contributions to the *Woman's Journal* reiterated her endorsement of that paper: "I read it, lend it to my neighbors, and send it to hospitals, prisons, country libraries."

Louisa Alcott and her father both died in March 1888. The *Woman's Journal* commented in a joint obituary: "It seemed her destiny to fill the gaps in life; a wife to her father; a husband to her widowed sister; a mother to May's daughter."[28] At the twentieth meeting of the suffragists held in Cincinnati, Ohio, in November, a memorial resolution was adopted for Louisa M. Alcott.[29]

She had indeed been many things to many people, and neither children nor children's literature had been her exclusive preoccupation. Reform in general and feminist reform in particular had fired her imagination. In a letter of October 1885 to the American Woman Suffrage Association she had signed herself "Yours for woman suffrage and all other reforms," and earlier, in October 1879, she had ended a letter to the *Woman's Journal,* "Yours for reforms of all kinds."

The roster of reforms to which emancipated thinkers of the nineteenth century subscribed was long indeed, and Louisa Alcott endorsed most of them: dress reform and natural foods, homeopathy and temperance, peace and freedom. The emancipation of the slave aroused her sympathy consistently whether the slave was male or female, red, black, or white.

In the 1870s and 1880s, when she was in a position to support reform measures effectively, the outstanding cause was a feminist one. Woman suffrage had become "this most vital question of the age," and "the emancipation of the white slaves of America" demanded active attention. Louisa Alcott gave it such attention. It becomes clear from a study of her feminist letters that her feminism was dynamic without being militant. It reflected the traditional attitudes of her family, although her own espousal—clear and direct—was never lost in "transcendental mist." Louisa Alcott's feminism was the feminism of a human being impatient with indifference, apathy, and intolerance. Neither humorless nor overly aggressive, hers was a firm and convincing advocacy that advanced a cause while it enriched a life.

———

I.

Petition of Abby May Alcott and others to the citizens of Massachusetts on equal political rights of woman.[30]   *1853*

Fellow-Citizens:—In May next a Convention will assemble to revise the Constitution of the Commonwealth.

At such a time it is the right and duty of every one to point out whatever he deems erroneous and imperfect in that instrument, and press its amendment on public attention.

We deem the extension to woman of all civil rights, a measure of vital importance to the welfare and progress of the State. On every principle of natural justice, as well as by the nature of our institutions, she is as fully entitled as man to vote, and to be eligible to office. In governments based on force, it might be pretended with some plausibility, that woman being supposed physically weaker than man, should be excluded from the State. But ours is a government professedly resting on the consent of the governed. Woman is surely as competent to give that consent as man. Our Revolution claimed that taxation and representation should be co-extensive. While the property and labor of women are subject to taxation, she is entitled to a voice in fixing the amount of taxes, and the use of them when collected, and is entitled to a voice in the laws that regulate punishments. It would be a disgrace to our schools and civil institutions, for any one to argue that a Massachusetts woman who has enjoyed the full advantage of all their culture, is not as competent to form an opinion on civil matters, as the illiterate foreigner landed but a few years before upon our shores—unable to read or write—by no means free from early prejudices, and little acquainted with our institutions. Yet such men are allowed to vote.

Woman as wife, mother, daughter, and owner of property, has important rights to be protected. The whole history of legislation so unequal between the sexes, shows that she can not safely trust these to the other sex. Neither have her rights as mother, wife, daughter, laborer, ever received full legislative protection. Besides, our institutions are not based on the idea of one class receiving protection from another; but on the well-recognized rule that each class, or sex, is entitled to such civil rights, as will enable it to protect itself. The exercise of civil rights is one of the best means of education. Interest in great questions, and the discussion of them under momentous responsibility, call forth all the faculties and nerve them to their fullest strength. The grant of these rights on the part of society, would quickly lead to the enjoyment by woman, of a share in the higher grades of professional employment. Indeed, without these, mere book study is often but a waste of time. The learning for which no use is found or anticipated, is too frequently forgotten, almost as soon as acquired. The influence of such a share, on the moral condition of society, is still more important. Crowded now into few employments, women starve each other by close competition; and too often vice borrows overwhelming power of temptation from poverty. Open to women a great variety of employments, and her wages in each will rise; the energy and enterprise of the more highly endowed, will find full scope in honest effort, and the frightful vice of our cities will be stopped at its fountain-head. We hint very briefly at these matters. A circular like this will not allow room for more. Some may think it too soon to expect any action from the Convention. Many facts lead us to think that public opinion is more advanced on this question than is generally supposed. Beside, there can be no time so proper to call public attention to a radical change in our civil polity as now, when the whole framework of our government is to be subjected to examination and discussion. It is never too early to begin the discussion of any desired change. To urge our claim on the Convention, is to bring our question before the proper tribunal, and secure at the same time the immediate attention of the general public. Massachusetts, though she has led the way in most other reforms, has in this fallen behind her rivals, consenting to learn, as to the protection of the property of married women, of many younger States. Let us redeem for her the old pre-eminence, and urge her to set a noble example in this the most important of all civil reforms. To this we ask you to join with us in the accompanying petition to the Constitutional Convention.

2.

[Louisa M. Alcott to Lucy Stone][31]   Concord, October 1, 1873

Dear Mrs. Stone:—I am so busy just now proving "woman's right to labor," that I have no time to help prove "woman's right to vote."

When I read your note aloud to the family, asking "What shall I say to Mrs Stone?" a voice from the transcendental mist which usually surrounds my honored father instantly replied, "Tell her you are ready to follow her as leader, sure that you could not have a better one." My brave old mother, with the ardor of many unquenchable Mays shining in her face, cried out, "Tell her I am seventy-three, but I mean to go to the polls before I die, even if my three daughters have to carry me." And two little men, already mustered in, added the cheering words, "Go ahead, Aunt Weedy, we will let you vote as much as ever you like."

Such being the temper of the small Convention of which I am now president, I can not hesitate to say that though I may not be with you in body, I shall be in spirit, and am as ever, hopefully and heartily yours,

Louisa May Alcott

3.

LETTER OF MISS LOUISA ALCOTT[32]

The following letter of Miss Alcott was accidentally omitted in our report of the Annual Meeting of the American Woman Suffrage Association at Detroit.

Dear Mrs. Stone.—I am sorry that I cannot accept the invitation to be one of the elect precious at the Convention. But my engagements prevent my accepting the honor.

I can write nothing that would be worth reading after the brave and good words which will be uttered on that occasion. I can only wish that every one may be especially inspired, and a forward step taken toward the goal of our desire.

With a firm belief in the good time coming, I am cordially yours,

L. M. Alcott

Boston, Oct. 6, 1874.

———

4.

WOMAN'S PART IN THE CONCORD CELEBRATION[33]

Being frequently asked "what part the women took in the Concord Centennial celebration?" I give herewith a brief account of our share on that occasion.

Having set our houses in order, stored our larders, and filled our rooms with guests, we girded up our weary souls and bodies for the great day, feeling that we must do or die for the honor of old Concord.

We had no place in the procession, but such women as wished to hear the oration were directed to meet in the town hall at half past nine, and there wait till certain persons, detailed for the service, should come to lead them to the tent, where a limited number of seats had been provided for the weaker vessels.

This seemed a sensible plan, and as a large proportion of ladies chose the intellectual part of the feast the hall was filled with a goodly crowd at the appointed hour. No one seemed to know what to do except wait, and that we did with the patience born of long practice. But it was very trying to the women of Concord to see invited guests wandering forlornly about or sitting in chilly corners meekly wondering why the hospitalities of the town were not extended to them as well as to their "men folks" who were absorbed into the pageant in one way or another.

For an hour we women waited, but no one came, and the sound of martial music so excited the patient party that with one accord we moved down to the steps below, where a glimpse of the approaching procession might cheer our eyes. Here we stood, with the north wind chilling us to the marrow of our bones, a flock of feminine Casabiancas with the slight difference of freezing instead of burning at our posts.

Some wise virgins, who put not their trust in men, departed to shift for themselves, but fifty or more obeyed orders and stood fast till, just as the procession appeared, an agitated gentleman with a rosette at his buttonhole gave the brief command,

"Ladies cross the common and wait for your escort:"

Then he vanished and was seen no more.

Over we went, like a flock of sheep, leaving the show behind us, but comforting ourselves with the thought of the seats "saving up" for us and of the treat to come. A cheerful crowd, in spite of the bitter wind, the rude comments of the men swarming by, and the sad certainty which slowly dawned upon us that we were entirely forgotten. The gay and gallant presence of a granddaughter of the Dr. Ripley who watched the fight from the Old Manse, kept up our spirits; for this indomitable lady circulated among us like sunshine, inspiring us with such confidence that we rallied round the little flag she bore, and followed where it led.

Patience has its limits, and there came a moment when the revolutionary spirit of '76 blazed up in the bosoms of these long suffering women; for, when some impetuous soul cried out "Come on and let us take care of ourselves!" there was a general movement; the flag fluttered to the front, veils were close reefed, skirts kilted up, arms locked, and with one accord the Light Brigade charged over the red bridge, up the hill, into the tented field, rosy and red-nosed, disheveled but dauntless.

The tent was closely packed, and no place appeared but a corner of the platform. Anxious to seat certain grey-haired ladies weary with long waiting, and emboldened by a smile from Senator Wilson, a nod from Representative May, and a pensive stare from Orator Curtis, I asked the President of the day if a few ladies could occupy that corner till seats could be found for them?

"They can sit or stand anywhere in the town except on this platform; and the quicker they get down the better, for gentlemen are coming in to take these places."

This gracious reply made me very glad to descend into the crowd again, for there at least good-nature reigned; and there we stood, placidly surveyed by the men (who occupied the seats set apart for us,) not one of whom stirred, though the grandmother of Boston waited in the ranks.

My idea of hospitality may be old-fashioned, but I must say I felt ashamed of Concord that day, when all I could offer my guests, admiring pilgrims to this "Mecca of the mind," was the extreme edge of an unplaned board; for, when the gods were settled, leave was given us to sit on the rim of the platform.

Perched there, like a flock of tempest tossed pigeons, we had the privilege of reposing among the sacred boots of the Gamalials at whose feet we sat, and of listening to the remarks of the reporters, who evidently felt that the elbow room of the almighty press should not be encroached upon even by a hair's breadth.

"No place for women," growled one.

"Never was a fitter," answered a strong-minded lady standing on one foot.

"Ought to have come earlier, if they come at all."

"So they would, if they had not obeyed orders. Never will again."

"Don't see why they couldn't be contented with seeing the procession."

"Because they preferred poetry and patriotism to fuss and feathers."

"Better have it all their own way, next time."

"No doubt they will, and I hope we shall all be there to see."

So the dialogue ended in a laugh, and the women resigned themselves to cold shoulders all around. But as I looked about me, it was impossible to help thinking that there should have been a place for the great granddaughters of Prescott, William Emerson, John Hancock and Dr. Ripley, as well as for Isaac Davis's old sword, the scissors that cut the immortal cartridges, and the ancient flag some woman's fingers made. It seemed to me that their presence on that platform would have had a deeper significance than the gold lace which adorned one side, or the senatorial ponderosity under which it broke down on the other; and that the men of Concord had missed a grand opportunity of imitating those whose memory they had met to honor.

The papers have told the tale of that day's exploits and experiences, but the papers did not get all the little items, and some of them were rather funny. Just before the services began, a distracted usher struggled in to inform Judge Hoar that the wives of several potentates had been left out in the cold, and must be accommodated. Great was the commotion then, for these ladies being bobs to political kites, could not be neglected; so a part of the seats reserved for women were with much difficulty cleared, and the "elect precious" set thereon. Dear ladies! how very cold and wretched they were when they got there, and how willingly the "free and independent citizenesses" of Concord forgave them for reducing their limited quarters to the point of suffocation, as they spread their cloaks over the velvet of their guests, still trying to be hospitable under difficulties.

When order was restored, what might be called "the Centennial Break Down" began. The President went first—was it an omen? and took refuge among the women, who I am happy to say received him kindly and tried to temper the wind to His Imperturbability, as he sat among them looking so bored that I longed to offer him a cigar.

The other gentleman stood by the ship, which greatly diversified the performances by slowly sinking with all on board but the captain. Even the orator tottered on the brink of ruin more than once, and his table would have gone over if a woman had not held up one leg of it for an hour or so. No light task, she told me afterward, for when the inspired gentleman gave an impressive thump, it took both hands to sustain the weight of his eloquence. Another lady was pinned down by the beams falling on her skirts, but cheerfully sacrificed them, and sat still, till the departure of the presidential party allowed us to set her free.

Finding us bound to hear it out, several weary gentlemen offered us their seats, after a time; but we had the laugh on our side now, and sweetly declined, telling them their platform was not strong enough to hold us.

It was over at last, and such of us as had strength enough left went to the dinner, and enjoyed another dish of patriotism "cold without;" others went home to dispense hot comforts, and thaw the congealed visitors who wandered to our doors.

Then came the ball, and there all went well, for Woman was in her sphere, her "only duty was to please," and the more there were, the merrier; so the deserted damsels of the morning found themselves the queens of the evening, and, forgetting and forgiving, bore their part as gaily as if they had put on the vigor of their grandmothers with the old brocades that became them so well.

Plenty of escorts, ushers and marshals at last, and six chairs apiece if we wanted them. Gentlemen who had been as grim as griffins a few hours before were all devotion now, and spectacles that had flashed awful lightning on the women who dared prefer poetry to polkas now beamed upon us benignly, and hoped we were enjoying ourselves, as we sat nodding along the walls while our guests danced.

That was the end of it, and by four A.M., peace fell upon the exhausted town, and from many a welcome pillow went up the grateful sigh:

"Thank heaven we shall not have to go through this again!"

No, not quite the end; for by and by there will come a day of reckoning, and then the tax-paying women of Concord will not be forgotten I think, will not be left to wait uncalled upon, or be considered in the way; and *then*, I devoutly wish that those who so bravely bore their share of that day's burden without its honor, will rally round their own flag again, and, following in the footsteps of their forefathers, will utter another protest that shall be "heard round the world."

Louisa M. Alcott.

Concord, Mass.

5.

LETTER FROM LOUISA M. ALCOTT[34]

Dear Mrs. Stone:—One should be especially inspired this Centennial year before venturing to speak or write. I am not so blest, and find myself so busy trying to get ready for the good time that is surely coming, I can only in a very humble way, help on the cause all women should have at heart.

As reports are in order, I should like to say a word for the girls, on whom in a great measure, depends the success of the next generation.

My lines fell in pleasant places last year, and I looked well about me as I went among the young people, who unconsciously gave me some very cheering facts in return for very poor fictions.

I was both surprised and delighted with the nerve and courage, the high aims and patient persistence which appeared, not only among the laborious young women whose teacher is necessity, but among tenderly nurtured girls who cherished the noblest ambitions and had learned to earn the happiness no wealth could buy them.

Having great faith in young America, it gave me infinite satisfaction to find such eager interest in all good things, and to see how irresistibly the spirit of our new revolution, stirring in the hearts of sisters and daughters, was converting the fathers and brothers who loved them. One shrewd, business man said, when talking of Woman Suffrage, "How *can* I help believing in it, when I've got a wife and six girls who are *bound* to have it?"

And many a grateful brother declared he could not be mean enough to shut any door in the face of the sister who had made him what he was.

So I close this hasty note by proposing three cheers for the girls of 1876—and the hope that they will prove themselves worthy descendants of the mothers of this Revolution, remembering that

> "Earth's fanatics make
> Too often Heaven's saints."

L. M. Alcott.

Concord, June 29.

6.

LETTER FROM LOUISA M. ALCOTT[35]

Editors Journal. Some time ago you asked for a report from Concord as to what was being done about preparing to vote for school committee. So little has been done that it is hardly worth recording, yet honor is due to the few brave and sensible women who have done their duty at the cost of time, money and feeling.

Three meetings were held at our house. Half-a-dozen were expected, and twenty-five came to hear what Mrs. Cheney, Mrs. Dr. Talbot and Mrs. Shattuck could tell us of the proper ways and means. Very informal meetings, where we met and talked over the matter, asked questions, compared notes and got ready to go and register.

I had already been to see the Assessor, and as my interview has been very untruly reported by the gossips, it is only fair to the gentlemen in office to clear them of the absurd blunders they are said to have made. At my first call I was kindly received, and having asked my question, "What must I do?" was told that as a woman paying a property tax I need only take my last year's receipted bill and go to the Registrar.

I did so July 23d, and the interview was as simple and brief as possible. I told what I wanted, showed my bill, was asked where I was born, age and profession; requested to read a few words from the Constitution to prove that I could read, to sign my name to the paper to prove that I could write, and that was all.

The Assessor did not make out my new tax bill, nor did I pay it to him, as the Collector is the person to receive it, and none of the reported conversation took place, except that I said I never felt that my tax was just before, and though not wholly so now I should pay it with pleasure.

Both gentlemen have been very courteous and made matters as easy as they could, though as no one seems to know just how things stand there is some confusion, and each new case has to be settled as well as they can.

Letters were written to Mr. Higginson and Hon. George Hoar, asking them to give us a public meeting; but politics absorbed them and they could not be had till after the 15th of September. We still hope to have a meeting, for it is not too late to stir up the class of women who seem slowest to register. I am ashamed to say that out of a hundred women who pay taxes on property in Concord, only seven have as yet registered, while fourteen have paid a poll tax and put their names down in time.

A very poor record for a town which ought to lead if it really possesses all the intelligence claimed for it.

Yours for reforms of all kinds,

L. M. Alcott.

7.

LETTER FROM LOUISA M. ALCOTT[36]

Editors Journal:—As other towns report their first experience of women at the polls, Concord should be heard from, especially as she has distinguished herself by an unusually well conducted and successful town meeting.

Twenty-eight women intended to vote, but owing to the omission of some formality several names could not be put upon the lists. Three or four were detained at home by family cares and did not neglect their domestic duties to rush to the polls as has been predicted. Twenty, however, were there, some few coming alone, but mostly with husbands, fathers or brothers as they should; all in good spirits and not in the least daunted by the awful deed about to be done.

Our town meetings I am told are always orderly and decent, this one certainly was; and we found it very like a lyceum lecture only rather more tedious than most, except when gentlemen disagreed and enlivened the scene with occasional lapses into bad temper or manners, which amused but did not dismay the women-folk, while it initiated them into the forms and courtesies of parliamentary debate.

Voting for school committee did not come till about three, and as the meeting began at one, we had ample time to learn how the mystic rite was performed, so, when at last our tickets were passed to us we were quite prepared to follow our leader without fear.

Mr. Alcott with a fatherly desire to make the new step as easy as possible for us, privately asked the moderator when the women were to vote, and on being told that they could take their chance with the men or come later, proposed that they should come first as a proper token of respect and for the credit of the town. One of the selectmen said "By all means;" and proved himself a tower of strength by seconding the philosopher on this momentous occasion.

The moderator (who is also the registrar and has most kindly and faithfully done his duty to the women in spite of his own difference of opinion) then announced that the ladies would prepare their votes and deposit them before the men did. No one objected, we were ready, and filed out in good order, dropping our votes and passing back to our seats as quickly and quietly as possible, while the assembled gentlemen watched us in solemn silence.

No bolt fell on our audacious heads, no earthquake shook the town, but a pleasing surprise created a general outbreak of laughter and applause, for, scarcely were we seated when Judge Hoar rose and proposed that the polls be closed. The motion was carried before the laugh subsided, and the polls were closed without a man's voting; a perfectly fair proceeding we thought since we were allowed no voice on any other question.

The superintendent of schools expressed a hope that the whole town would vote, but was gracefully informed that it made no difference as the women had all voted as the men would.

Not quite a correct statement by the way, as many men would probably have voted for other candidates, as tickets were prepared and some persons looked disturbed at being deprived of their rights. It was too late, however, for the joke became sober earnest, and the women elected the school committee for the coming year, feeling satisfied, with one or two exceptions, that they had secured persons whose past services proved their fitness for the office.

The business of the meeting went on, and the women remained to hear the discussion of ways and means, and see officers elected with neatness and dispatch by the few who appeared to run the town pretty much as they pleased.

At five the housewives retired to get tea for the exhausted gentlemen, some of whom certainly looked as if they would need refreshment of some sort after their labors. It was curious to observe as the women went out how the faces which had regarded them with disapproval, derision or doubt when they went in now smiled affably, while several men hoped the ladies would come again, asked how they liked it, and assured them that there had not been so orderly a meeting for years.

One of the pleasant sights to my eyes was a flock of school-boys watching with great interest their mothers, aunts and sisters, who were showing them how to vote when their own emancipation day came. Another was the spectacle of women sitting beside their husbands, who greatly enjoyed the affair though many of them differed in opinion and had their doubts about the Suffrage question.

Among the new voters were descendants of Major Buttrick of Concord fight renown, two of Hancock and Quincy, and others whose grandfathers or great grandfathers had been among the first settlers of the town. A goodly array of dignified and earnest women, though some of the "first families" of the historic town were conspicuous by their absence.

But the ice is broken, and I predict that next year our ranks will be fuller, for it is the first step that counts, and when the timid or indifferent, several of whom came to look on, see that we still live, they will venture to express publicly the opinions they held or have lately learned to respect and believe.

L.M.A.

Concord, March 30, 1880.

8.

LETTER FROM LOUISA M. ALCOTT[37]

Editor Journal:—You ask what we are going to do about Municipal Suffrage for women in Concord? and I regret to be obliged to answer, as before—"Nothing but make a motion asking for it at town meeting, and see it promptly laid upon the table again."

It is always humiliating to have to confess this to outsiders, who look upon Concord as a representative town, and are amazed to learn that it takes no active part in any of the great reforms of the day, but seems to be content with the reflected glory of dead forefathers and imported geniuses, and falls far behind smaller but more wide awake towns with no pretensions to unusual intelligence, culture, or renown.

I know of few places where Municipal Suffrage might more safely be granted to our sex than this, for there is an unusually large proportion of tax-paying, well-to-do and intelligent women, who only need a little training, courage, and good leadership to take a helpful and proper share in town affairs. They would not ask or accept town offices, but would be glad to work in their own efficient and womanly way, as they have proved they could work by the success of their church, charity and social labors for years past.

To those who see what brave and noble parts women elsewhere are taking in the larger and more vital questions of the time, the thought very naturally comes: "What a pity that so much good sense, energy, time, and money could not be used for more pressing needs than church-fairs, tea-parties, or clubs for the study of pottery, Faust, and philosophy!"

While a bar room door stands open between two churches, and men drink themselves to death before our eyes, it seems as if Christian men and women should bestir themselves to try at least to stop it; else the commandment "Thou shalt love thy neighbor as thyself" is written over the altars in vain, and the daily prayer "Lead us not into temptation" is but empty breath.

If the women could vote on the license question I think the bar-room would be closed; but while those who own the place say, "It would lessen the value of the property to make a temperance house of it," and the license matter is left to the decision of those men who always grant it, the women can only wait and hope and pray for the good time when souls are counted of more value than dollars, and law and gospel can go hand in hand.

A forty years acquaintance with the town leads me to believe that as the conservative elders pass away, the new generation will care less for the traditions of the past, more for the work of the present, and taking a brave part in it, will add fresh honors to the fine old town, which should be marching abreast with the foremost, not degenerating into a museum for revolutionary relics, or a happy hunting-ground for celebrity-seekers.

A rumor has just reached me that some of the husbands of our few Suffrage women intend to settle the license question in the right way, and perhaps say a good word for our petition before it is shelved. This is encouraging, for it shows that the power behind the throne is gently working, and though the good women have little to say in public, they do know how to plead, advise, and convince in private. So, even if fewer should vote this year than last, and if nothing seems to come of our effort to secure Municipal Suffrage this time, we shall not be disheartened, but keep stirring our bit of leaven, and wait, as housewives know how to do, for the fermentation which slowly but surely will take place, if our faith hope and charity are only strong, bright, and broad enough.

L. M. Alcott.

Concord, Mass., Feb. 4, 1882.

9.

LETTER FROM MISS ALCOTT[38]

My attention having been called to the fact that a letter of mine, sent to the annual woman suffrage meeting, has been entirely misunderstood by the opponents of the cause, I wish to set the matter right, being as anxious as Mrs. Howe to have it clearly understood that, though a "well-descended woman," I am heart and soul on the unpopular side of the question.

Those to whom the letter was addressed made no mistake in its meaning, knowing well that while home duties kept me from a festival where I was not needed, nothing but the most pressing care or calamity would prevent me from discharging the duties I owe the cause. I had no time for pleasure, but when our town meeting comes I shall be there, glad of a chance to help secure good schools for my neighbors' children. Surely this will be as feminine and worthy an act as standing behind a stall in a charity fair or dancing in a ballroom.

The assertion that suffragists do not care for children, and prefer notoriety to the joys of maternity, is so fully contradicted by the lives of the women who are trying to make the world a safer and a better place for both sons and daughters, that no defence is needed. Having spent my own life, from fifteen to fifty, loving and laboring for children, as teacher, nurse, story-teller and guardian, I know whereof I speak, and value their respect and confidence so highly that for their sakes, if for no other reason, I desire them to know that their old friend never deserts her flag.

So far from losing interest in this question, every year gives me greater faith in it, greater hope of its success, a larger charity for those who cannot see its wisdom and a more earnest wish to use what influence I possess for its advancement.

Louisa May Alcott.

Concord, March 6, 1883.

10.

LETTER FROM MISS LOUISA M. ALCOTT— WOMEN IN CONCORD TOWN MEETING[39]

Concord, Mass., May 8, 1884.

Editors Woman's Journal:

There is very little to report about the woman's vote at Concord Town Meeting, as only eight were there in time to do the one thing permitted them.

With the want of forethought and promptness which shows how much our sex have yet to learn in the way of business habits, some dozen delayed coming till the vote for school committee was over. It came third on the warrant, and a little care in discovering this fact would have spared us much disappointment. It probably made no difference in the choice of officers, as there is seldom any trouble about the matter, but it is to be regretted that the women do not give more attention to the duty which they really care for, yet fail, as yet, to realize the importance of, small as it is at present.

Their delay shows, however, that home affairs are *not* neglected, for the good ladies remained doubtless to give the men a comfortable dinner and set their houses in order before going to vote.

Next time I hope they will leave the dishes till they get home, as they do when in a hurry to go to the sewing-society, Bible-class, or picnic. A hasty meal once a year will not harm the digestion of the lords of creation, and the women need all the drill they can get in the new duties that are surely coming to widen their sphere, sharpen their wits, and strengthen their wills, teaching them the courage, intelligence and independence all should have, and many sorely need in a world of vicissitudes. A meeting should be called before the day for action comes, to talk over matters, to get posted as to time, qualification of persons, and the good of the schools; then the women can act together, know what they are doing, and keep up the proper interest all should feel in so important a matter.

"I come, but I'm lukewarm," said one lady, and that is the spirit of too many.

"We ought to have had a meeting, but you were not here to call it, so no one did," said another, as if it were not a very simple thing to open any parlor and ask the twenty-eight women voters to come and talk an hour.

It was a good lesson, and we hope there will be energy and foresight enough in Concord to register more names, have a quiet little caucus, and send a goodly number of earnest, wide-awake ladies to town-meeting next year.

Louisa M. Alcott.

Concord, May 8, 1884.

———

II.

KIND WORDS FROM MISS ALCOTT[40]

A letter just received from Miss Alcott, which we are permitted to print, contains the following very pleasant words about the WOMAN'S JOURNAL:

It is the only paper I take, and I find it invaluable to me in many ways. It gives the information about women's work and wants which we all need; inspires the weak and doubting with fresh courage and hope by its record of unfailing loyalty in the faithful few who stand fast year after year, and is a part of the education which is to fit us for the duties, honors, and liberties which will surely come when we are ready for them.

I read it, lend it to my neighbors, and send it to hospitals, prisons, country libraries, or lonely souls longing for encouragement as they sit waiting hopefully in the quiet corners of the world out of which often come brave workers and noble lives.

When pen-work is allowed, I shall try to carry out my long-cherished plan of a story for women told in the columns of their paper. Meanwhile I wish it all success, more generous bequests, and a wider field of usefulness.

Cordially yours,
L. M. Alcott.

Concord, Mass., May 12, 1885.

———————

12.

[LOUISA M. ALCOTT TO THE AMERICAN WOMAN SUFFRAGE ASSOCIATION][41]

Concord [October 1885]

I should think it was hardly necessary for me to say that it is impossible for me ever to "go back" on woman suffrage. I earnestly desire to go forward on that line as far and as fast as the prejudices, selfishness and blindness of the world will let us, and it is a great cross to me that ill-health and home duties prevent my devoting heart, pen and time to this most vital question of the age. After a fifty years' acquaintance with the noble men and women of the anti-slavery cause and the sight of the glorious end to their faithful work, I should be a traitor to all I most love, honor and desire to imitate if I did not covet a place among those who are giving their lives to the emancipation of the white slaves of America.

If I can do no more, let my name stand among those who are willing to bear ridicule and reproach for the truth's sake, and so earn some right to rejoice when the victory is won.

Most heartily yours for woman suffrage and all other reforms.

NOTES

1. *Behind a Mask: The Unknown Thrillers of Louisa May Alcott*, ed. Madeleine B. Stern (New York: William Morrow, 1975); *Plots and Counterplots: More Unknown Thrillers of Louisa May Alcott*, ed. Madeleine B. Stern (New York: William Morrow, 1976).

2. "Petition of Abby May Alcott and others," *Una* (November 1853); see item No. 1 for the full text.

3. *History of Woman Suffrage*, ed. Elizabeth Cady Stanton et al., 6 vols. (New York and Rochester: Fowler & Wells—S. B. Anthony, 1881–1922), vol. 1, 253; Harriet H. Robinson, *Massachusetts in the Woman Suffrage Movement* (Boston: Roberts, 1881), 92, 232.

4. *History of Woman Suffrage*, vol. 3, 193. See also Eleanor Flexner, *Century of Struggle: The Woman's Rights Movement in the United States* (Cambridge: Harvard University Press, 1959), 80; Robinson, *Massachusetts in the Woman Suffrage Movement*, 37.

5. Bronson Alcott to Lucy Stone, 13 September 1867, in *The Letters of A. Bronson Alcott*, ed. Richard L. Herrnstadt (Ames: Iowa State University Press, 1969), 411–12. The Lucy Stone "Appeal" probably solicited support for a state woman suffrage amendment in Kansas, the campaign for which Lucy Stone was involved in at the time.

6. Bronson Alcott to Lucy Stone, 11 April 1874, in *Letters of Bronson Alcott*, 629–30; also printed in part in *History of Woman Suffrage*, vol. 3, 519–20.

7. *Rose in Bloom* (Boston: Roberts, 1876) conveyed in a mild way the author's thoughts on woman's rights: "Phebe and I believe that it is as much a right and a duty for women to do something with their lives as for men. . . . We want to live and learn as well as love and be loved" (11–12). Earlier, Louisa Alcott had applauded those "superior women who . . . remain single, and devote themselves to some earnest work" ("Happy Women," *New York Ledger* 24 [11 April 1868]).

8. Shortly after the *Woman's Journal* was projected, the *Agitator*, then published in Chicago by Mary Livermore, was merged with it, and Mary Livermore served as editor for one year. For details of the *Woman's Journal*, see Alice Stone Blackwell, *Lucy Stone* (Boston: Little, Brown, 1930), 236–37, 246, 300 f; Frank Luther Mott, *A History of American Magazines 1865–1885* (Cambridge: Harvard University Press, 1957), 94; Robinson, *Massachusetts in the Woman Suffrage Movement*, 51, 62–64.

9. Louisa Alcott's eighteen contributions to the *Woman's Journal* are: "Letter of Miss Louisa May Alcott," 5 (14 November 1874); "An Advertisement" (poem), 6 (23 January 1875); "Woman's Part in the Concord Celebration," 6 (1 May 1875); "Letter

from Louisa M. Alcott," 7 (15 July 1876); "Mrs. Gay's Prescription," 9 (24 August 1878); "Letter from Louisa M. Alcott," 10 (11 October 1879); "Letter from Louisa M. Alcott," 11 (3 April 1880); "Letter from Louisa M. Alcott," 13 (11 February 1882); "Mr. Alcott's True Condition," 14 (6 January 1883); "Letter from Miss Alcott," 14 (10 March 1883); "Letter from Miss Louisa M. Alcott—Women in Concord Town Meeting," 15 (17 May 1884); "In Memoriam Sophia Foord," 16 (11 April 1885); "Miss Alcott on Mind-Cure," 16 (18 April 1885); "Old Times at Old Concord," 16 (18 April 1885); "Kind Words from Miss Alcott," 16 (16 May 1885); "To My Father on His 86th Birthday" (poem), 16 (12 December 1885); "The Lay of a Golden Goose" (poem), 17 (8 May 1886); "A Flower Fable," 18 (26 February 1887).

10. Frances Dana Gage (1808–84), reformer, lecturer, author, active in woman's rights movement; Hannah Tracy Cutler (1815–96), woman's rights leader and physician, author of *Woman as She Was, Is, and Should Be* (1846) and of *Phillipia, or a Woman's Question* (1886).

11. Quoted in the *Woman's Journal*; see, e.g., 18 (26 February 1887): 20.

12. Madeleine B. Stern, *Louisa May Alcott* (Norman: University of Oklahoma Press, 1971), 243–44, 394; see also *Letters of Bronson Alcott*, 657.

13. Mary A. Livermore, "The Third Congress of Women," *Woman's Journal* 6 (23 October 1875): 341.

14. Louisa M. Alcott, "My Girls," *Aunt Jo's Scrap-Bag IV* (Boston: Roberts, 1878), 25–26.

15. Robinson, *Massachusetts in the Woman Suffrage Movement*, 240.

16. Ednah D. Cheney, ed., *Louisa May Alcott: Her Life, Letters, and Journals* (Boston: Roberts, 1889), 321. Hereinafter "Cheney."

17. Ibid., 321.

18. Ibid., 327. Judge Hoar was Ebenezer Rockwood Hoar of Concord, Mass.

19. Ibid., 337.

20. Ibid., 340.

21. Ibid., 353.

22. Ibid., 318, 398.

23. Ibid., 341–42.

24. Ibid., 342.

25. Robinson, *Massachusetts in the Woman Suffrage Movement*, xi; see also Raymond L. Kilgour, *Messrs. Roberts Brothers Publishers* (Ann Arbor: University of Michigan Press, 1952), 197.

26. *Woman's Journal* 19 (10 March 1888): 78–79.

27. *History of Woman Suffrage*, vol. 4, 702.

28. *Woman's Journal* 19 (10 March 1888): 78.

29. *History of Woman Suffrage*, vol. 4, 431.

30. First published in *Una* (November 1853), the first "pronounced Woman Suffrage paper," founded in Providence, R.I., by Paulina Wright Davis in February 1853, and reprinted in *History of Woman Suffrage*, vol. 1, 247–48.

31. *History of Woman Suffrage*, vol. 2, 831–32. The letter was read at the second session of the Woman Suffrage Convention in Brooklyn's Plymouth Church.

32. *Woman's Journal* 5 (14 November 1874).

33. *Woman's Journal* 6 (1 May 1875). References are to Henry Wilson (1812–75), United States senator from Massachusetts and vice-president, 1873–75; State Representative Samuel May, Jr., of Leicester, son of Louisa Alcott's relative Samuel May; George William Curtis (1824–92), orator, author of *Prue and I;* Samuel Prescott of Concord (1751–77), one of the "warners" of 18 April 1775; the Reverend William Emerson (1769–1811), Unitarian clergyman, father of Ralph Waldo Emerson; John Hancock (1736/7–93), Signer, first governor of Massachusetts; Dr. Ezra Ripley (1751–1841), pastor of the First Church in Concord; for Judge Hoar see note 18. For further details of the centennial celebration in Concord, see Stern, *Louisa May Alcott*, 240–43, 394.

34. *Woman's Journal* 7 (15 July 1876).

35. *Woman's Journal* 10 (11 October 1879). This letter was in part a reply to the following notice, which had appeared in the *Woman's Journal* of 23 August 1879:

MISS ALCOTT BEFORE THE REGISTRAR.

An eye witness reports the appearance of Louisa M. Alcott before the Selectmen of Concord to secure registration for herself. It was several weeks ago. Miss Alcott meant to register early. She said to the authority, "I want to have my name put on the register that I may vote for School Committee." "Very well," said the Selectman. "Have you brought your receipt for your last year's tax?" "No," said Miss Alcott, "I did not know it was necessary." "You will have to bring it." "Won't this year's tax receipt do just as well?" "Oh, yes, but you have not paid it."

Miss Alcott runs over with mirth. A little comical look came on her face, as she said, "I never did hanker to pay my taxes, but now I am in a hurry to pay them." The Selectman, as much amused as Miss Alcott, got the tax bill made out by the Assessor, and then and there Miss Alcott paid it. When they put her name on the Register, it was found that Miss Alcott had been the first woman to register in the old town of Concord. Since that time several meetings have been held, and other names added. But it seemed right that that of Miss Alcott should lead all the rest.   W.

References are to Ednah Dow Cheney (1824–1904), Boston writer, reformer, philanthropist, and suffragist; Emily Fairbanks Talbot (1834–1900), philanthropist and co-worker with her husband, the homeopathic physician Israel Tisdale Talbot; Harriette Robinson Shattuck (1818–76), daughter of the journalist William S. Robinson ("Warrington") and "first woman in Massachusetts to express publicly her desire to vote under the new law"; Thomas Wentworth Higginson (1823–1911), Massachusetts reformer especially in the field of woman's rights, author, and biographer of Margaret Fuller; George Frisbie Hoar (1826–1904), lawyer, representative, and senator, born in Concord, who in 1879 was representing Massachusetts in the Senate.

36. *Woman's Journal* 11 (3 April 1880).

37. *Woman's Journal* 13 (11 February 1882).

38. *Woman's Journal* 14 (10 March 1883). At the time of the annual meeting of

the Massachusetts Woman Suffrage Association, Louisa Alcott was indeed over-whelmed with "pressing care." Between her father's stroke and care of her niece Lulu, she was "too busy to keep a diary." Julia Ward Howe was a "leading spirit in the American Woman Suffrage Association."

39. *Woman's Journal* 15 (17 May 1884).

40. *Woman's Journal* 16 (16 May 1885). Louisa Alcott's "long-cherished plan of a story for women told in the columns of their paper" was not realized. The closest she came to it was "A Flower Fable," printed in the Children's Column of the *Woman's Journal* 18 (26 February 1887), in which, as election time drew near, the opinion was "We have had kings long enough; let us try a queen now."

41. *History of Woman Suffrage*, vol. 4, 412. The letter was written for the seven-teenth annual meeting of the American Woman Suffrage Association held in Min-neapolis, 13–15 October 1885, after persistent and false rumors that Julia Ward Howe and Louisa M. Alcott had renounced their belief in equal suffrage.

Appraisals & Reputation

Louisa Alcott's Self-Criticism

The self-portrait of a writer is a comparatively rare phenomenon; yet, to the literary critic, it provides insights available nowhere else. Unlike most major—or minor—writers, Louisa May Alcott had few illusions about herself, and when she wrote about the development of her own craft she wore no rose-colored glasses. Her literary self-criticism reveals a consciousness of her limitations, an awareness of her experimentations and growth, her use of source materials, her techniques, her attitude toward language, and her ultimate professionalism. That self-criticism is to be found in her letters, published and unpublished, in her journals, prefaces, and narratives. Excerpted from those sources, her comments upon her literary purposes and style form a revealing self-portrait of one who essayed many genres, learned to heed the public pulse, and became a professional American writer in the second half of the nineteenth century.

Almost from the start, Alcott was aware that she was experimenting and, as she moved from style to style, that she was developing. Inscribing her first book, *Flower Fables* (1855), to her mother, she wrote prophetically: "I hope to pass in time from fairies and fables to men and realities."[1] And this, of course, she did in *Hospital Sketches* (1863), which she described in the preface to a later edition as "simply a brief record of one person's hospital experience." When, about the same time, she tried her hand at sensationalism, her consciousness of experimentation was as sharp as her ambivalence about the results. She wrote her thrillers for money and also, as she confided to her journal, in the hope that they were "good drill for fancy and language."[2] Whether she was cognizant of the emotional catharsis they gave her is uncertain, but the zest with which she produced "Behind a Mask" and "A Marble Woman," "Pauline's Passion and Punishment" and "The Abbot's Ghost" is reflected in the stories themselves. Louisa Alcott, however, was never proud of those sensational concoctions, and when she transferred their creation to her alter ego Jo March in *Little Women,* she tempered her enthusiasm with remorse. There Jo's rash "plunge into the frothy sea of sensational literature" is described in some detail, along with her use of exotic characters, her search for unusual sources, her disregard of "grammar, punctuation, and probability." But there too the authoritarian Professor Bhaer plays the role of censor, points out the "poison in the sugarplum" of sensationalism, and causes Jo March to burn her "inflammable nonsense" as she muses: "I'd better burn the house down, I suppose, than let other people blow themselves up with my gunpowder."

The righteous censorship continued in *Eight Cousins* (1875). There, mindful less perhaps of her own plunge into the "frothy sea" of sensationalism than of the work of Horatio Alger or even of Mark Twain, of whom she is said to have disapproved,[3] Louisa Alcott lashed out against sensational stories for boys. Using Aunt Jessie as a mouthpiece, she deplored the "popular stories" whose "motto is, 'Be smart, and you will be rich,' instead of 'Be honest, and you will be happy,'" whose "hairbreadth escapes and adventures" gave readers "wrong ideas of life."

And yet, and yet—as late as 1877 Alcott incorporated several sensational themes and episodes into her anonymous adult novel, *A Modern Mephistopheles,* and in the course of a conversation with LaSalle C. Pickett confessed that her "natural ambition is for the lurid style. I indulge in gorgeous fancies and wish that I dared inscribe them upon my pages and set them before the public." In 1882, however, when her collection *Proverb Stories* was published, the author included a fairly mild thriller, "The Baron's Gloves," "as a sample of the romantic rubbish which paid so well once upon a time. If it shows . . . what *not* to write it will not have been rescued from oblivion in vain." The pendulum had swung again.

While she was experimenting with her sensational stories, Louisa Alcott was also working on her first novel, *Moods,* published by A. K. Loring of Boston in 1865. Loring, who had advised the author to be concise in introducing her characters, to produce a "story of constant action," and to "teach some lesson of life," had also advised her to prune her first chapter, shorten the tenth, and make the eleventh less cold.[4] As a result, Alcott revised her novel about the relations of Warwick, Moor, and Sylvia, attempting to delineate a life affected by the moods of her heroine. When it appeared, she apparently studied the reviews with care, especially one in an English periodical which classified *Moods* as "Transcendental Fiction."[5] Her reaction was bristling: "My next book shall have no *ideas* in it, only facts, and the people shall be as ordinary as possible; then critics will say it's all right." As it turned out, Alcott's forte *was* to lie less in the exposition of ideas than in the depiction of "ordinary" people. In 1882, when she again revised her first novel for a new edition, she made her narrative more conventional and her heroine met "a wiser if less romantic fate than in the former edition."

By 1868, when she wrote *Little Women*, Alcott was aware that its value lay in its truth and simplicity, "for we really lived most of it," and to her publisher Thomas Niles she later commented, "The success of L. W. comes from just that . . . use of real life and one's own experience." The "use of real life and one's own experience" would dominate most of the Alcott oeuvre during the remainder of her life, and this was purposeful. In 1881, in "A Country Christmas," she has a character remark, "I do feel as if books was more sustainin' ef they was full of every-day people and things, like good bread and butter." And paraphrasing her early mentor A. K. Loring, who assured her "Stories of the *heart* are what live in the memory," Alcott continues, "Them that goes to the heart and ain't soon forgotten is the kind I hanker for."[6] Later, writing of *Jo's Boys*, she reiterated to Thomas Niles, "the best liked episodes are the real ones." In that last of the March novels, she elected to describe the "simple domestic scenes that touch people's hearts, and make them laugh and cry and feel better." Like Jo March, Louisa Alcott had "found her style at last" in *Little Women*, and her adherence to that style during the better part of the next twenty years was clearly a conscious effort. The consciousness of that effort is threaded through Louisa Alcott's self-criticism.

Discernible also in the documents that follow is the author's selection of her source material. This consisted primarily of episodes from her own life, episodes from the lives of those around her, and her readings.

In describing her methods of work to the journalist Frank Carpenter, she enunciated her reliance upon "real life": "Material for the children's tales I find in the lives of the little people about me. . . . In the older books the events are mostly from real life, the strongest the truest." She was early an observer, the child among them taking notes, and aware too that at times she could not observe as closely as she wished. In 1863, writing of her story "My Contraband" to Thomas Wentworth Higginson, she remarked, "I knew that my contraband did not talk as he should, for even in Washington I had no time to study the genuine dialect." As a result, she had relied upon a secondary, more literary source: "The hospital ship & the row of dusky faces were taken from a letter of Mrs Gage's describing her visit . . . with the Wagner heroes in Hilton Head Harbor." Thus, this extraordinary letter to Higginson reveals not only Alcott's source material but her awareness of her own imperfections. As she wrote to another abolitionist, James Redpath, of herself: "people mustn't talk about genius—for I drove that idea away years ago. . . . The inspiration of necessity is all I've had, & it is a safer help than any other."

The "inspiration of necessity" was not all she had, however. Louisa Alcott was also equipped with a bagful of devices and techniques that made her a literary craftsman. That she was alive to those techniques is evident especially in her remarkable letter of advice to Mrs. J. E. Sweet of Montana, written in 1885 in response to a tentative story outline submitted to her. Every suggestion made by Alcott to Mrs. Sweet reveals some facet of her own craftsmanship: "We write it in the form of a child's story, & let their impressions, words & adventures be the main thread. Give them names, & let them talk as yours did. . . . Imagine you are telling it to children & the right words will come." Alcott goes on to sketch the sequence of events, a sequence that will make for a dramatic narrative. Especially interesting is her advice regarding those slight touches that should be used to adumbrate character and develop plot: "I should open with the father going away, & his good bye, with a hint that it was his last. A few anxious words of the mother's, & happy little plans of the children. . . . A fine bit might be made of the hiding in the reeds." Here surely the key words are *hint, few, little, bit*—words that disclose the device of suggestion to animate characters and describe events, a craft in which Louisa Alcott excelled. With such brief touches as those outlined to Mrs. Sweet, she wove her own narratives, most of which were written in episodic form. As she wrote of *Little Men:* "As there is no particular plan to this story, except to describe a few scenes in the life at Plumfield . . . we will gently ramble along." The ramble—a series of episodes by a short-story writer turned novelist—may have included an occasional invented scene, such as the earring episode in *Eight Cousins,* but for the most part, as Alcott informed her public, "most of the incidents are taken from real life, and . . . the oddest are the truest."

One device consciously used by Alcott to convey a sense of verisimilitude was her language, which was always simple and often ungrammatical. As editor of the juvenile periodical *Merry's Museum* in 1868 she advised contributors: "Never use a *long* word, when a short one will do as well" and "Learn to write prose, before you attempt poetry." In *An Old-Fashioned Girl* (1870) she candidly explained: "I deeply regret being obliged to shock the eyes and ears of such of my readers as have a prejudice in favor of pure English, . . . but, having rashly undertaken to write a little story about Young America, for Young America, I feel bound to depict my honored patrons as faithfully as my limited powers permit; otherwise, I must expect the crushing criticism, 'Well, I dare say it's all very prim and proper, but it isn't a bit like us,' and never hope to arrive at the distinction of finding the covers of 'An Old-Fashioned Girl' the dirtiest in the library." In 1882 she wrote regarding her revision of *Moods* that certain chapters had been "pruned of as much fine writing as could be done without destroying the youthful spirit of the little romance." "Fine writing," in other words, was to be eschewed when realism and not romance was the object. As Alcott advised the young writer J. P. True: "use short words, and express as briefly as you can your meaning. Young people use too many adjectives and try to 'write fine.' The strongest, simplest words are best."

All this conscious experimentation, this exploitation of various techniques, this selection of sources, this use of language developed in Louisa Alcott the professionalism that may have been her outstanding literary attribute. It consisted in part of learning the public taste and then being able to cater to it. It included compromise as well as skill, and mature attitudes toward many minor aspects of literary work. In several of her unpublished letters Louisa Alcott gave evidence that she was cognizant of her own professionalism. Trained as she had been early in her career by those publishers of sensational periodicals, Elliott, Thomes and Talbot of Boston,[7] Alcott had learned to tailor her narratives to fit certain requirements: to adapt plot and character to a specific readership; to shape a story for installment appearance; to supply a specified number of words; to meet the deadlines. Another publisher, A. K. Loring of Boston, had emphasized the heart and action of a story, and taught her to prune. All these skills were intensified as Alcott pursued her literary career. That she knew she possessed them is evidenced by her letter to Frank Stockton in which she discussed serial publication of *Eight Cousins,* assuring him, "I can easily take out two chapters, which will bring the tale to the right length for St. Nicholas; & they can be put back again when the book appears. . . . There were 24 chapters, but I can make 20 by shortening some & removing two that can be spared." These surely are the remarks of one whose guide was the "inspiration of necessity," and whose attitude toward her craft was strictly professional.

One ingredient of Alcott's professionalism was her commonsensical attitude toward her writing. When, for example, her use of the name of a living individual for a character in *Eight Cousins* was challenged, Alcott wrote in 1875: "The name cannot be changed in the book now; in the sequel of course it will be. . . . Any further discussion of the affair seems to me unwise as everything in this busy world is so soon forgotten if let alone." Technical matters related to the writer's craft concerned her as a professional, along with the matter of fees, as when she informed Daniel Ford, editor of the *Youth's Companion,* that she wished to see proofs of her sloppy manuscript, along with "a nice little check for $100, so that I can make my Xmas story pay for my Xmas shopping."

These and other aspects of Alcott's professionalism emerge from three additional groups of letters: the first to the principal publisher of her Civil War days; the second to the editor of *St. Nicholas;* the third to the leading spirit of Roberts Brothers, Boston. The first group (Letters 1–11) yield insights into the early stages of her developing professionalism. The second (Letters 12–23) concern the writer's later short stories and serials for periodical publication; the third (Letters 24–35) concern her major books, and together those two groups reveal her knowledge of the demands of two distinct readerships, and her ability to supply those demands.

James Redpath, journalist, editor, and lecture promoter, published books in Boston for a short period (1863–64), and since he was a fiery abolitionist, his list reflected his commitment. On the day of John Brown's death, Louisa Alcott, age twenty-seven, wrote a poem, "With a Rose, That Bloomed on the Day of John Brown's Martyrdom," which was published in the *Liberator* on 20 January 1860. James Redpath, who had come to Concord seeking information for his *The Public Life of Captain John Brown* (1860), asked permission to reprint Louisa's poem in another volume on John Brown, *Echoes of Harper's Ferry* (1860).

After serial publication of Alcott's "Hospital Sketches" in the *Boston Commonwealth* three years later, both James Redpath and the firm of Roberts Brothers requested reprint permission, which the author granted to the abolitionist Redpath. After his publication in book form of *Hospital Sketches* he added two other Alcott titles to his list: *The Rose Family. A Fairy Tale* (1864) and *On Picket Duty, and Other Tales* (1864). His publishing program limited to two Civil War years, Redpath ventured into other fields after 1864.

During those two years, however, Alcott was deeply involved with the abolitionist publisher, and the series of her letters to him throws light upon the attitudes of an author learning the diverse aspects of her trade. She sees *Hospital Sketches* and *On Picket Duty* through the press, she studies contracts, she learns something of the laws of copyright, she appreciates the value of good notices and the joy of an enthusiastic reception. What is more, she is driven by the necessity of following one publication with another, and the inspiration of that necessity leads her to work on *Moods* and *Work*, to indite hospital scenes and fairy tales at approximately the same time. Here too are reflected her opinions of the prestigious *Atlantic Monthly* and of various editors as well as her reactions to the growing demands upon her pen. In short, the Alcott-Redpath letters crystallize Alcott's professionalism in the making.

A decade later, in 1873, Mary Mapes Dodge, author of *Hans Brinker or the Silver Skates*—a juvenile whose popularity was comparable with that of *Little Women*—agreed to edit a magazine for children launched by the firm of Scribner & Company. Dodge's editorial demands accorded with Louisa Alcott's special skills, for she wished no sermonizing, no wearisome recital of facts, no rattling of dry bones. Rather, she hoped to provide in *St. Nicholas* a pleasure ground for children's minds. Nonetheless, at first Alcott, busy with other matters, refused to provide a serial for the new periodical. In time, however, from 1874 on, she was to supply for *St. Nicholas* thirty-two narratives including three serials. Her payment for single stories, such as "Jimmy's Cruise in the 'Pinafore,'" was one hundred dollars.[8] Her payment for serials was three thousand dollars, and of these she contributed *Under the Lilacs* and *Jack and Jill* to the magazine *Eight Cousins*.[9] Of *Jack and Jill*, Alcott wrote in her journal in September 1879: "Home from the seaside refreshed, and go to work on a new serial for 'St. Nicholas,'—'Jack and Jill.' Have no plan yet but a boy, a girl, and a sled, with an upset to start with. Vague idea of working in Concord young folks and their doings. . . . A chapter a day is my task."[10]

Long before the writing of *Jack and Jill*, Louisa Alcott had met Mary Mapes Dodge. During a visit to New York in 1875, they had both attended a Fraternity Club meeting, and the two successful women had shared confidences, Dodge recalling how the Mapes girls—much like the March girls—had dramatized their childhood readings.[11] As the years passed, they shared their professional skills as well, and the letters, published and previously unpublished, that Alcott wrote to her editor between 1874 and 1887 yield further insights into her professional concerns.

The reliance upon real or live subjects, which Alcott mentioned to Frank Carpenter, had earlier been noted in her letters to Dodge. Writing about *Jack and Jill*, for example, she remarked, "We have many little romances going on among the Concord boys and girls, and all sorts of queer things, which will work into 'Jack and Jill' nicely," and again, "Jack and Jill are right out of our own little circle, and the boys and girls are in a twitter to know what is going in; so it will be a 'true story' in the main." In her journal she recorded, after receiving the first proof of the serial, "The nearer I keep to nature, the better the work is. Young people much interested in the story, and all want to 'go in.' I shall have a hornet's nest about me if all are not *angels*."[12] From her father's recollections, as well as his letters and journals, she hoped to write a narrative of his life, "An Old-Fashioned Boy," but this was never produced.

As she relied upon life for her characters, she relied heavily upon the suggestions and desires of her young readers. As she informed Dodge in 1879: "I have casually asked many of my young folks, when they demand a new story, which they would like, one of that sort [a Revolutionary tale], or the old 'Eight Cousin' style, and they all say the latter." As a result, *Jack and Jill* rather than a story of the American Revolution issued from her inkstand. Even one-year-old Lulu, her niece, might offer "hints and . . . studies of character" for her work. Writing from Nonquitt in 1881, she mentioned to her editor that "the twenty boys & girls here at the beach clamor for more stories & suggest many plans." Toward the end of her life she reiterated to Dodge, "There are usually about forty young people at N[onquitt]., and I think I can get a hint from some of them."[13]

If children sat for their portraits in Alcott's work, and if their demands helped shape her narratives, she thanked them in her own way, often by serving as their literary agent. "A little cousin, thirteen years old has written a story & longs to see it in print. It is a well-written bit & pretty good for a beginning, so I send it to you hoping it may find a place in the children's corner."

In Alcott's letters to Dodge, the "simmering" process she described to Frank Carpenter—"My head is my study, & there I keep the various plans of stories for years sometimes, letting them grow as they will till I am ready to put them on paper"—is referred to. She mentions, for example, her intermittent work on *Jo's Boys* and "the tales 'knocking at the sauce pan lid & demanding to be taken out,'" and she promises to "simmer" on a serial for *St. Nicholas.*

These letters also reflect Alcott's consciousness of the differing requirements for a magazine serial and a book, an awareness she indicated in her letter to Frank Stockton. Writing to Dodge in June 1877 about *Under the Liliacs,* she stated, "Twelve chapters are done, but are short ones, and so will make about six or seven numbers in 'St. Nicholas.' I will leave them divided in this way that you may put in as many as you please each month; for trying to suit the magazine hurts the story in its book form, though this way does no harm to the monthly parts, I think."

The Alcott correspondence with the editor of *St. Nicholas* is of considerable interest for the light it casts upon the author's attention to the mechanics of writing and publishing. She is concerned, for instance, with matters of copyright. The British periodical *Good Things: A Picturesque Magazine for the Young of All Ages* serialized *Eight Cousins* between December 1874 and November 1875. The novel was also serialized, between January and October 1875, in *St. Nicholas,* and in the same year Roberts Brothers published it in book form. As Alcott wrote in her journal in November 1874: "Funny time with the publishers about the tale; for all wanted it at once, and each tried to outbid the other for an unwritten story. I rather enjoyed it, and felt important with Roberts, Low [Sampson Low of London], and Scribner [publisher of *St. Nicholas*] all clamoring for my " 'umble works."[14] She also felt somewhat concerned regarding her rights as her letter of 2 December to Dodge indicates. There she writes: "To me the matter appears thus. I make an agreement with S[cribner]. & Co. about Eight Cousins exactly as I have always done with other serials. Reserving all rights to the tale outside of thier [*sic*] magazine. Among these rights is that of selling it as a serial in England which gives me my copyright there & secures the book hereafter. Of course I protect S. & Co. by forbidding the tale to appear in this country in any English magazine, & if it *does* I have the power to stop it."

Even more professional than her concern about copyright was Alcott's punctiliousness about deadlines, a characteristic revealed in her letter of 22 December 1887 to Dodge: "I send you the story your assistant editor asked for. As it is needed at once I do not delay to copy it. . . . You are used to my wild Mss. & will be able to read it."

Still another facet of Alcott's professionalism appears in these letters to Dodge—her deep interest in the illustration of her stories. She had many illustrators, from her first, her sister May, whose unfortunate sketches adorned part 1 of *Little Women,* to Frank Merrill, whose pen-and-ink drawings were used for a late edition of that novel. In an early letter to Mary Mapes Dodge, Alcott compared the drawings of Mrs. Innis with those of Elizabeth B. Greene, who had illustrated *Morning-Glories, and Other Stories:* "I like Mrs Innis' drawing better than Miss Greene's. Mrs I. is illustrating a book for me now. . . . Her children are altogether charming, thier [*sic*] little fat legs captivate me entirely. But I love E. B. G. & dont mind her infant's dropsical heads very much." Later, considering illustrations by Mrs. Foote for *Under the Lilacs,* Alcott wrote to her editor: "I will send you the first few chapters during the week for Mrs. Foote, and with them the schedule you suggest, so that my infants may not be drawn with whiskers, and my big boys and girls in pinafores, as in 'Eight Cousins.' . . . I do feel a natural wish to have one story prettily adorned with good pictures, as hitherto artists have much afflicted me." As late as 1883, when *Spinning-Wheel Stories* was conceived—to be published first as individual tales in *St. Nicholas* and then in book form by Roberts Brothers—the author was mindful of the relationship between illustration and text, writing to Mrs. Dodge: "A Christmas party of children might be at an old farm-house . . . grandma spins and tells the first story. . . . The mother and child picture would come in nicely for the first tale."

Alcott's professional concern with book illustration also punctuates her letters to her book publisher, Thomas Niles of Roberts Brothers. Her business relations with Niles antedated those with Mary Mapes Dodge. Trained in the Old Corner Bookstore, Thomas Niles had been active in the firm of Whittemore, Niles and Hall before joining Roberts Brothers. As partner of Roberts, he had in September 1867 suggested that Louisa Alcott write the "girls' book," which in 1868 and 1869 became *Little Women,* over the Roberts imprint. Around the same time the firm issued Bronson Alcott's *Tablets,* and for the remainder of her life the fortunes of Louisa Alcott would be linked with the enterprise of Thomas Niles of Roberts Brothers. According to Bronson Alcott, Niles early "spoke in terms of admiration" of Louisa Alcott's "literary ability, thinking most highly of . . . [her] rising fame and prospects."[15] With this admiration he offered an honesty rare among publishers for, when Roberts made their offer for *Little Women,* the firm advised the author to "keep the copyright."[16] That Louisa Alcott appreciated the ability and integrity of Thomas Niles is indicated by her modest acknowledgment of his creative role in that book, and by her characterization of him in *Jo's Boys,* where he is metamorphosed into Mr. Tiber, "one of the most successful men in the business; also generous, kind, and the soul of honor. . . . Mr. Tiber sits at his desk like a sort of king, receiving his subjects; for the greatest authors are humble to him and wait his Yes or No with anxiety."[17]

Alcott's letters to Niles, reprinted here, are scarcely humble, for the majority date from the latter period of their relationship, between 1880 and 1887. Substantiating the professionalism found in her letters to Dodge, they are concerned with such matters as shaping collections from contributions to periodicals, choosing illustrations, and combining illustrations with collections. On 23 June 1883, Alcott writes to Niles that "Mrs. Dodge begged me to consider myself mortgaged to her for tales, etc., and as I see no prospect of any time for writing books, I may be able to send her some short stories from time to time, and so be getting material for a new set of books like 'Scrap-bag,'[18] but with a new name." Indeed, as it turned out, it was in just that manner that *Spinning-Wheel Stories* was compiled. Later, the writer, whose desire to produce far exceeded her physical ability to do so, suggested to her publisher a "companion volume" for *Spinning-Wheel Stories*—her *Garland for Girls*. Still another anthology, *Lulu's Library*,[19] could be assembled, she informed Niles, "to match the pictures we bought," adding, "Old ladies come to this twaddle when they can do nothing else." Alcott's continued interest in book illustration is apparent in several of her letters to Niles. Of the Frank Merrill illustrations for *Little Women* she wrote in 1880: "The drawings are all capital. . . . Mr. Merrill certainly deserves a good penny for his work. Such a fertile fancy and quick hand as his should be well paid, and I shall not begrudge him his well-earned compensation, nor the praise I am sure these illustrations will earn. . . . I am much obliged to him for so improving on my hasty pen-and-ink sketches." Five years later she submitted "some funny sketches by Mrs. L." to illustrate a fairy book, and as late as 1886 she considered the possibility of issuing *Jo's Boys* without any illustrations. "Why have any illustrations? The book is not a child's book . . . and pretty pictures are not needed." Having submitted a bas-relief of herself for the frontispiece of *Jo's Boys* instead of illustrations, Louisa wrote to Niles: "Sorry you don't like the bas-relief; I do. A portrait, if bright and comely, wouldn't be me, and if like me would disappoint the children; so we had better let them imagine 'Aunt Jo young and beautiful, with her hair in two tails down her back,' as the little girl said."[20]

From the corpus of letters and journal entries, prefaces and excerpts from narratives here assembled, another portrait of Aunt Jo is developed—the self-portrait of a professional writer who, neither a perfectionist nor a purist, became one of the most popular American authors of the latter half of the nineteenth century.[21]

NOTES

1. All quotations, unless otherwise indicated, are from the documents that follow.

2. Ednah D. Cheney, ed., *Louisa May Alcott: Her Life, Letters, and Journals* (Boston: Roberts, 1889), 131. Hereinafter "Cheney."

3. See, for example, Frank Luther Mott, *Golden Multitudes: The Story of Best Sellers in the United States* (New York: Macmillan, 1947), 249.

4. A. K. Loring to Louisa May Alcott, [Boston, 1864], in *Publishers for Mass Entertainment in Nineteenth Century America*, ed. Madeleine B. Stern (Boston: G. K. Hall, 1980), 192. See also Stern, *Louisa May Alcott* (Norman: University of Oklahoma Press, 1971), 140.

5. "Transcendental Fiction," *Reader* 5 (15 April 1865): 422–23.

6. Loring had written: "Stories of the *heart* are what live in the memory" (see note 4).

7. See Leona Rostenberg, "Some Anonymous and Pseudonymous Thrillers of Louisa M. Alcott," reprinted in this collection.

8. Cheney, 320. "Jimmy's Cruise in the 'Pinafore' " appeared in *St. Nicholas* for October 1879.

9. Cheney, 295. *The Letters of A. Bronson Alcott*, ed. Richard L. Herrnstadt (Ames: Iowa State University Press, 1969), 697. "Eight Cousins" appeared in *St. Nicholas* for January–October 1875; "Under the Lilacs" in December 1877–October 1878; "Jack and Jill" in December 1879–October 1880.

10. Cheney, 321.

11. Stern, *Louisa May Alcott*, 249.

12. Cheney, 322.

13. Ibid., 373.

14. Ibid., 274–75.

15. *The Letters of A. Bronson Alcott*, 427.

16. Cheney, 199.

17. Louisa May Alcott, *Jo's Boys* (Cleveland: World, 1957), 181.

18. Six volumes of *Aunt Jo's Scrap-Bag* appeared over the Roberts Brothers imprint between 1872 and 1882.

19. Three volumes of *Lulu's Library* appeared over the Roberts Brothers imprint between 1886 and 1889.

20. Cheney, 376.

21. For a far less comprehensive compilation of Alcott self-criticism, see Madeleine B. Stern, "Louisa M. Alcott's Self-Criticism," *More Books* 20 (October 1945): 339–46.

D 1
FLOWER FABLES

Into your Christmas stocking I have put my "first-born," knowing that you will . . . look upon it merely as an earnest of what I may yet do; for, . . . I hope to pass in time from fairies and fables to men and realities.[1]

1. Alcott to her mother, with a copy of *Flower Fables*, Boston, 25 December 1854, in Cheney, 76–77.

D 2
"MY CONTRABAND"[1]

Concord Nov 12th 1862 [i.e., 1863]

My Dear Mr Higginson,

To receive a letter with Beaufort[2] at the beginning & Higginson at the end was both a surprise & honor for which I thank you, as for the commendation & the criticism.

I knew that my contraband did not talk as he should, for even in Washington I had no time to study the genuine dialect, & when the story was written here I had no one to tell me how it should be.

The hospital ship & the row of dusky faces were taken from a letter of Mrs Gage's describing her visit & interview with the Wagner heroes in Hilton Head Harbor.[3] Perhaps she was mistaken, in the locality, women often are inaccurate when their sympathies are at work.

I should like of all things to go South & help the blacks as I am no longer allowed to nurse the whites. The former seems the greater work, & would be most interesting to me. I offered to go as teacher on one of the Islands but Mr Philbrey objected because I had no natural protector to go with me, so I was obliged to give that up.[4]

Fields spoke of engaging some letters for his Magazine[5] if I did go, & I was much disappointed as I was willing to rough it anywhere for a time both for the sake of the help it would be to me in many ways, & the hope that I might be of use to others.

Dont you want a cook, nurse, or somewhat venerable "Child" for your regiment? I am willing to enlist in any capacity for the blood of old Col. May[6] asserts itself in his granddaughter in these martial times & she is very anxious to be busied in some more loyal labor than sitting quietly at home spinning fictions when such fine facts are waiting for all of us to profit by & celebrate.

Father & mother desire to be remembered.

Very Truly Yours
L. M. Alcott.

1. "My Contraband," a story of race relations that probes into problems of miscegenation, was written in August 1863 after Alcott had briefly served as a nurse in the Union Hotel Hospital, Georgetown, D.C. It was sent to James T. Fields of the *Atlantic Monthly*, who accepted it and paid fifty dollars for it, "with much approbation for it." According to Alcott's journal, "My Contraband; or, The Brothers" came out in September 1863 and "was liked." Actually, it was published in the *Atlantic Monthly* for November 1863. The story "called forth a letter of commendation and frank criticism from Col. T. W. Higginson, which was very encouraging to the young writer." Alcott's letter of 12 November to the reformer, soldier, and author Thomas Wentworth Higginson is obviously her reply to that "letter of commendation" (see Cheney, 139, 153, 154). The letter is printed here for the first time from the original in the Louisa May Alcott Collection, Brigham Young University, Provo, Utah.

2. Beaufort, S.C., where Higginson was encamped. He was colonel of the first Negro regiment in the Union Army (First South Carolina Volunteers) between November 1862 and May 1864.

3. Frances Dana Barker Gage (1808–84), reformer and abolitionist, went to the Sea Islands of South Carolina in October 1862. Alcott refers to Fort Wagner and Hilton Head.

4. According to her journal, in October 1863 Alcott "thought much about going to Port Royal to teach contrabands" (Cheney, 154).

5. James T. Fields of the *Atlantic Monthly*.

6. Colonel Joseph May, father of Louisa's mother, Abigail May Alcott, and of Samuel Joseph May.

D 3
HOSPITAL SKETCHES

These sketches, taken from letters hastily written in the few leisure moments of a very busy life, make no pretension to literary merit, but are simply a brief record of one person's hospital experience. . . .[1]

1. Alcott, preface to *Hospital Sketches and Camp and Fireside Stories* (Boston:

Roberts, 1869), i. *Hospital Sketches* originally appeared over the imprint of James Redpath in 1863. The preface to the later edition is dated March 1869.

D 4
ON SENSATIONAL STORIES

. . . Jo rashly took a plunge into the frothy sea of sensational literature, but thanks to the life preserver thrown her by a friend, she came up again not much the worse for her ducking.

Like most young scribblers, she went abroad for her characters and scenery. . . .

Her readers were not particular about such trifles as grammar, punctuation, and probability, and Mr. Dashwood graciously permitted her to fill his columns at the lowest prices, not thinking it necessary to tell her that the real cause of his hospitality was the fact that one of his hacks, on being offered higher wages, had basely left him in the lurch. . . .

But Mr. Dashwood rejected any but thrilling tales. . . .

Jo soon found that her innocent experience had given her but few glimpses of the tragic world which underlies society, so regarding it in a business light, she set about supplying her deficiencies with characteristic energy.[1]

1. Alcott, *Little Women* (New York: Collier Books, 1975 [1868–69]), 385–86.

D 5
ON SENSATIONAL STORIES

"All may not be bad, only silly, you know, and if there is a demand for it, I don't see any harm in supplying it. Many very respectable people make an honest living out of what are called sensational stories," said Jo, scratching gathers so energetically that a row of little slits followed her pin.

"There is a demand for whisky, but I think you and I do not care to sell it. If the respectable people knew what harm they did, they would not feel that the living *was* honest. They haf no right to put poison in the sugarplum, and let the small ones eat it. No, they should think a little, and sweep mud in the street before they do this thing." . . .

As soon as she went to her room, she got out her papers, and carefully reread every one of her stories. Being a little shortsighted, Mr. Bhaer sometimes used eyeglasses, and Jo had tried them once, smiling to see how they magnified the fine print of her book; now she seemed to have got on the Professor's mental or moral spectacles also, for the faults of these poor stories glared at her dreadfully and filled her with dismay.

"They *are* trash, and will soon be worse than trash if I go on, for each is more sensational than the last. I've gone blindly on, hurting myself and other people, for the sake of money. I know it's so, for I can't read this stuff in sober earnest without being horribly ashamed of it, and what *should* I do if they were seen at home or Mr. Bhaer got hold of them?"

Jo turned hot at the bare idea, and stuffed the whole bundle into her stove, nearly setting the chimney afire with the blaze.

"Yes, that's the best place for such inflammable nonsense. I'd better burn the house down, I suppose, than let other people blow themselves up with my gunpowder," she thought as she watched the *Demon of the Jura* whisk away, a little black cinder with fiery eyes.[1]

1. Conversation between Jo and Professor Bhaer and its aftermath, in Alcott, *Little Women*, 392–94.

D 6

ON SENSATIONAL STORIES

. . . The writers of these popular stories intend to do good . . . but it seems to me they fail because their motto is, 'Be smart, and you will be rich,' instead of 'Be honest, and you will be happy.' . . .

. . . is it natural for lads from fifteen to eighteen to command ships, defeat pirates, outwit smugglers, and so cover themselves with glory, that Admiral Farragut invites them to dinner, saying: 'Noble boy, you are an honor to your country!' Or, if the hero is in the army, he has hair-breadth escapes and adventures enough in one small volume to turn his hair white, and in the end he goes to Washington at the express desire of the President or Commander-in-Chief to be promoted to no end of stars and bars. Even if the hero is merely an honest boy trying to get his living, he is not permitted to do so in a natural way, by hard work and years of patient effort, but is suddenly adopted by a millionaire whose pocketbook he has returned; or a rich uncle appears from sea, just in the nick of time; or the remarkable boy earns a few dollars, speculates in pea-nuts or neck-ties, and grows rich so rapidly that Sinbad in the diamond valley is a pauper compared to him. . . .

. . . an illustration on the open page . . . [depicts] a small but virtuous youth . . . upsetting a tipsy giant in a bar-room, and under it the elegant inscription: 'Dick Dauntless punches the head of Sam Soaker.'

It gives boys such wrong ideas of life and business; shows them so much evil and vulgarity that they need not know about, and makes the one success worth having a fortune, a lord's daughter, or some worldly honor, often not worth the time it takes to win. It does seem to me that some one might write stories that should be lively, natural, and helpful,—tales in which the English should be good, the morals pure, and the characters such as we can love in spite of the faults that all may have. I can't bear to see such crowds of eager little fellows at the libraries reading such trash; weak, when it is not wicked, and totally unfit to feed the hungry minds that feast on it for want of something better. . . .

[Dr. Alec to Jessie]: "You have laid out a hard task for yourself, Jessie, in trying to provide good reading for boys who have been living on sensation stories. It will be like going from raspberry tarts to plain bread and butter; but you will probably save them from a bilious fever."[1]

1. Alcott, *Eight Cousins, or The Aunt-Hill* (Boston: Little, Brown, 1927 [1875]), 195, 196–98, 200.

D 7
ON SENSATIONAL STORIES

I think my natural ambition is for the lurid style. I indulge in gorgeous fancies and wish that I dared inscribe them upon my pages and set them before the public. . . . How should I dare to interfere with the proper grayness of old Concord? The dear old town has never known a startling hue since the redcoats were there. Far be it from me to inject an inharmonious color into the neutral tint. And my favorite characters!

Suppose they went to cavorting at their own sweet will, to the infinite horror of dear Mr. Emerson, who never imagined a Concord person as walking off a plumb line stretched between two pearly clouds in the empyrean. To have had Mr. Emerson for an intellectual god all one's life is to be invested with a chain armor of propriety. . . . And what would my own good father think of me . . . if I set folks to doing the things that I have a longing to see my people do? No, my dear, I shall always be a wretched victim to the respectable traditions of Concord.[1]

1. LaSalle Corbell Pickett, *Across My Path: Memories of People I Have Known* (New York: Brentano's, 1916), 107–8. The excerpt is from a conversation with Alcott.

D 8
ON SENSATIONAL STORIES

As many girls have asked to see what sort of tales Jo March wrote at the beginning of her career, I have added "The Baron's Gloves," as a sample of the romantic rubbish which paid so well once upon a time. If it shows them what *not* to write it will not have been rescued from oblivion in vain.[1]

1. Alcott, preface to *Proverb Stories* (Boston: Roberts, 1882).

D 9
ON LITERARY EXPERIMENTATION

Jo wrote no more sensational stories, deciding that the money did not pay for her share of the sensation, but going to the other extreme, as is the way with people of her stamp, she took a course of Mrs. Sherwood, Miss Edgeworth, and Hannah More, and then produced a tale which might have been more properly called an essay or a sermon, so intensely moral was it. She had her doubts about it from the beginning, for her lively fancy and girlish romance felt as ill at ease in the new style as she would have done masquerading in the stiff and cumbrous costume of the last century. She sent this didactic gem to several markets, but it found no purchaser, and she was inclined to agree with Mr. Dashwood that morals didn't sell.

Then she tried a child's story, which she could easily have disposed of if she had not been mercenary enough to demand filthy lucre for it. The only person who offered enough to make it worth her while to try juvenile literature was a worthy gentleman who felt it his mission to convert all the world to his particular belief. But much as she liked to write for children, Jo could not consent to depict all her naughty boys as being eaten by bears or tossed by mad bulls because they did not go to a particular Sabbath school, nor all the good infants who did go as rewarded by every kind of bliss, from gilded gingerbread to escorts of angels when they departed this life with psalms or sermons on their lisping tongues. So nothing came of these trials, and Jo corked up her inkstand, and said in a fit of very wholesome humility—

"I don't know anything; I'll wait till I do before I try again. . . ."[1]

    1. Alcott, *Little Women*, 394–95.

D 10
MOODS

English people don't understand "transcendental literature," as they call "Moods." My next book shall have no *ideas* in it, only facts, and the people shall be as ordinary as possible; then critics will say it's all right. I seem to have been playing with edge tools without knowing it. The relations between Warwick, Moor, and Sylvia are pronounced impossible; yet a case of the sort exists, and the woman came and asked me how I knew it. I did *not* know or guess, but perhaps felt it, without any other guide, and unconsciously put the thing into my book, for I changed the ending about that time. It was meant to show a life affected by *moods*, not a discussion of marriage, which I knew little about, except observing that very few were happy ones.[1]

    1. Alcott's journal entry of April 1865, in Cheney, 166. She is referring to an article, "Transcendental Fiction," in *Reader* 5 (15 April 1865): 422–23, which presented a lengthy review of *Moods*.

D 11
THE REVISION OF *MOODS*

When "Moods" was first published, an interval of some years having then elapsed since it was written, it was so altered, to suit the taste and convenience of the publisher, that the original purpose of the story was lost sight of, and marriage appeared to be the theme instead of an attempt to show the mistakes of a moody nature, guided by impulse, not principle. Of the former subject a girl of eighteen could know but little, of the latter most girls know a good deal; and they alone among my readers have divined the real purpose of the book in spite of its many faults, and have thanked me for it.

As the observation and experience of the woman have confirmed much that the instinct and imagination of the girl felt and tried to describe, I wish to give my first novel, with all its imperfections on its head, a place among its more successful sisters; for into it went the love, labor, and enthusiasm that no later book can possess.

Several chapters have been omitted, several of the original ones restored; and those that remain have been pruned of as much fine writing as could be done without destroying the youthful spirit of the little romance. At eighteen death seemed the only solution for Sylvia's perplexities; but thirty years later, having learned the possibility of finding happiness after disappointment, and making love and duty go hand in hand, my heroine meets a wiser if less romantic fate than in the former edition. . . .[1]

1. Alcott, preface to *Moods* (Boston: Roberts, 1882). The preface to this revised edition is dated January 1882.

D 12
MERRY'S MUSEUM

Your little story is hardly up to the standard. Never use a *long* word, when a short one will do as well.

Your lines will not do. Learn to write prose, before you attempt poetry.[1]

1. "Merry's Monthly Chat with His Friends," *Merry's Museum* (May, October 1868): 208, 420.

D 13
HER STYLE AT LAST

"Why don't you write? That always used to make you happy," said her mother once, when the desponding fit overshadowed Jo.

"I've no heart to write, and if I had, nobody cares for my things."

"We do. Write something for us, and never mind the rest of the world. Try it, dear, I'm sure it would do you good, and please us very much."

"Don't believe I can." But Jo got out her desk and began to overhaul her half-finished manuscripts.

An hour afterward her mother peeped in and there she was, scratching away, with her black pinafore on, and an absorbed expression, which caused Mrs. March to smile and slip away, well pleased with the success of her suggestion. Jo never knew how it happened, but something got into that story that went straight to the hearts of those who read it, for when her family had laughed and cried over it, her father sent it, much against her will, to one of the popular magazines, and, to her utter surprise, it was not only paid for, but others requested. Letters from several persons, whose praise was honor, followed the appearance of the little story, newspapers copied it, and strangers as well as friends admired it. For a small thing it was a great success, and Jo was more astonished than when her novel was commended and condemned all at once.

"I don't understand it. What *can* there be in a simple little story like that to make people praise it so?" she said, quite bewildered.

"There is truth in it, Jo, that's the secret; humor and pathos make it alive, and you have found your style at last. . . ."[1]

1. Alcott, *Little Women*, 481.

D 14
LITTLE WOMEN

It reads better than I expected. Not a bit sensational, but simple and true, for we really lived most of it; and if it succeeds that will be the reason of it.[1]

1. Alcott's journal entry of 26 August 1868. Cheney, 199.

D 15
AN OLD-FASHIONED GIRL

"M. E." writes to ask, if Tom marries Polly? No; there is no marrying in the story, for the "Old-Fashioned Girl" doesn't believe in nonsense of that sort for children, and they don't grow up. "M. E." does not understand why the story was written, if she thinks it "would be nice to have Polly flirt with Tom." . . .[1]

As the first part of "An Old-Fashioned Girl" was written in 1869, the demand for a sequel . . . rendered it necessary to carry my heroine boldly forward some six or seven years into the future. The domestic nature of the story makes this audacious proceeding possible. . . .

This explanation will, I trust, relieve those well-regulated minds, who cannot conceive of such literary lawlessness, from the bewilderment which they suffered when the same experiment was tried in a former book.

The "Old-Fashioned Girl" is not intended as a perfect model, but as a possible improvement upon the Girl of the Period, who seems sorrowfully ignorant or ashamed of the good old fashions which make woman truly beautiful and honored, and, through her, render home what it should be,—a happy place, where parents and children, brothers and sisters, learn to love and know and help one another.

If the history of Polly's girlish experiences suggests a hint or insinuates a lesson, I shall feel that, in spite of many obstacles, I have not entirely neglected my duty toward the little men and women, for whom it is an honor and a pleasure to write, since in them I have always found my kindest patrons, gentlest critics, warmest friends.[2]

I deeply regret being obliged to shock the eyes and ears of such of my readers as have a prejudice in favor of pure English . . . but, having rashly undertaken to write a little story about Young America, for Young America, I feel bound to depict my honored patrons as faithfully as my limited powers permit; otherwise, I must expect the crushing criticism, "Well, I dare say it's all very prim and proper, but it isn't a bit like us," and never hope to arrive at the distinction of finding the covers of "An Old-Fashioned Girl" the dirtiest in the library.[3]

1. "Merry's Monthly Chat with His Friends," *Merry's Museum* 2 (October 1869): 484.

2. Alcott, preface to *An Old-Fashioned Girl* (Boston: Roberts, 1870).

3. Alcott, *An Old-Fashioned Girl* (Boston: Little, Brown, 1920 [1870]), 231.

D 16

LITTLE MEN

As there is no particular plan to this story, except to describe a few scenes in the life at Plumfield for the amusement of certain little persons, we will gently ramble along. . . . I beg leave to assure my honored readers that most of the incidents are taken from real life, and that the oddest are the truest.[1]

1. Alcott, *Little Men* (Boston: Little, Brown, 1922 [1871]), 126.

D 17

EIGHT COUSINS

Boston Jan. 10th 1875

F. R. Stockton[1]
Dear Sir,

The story was finished with the old year & has been waiting for the last touches which are most effectually given after an author has got out of the composing "vortex."[2]

I can easily take out two chapters, which will bring the tale to the right length for St. Nicholas; & they can be put back again when the book appears.[3]

These changes can be made without damage to the little tale as a whole, because I have not attempted much in the serial but a few hints at Dr Alec's experiment with Rose, Pictures of boy & girl life & chara[c]ter with as much fun & as little preaching as possible; this is all the short space allowed will permit me to do, & if the young people get an idea or a laugh or two out of it I shall be satisfied.

There were 24 chapters, but I can make 20 by shortening some & removing two that can be spared, as the Christmas one will come in spring & so seem out of place perhaps, & the frolics of Jamie & Pokey do not help on the story in any way.[4]

Each chapter is fifteen Ms. pages, & the two for each month will make about six printed pages, that being the number Mrs Dodge mentioned as suiting St. Nick best.

Shall it be so? I will at once rearrange the chapters, & send a part if more is needed for the artist.

Yrs respectfully
L. M. Alcott

1. Francis R. Stockton was assistant editor of *St. Nicholas* between 1873 and 1881.

Alcott's letter to him is printed from the original in the Houghton Library, Harvard University.

2. In her journal of December 1874, Alcott wrote: "Finish 'Eight Cousins'" (Cheney, 275). "Eight Cousins" was serialized in *St. Nicholas* in January–October 1875 and published in book form by Roberts Brothers the same year. On 27 March 1875 Bronson Alcott wrote to Louisa from Akron, Ohio:

> Having a few hours this morning to my self, I ran through the published chapters of your story in "St. Nicholas." Everyone praises and delights to tell me how much they like the wit and sense of the writer. So I read, and offer her my impressions, with the rest.
>
> I infer you to have in mind to show the absurdities of our modern modes of training the young.—Rose is to be subjected to various tests to prove her strength of character.— The aunts each of them trying their theory on their victim. The Uncle begins well, and opens up the sequel to the tale.
>
> One thing in your stories I observe and admire—your sympathy with the lower and laboring class. The interview between Rose and Phebe over the andirons, is an example of this kind. You cannot urge this moral too strongly on your readers. There is still,—all professions to the contrary—a fearful prejudice concerning the dignity and duty of work. . . . I think you are doing more than you are aware to break down this dispar[a]gement, by showing in unsuspected positions the morality and duty of serving. . . . And you have an audiance [*sic*] that no preacher, not all preachers combined, command. You have won the prize. (*Letters,* 646–47)

3. Actually, twenty-four chapters were published in each version, periodical and book.

4. Jamie, the youngest of the Campbells, is six years old in *Eight Cousins;* his friend Pokey ("an inquisitive little body . . . always poking . . . into everything") is four.

D 18

EIGHT COUSINS

41 West 26th Street[1]

10 November 1875

Dear Mrs Dall,[2]

Having explained the matter to Miss Blish herself as soon as I learned that she was alive & troubled by my use of her name, I do not think it necessary to do anything more.[3]

The name cannot be changed in the book now; in the sequel of course it will be, & as I intended no unkindness or disrespect in using the peculiar name of a child whom I saw for a few days thirty five years ago I consider that in explaining the fact & apologizing for the liberty I have amended my carelessness in the only way possible.

No earring episode ever occurred, & I remember nothing about little Ariadne except that she was a very well behaved child who was held up to naughty Louisa as a model girl.

Any further discussion of the affair seems to me unwise as everything in this busy world is so soon forgotten if let alone.

Yrs in haste
L. M. Alcott.

Nov. 10th/75

Thanks for defending me, but do not trouble yourself about it for I am used to being misunderstood by a certain class of persons & have learned not to mind it if I honestly do what seems right both to those whom I unwittingly offend & those who offend me. One's best defence is one's life & character.

1. In November 1875, Alcott took a room at the Bath Hotel, New York City, run by Dr. Eli Peck Miller at Number 39. At adjoining Number 41, Dr. Miller provided his New Hygienic Institution and Turkish Bath.

2. Caroline Healey Dall, author and reformer. The letter to Mrs. Dall is printed from the original at the Massachusetts Historical Society.

3. In *Eight Cousins,* Ariadne Blish, the paragon of Alcott's childhood, becomes Annabel Bliss, a flaxen-haired, conventional show-off who "*looked* like a wax doll." In the chapter entitled "Ear-Rings," Annabel entices Rose to have her ears pierced for earrings, a vanity not condoned by Uncle Alec (see Stern, *Louisa May Alcott,* 9, 237).

D 19
EIGHT COUSINS

The Author is quite aware of the defects of this little story, many of which were unavoidable, as it first appeared serially. But, as Uncle Alec's experiment was intended to amuse the young folks, rather than suggest educational improvements for the consideration of the elders, she trusts that these short-comings will be overlooked by the friends of the *Eight Cousins,* and she will try to make amends in a second volume, which shall attempt to show *The Rose in Bloom.*[1]

1. Alcott, preface to *Eight Cousins* (Boston: Roberts, 1875).

D 20

"A NEW WAY TO SPEND CHRISTMAS"

Dec. 5th [1875]

Dear Mr Ford,[1]

Expecting to have much more time I have been obliged to hurry terribly to finish the story,[2] & it is not what I meant it to be after all. I cannot even copy it, & hope your printers can read the Ms. I should like to see the proof if possible, or be sure it was carefully over looked by some one, else there will be a jumble.

Now in return for my obliging scramble please send me a nice little check for $100, so that I can make my Xmas story pay for my Xmas shopping.

The Ms goes by tonight's mail, to Boston, so you will get it by Wed. I hope.

Yrs truly

L. M. A.

1. Daniel Sharp Ford, editor, publisher, and philanthropist, edited the *Youth's Companion* between 1857 and 1899. Alcott's letter to him is printed from the original in the Overbury Collection, Barnard College, New York.

2. "A New Way to Spend Christmas"—Alcott's account of Randall's Island— was published in the *Youth's Companion* for 9 March 1876.

D 21

ROSE IN BLOOM

As authors may be supposed to know better than any one else what they intended to do when writing a book, I beg leave to say that there is no moral to this story. Rose is not designed for a model girl: and the Sequel was simply written in fulfilment of a promise; hoping to afford some amusement, and perhaps here and there a helpful hint, to other roses getting ready to bloom.[1]

1. Alcott, preface to *Rose in Bloom* (Boston: Roberts, 1876).

D 22

A MODERN MEPHISTOPHELES

It has been simmering ever since I read Faust last year. Enjoyed doing it, being tired of providing moral pap for the young.[1]

1. Alcott's journal entry of January, February 1877, in Cheney, 296.

D 23

"A COUNTRY CHRISTMAS"

I ain't no great of a jedge about anything but nat'ralness of books, and it really does seem as if some of your men and women was dreadful uncomfortable creaters. 'Pears to me it ain't wise to be always pickin' ourselves to pieces and pryin' into things that ought to come gradual by way of experience and the visitations of Providence. Flowers won't blow worth a cent ef you pull'em open. Better wait and see what they can do alone. . . . we can't live on spice-cake and Charlotte Ruche, and I do feel as if books was more sustainin' ef they was full of every-day people and things, like good bread and butter. Them that goes to the heart and ain't soon forgotten is the kind I hanker for. . . . I'd let my oven cool a spell, and hunt up some homely, happy folks to write about; folks that don't borrer trouble and go lookin' for holes in their neighbors' coats, but take their lives brave and cheerful. . . . That sort of a book would do a heap of good. . . .[1]

1. Alcott, "A Country Christmas," *Proverb Stories* (Boston: Roberts, 1882), 96–97. The story first appeared in *The Independent* for 15 and 22 December 1881.

D 24

AN INDIAN STORY[1]

[11 September 1885]

Mrs Sweet,[2]
My Dear Madame,

In reply to your touching letter I am happy to say that I think the outline of a story sent me may be filled up & make an interesting tale for some magazine or paper.

If I may suggest this is what I should do with it.

We write it in the form of a child's story, & let their impressions, words & adventures be the main thread. Give them names, & let them talk as yours did. There is enough in the facts to make a thrilling tale told briefly & dramatically as I am sure you are able to do it. Imagine you are telling it to children & the right words will come, for your language is both picturesque & elegant.

I should open with the father going away, & his good bye, with a hint that it was his last. A few anxious words of the mother's, & happy little plans of the children, with some incident to introduce the Indians & tell a little about their dangerous state just then, in a few words. Then the attack, & the journey & escape, ending with the return to the Fort to find the father dead. A fine bit might be made of the hiding in the reeds, & the brave children, & the sick one, & the mother's hope & heroism. So too, the canoe scene, where she goes down the river with her baby on her lap in the leaky boat.

When you have done it send it to me, & I will add a word of introduction & try to dispose of it.[3] Just now the death of "H. H." (Mrs. H. Jackson, the writer,) gives a special interest to all Indian tales, so it is a good time for yours. We will see.

Thank you for honoring me with your confidence. For what is success given me after years of hard work if I cannot feel tenderly for others in need, & gladly help all I can. There is no more beautiful tribute to my books than the appeals that come to me from strangers who call me "friend." I wish you were nearer me. Write & tell me about the son. How old—does he like books, &c. I am 52, & an invalid but still able to do something thank God.

Hold fast, dear woman, to your faith, else all is lost. God does not forget us, & in time we see *why* the trials come. May He bless your loving effort & let me aid in its success:

Yr friend

L. M. Alcott[4]

1. At this period Alcott was deeply interested in the American Indians. Her Indian story, "Onawandah," appeared in *St. Nicholas* for April 1884; on 18 September 1885 she wrote to Thomas Niles of Helen Hunt Jackson's *Ramona* as "a noble record of the great wrongs of her chosen people. . . . It recalls the old slavery days, only these victims are red instead of black"; she was working on *Jo's Boys*, which included Dan's death defending "his chosen people," the Indians.

2. Jannette E. Sykes was born near Lockport, N.Y., in 1833, married Joseph Warren De Camp in 1852, and in 1855 settled in Shakopee, Minnesota, where she remained until 1861, when she and her husband went to the Red Wood Sioux agency. They were caught in the massacre of 18 August 1862, and she was held captive by the Sioux Indians. In 1866 she returned to Fort Ridgely as the wife of the Reverend J. Sweet, chaplain of the garrison.

3. "Mrs. J. E. De Camp Sweet's Narrative of Her Captivity in the Sioux Outbreak of 1862" was not published until 1894, when it appeared in the *Minnesota Historical Society Collections* 6 (1894): 354–80.

4. Alcott's letter to Mrs. J. E. Sweet is addressed to her at Marysville, Montana, Lewis & Clarke Co.; it is postmarked 11 September in Concord, Massachusetts, and 17 September in Marysville. It is printed from the original in the Louisa May Alcott Collection, Brigham Young University, Provo, Utah. Many years ago, this letter was owned by the New York antiquarian bookseller Arthur Pforzheimer, who allowed me to examine it when I was researching my biography of Alcott; the firm of Leona Rostenberg and Madeleine B. Stern purchased it at auction for the Alcott collection of Brigham Young University. "Habent sua fata epistolae!"

D 25

JO'S BOYS

Having been written at long intervals during the past seven years, this story is more faulty than any of its very imperfect predecessors; but the desire to atone for an unavoidable disappointment, and to please my patient little friends, has urged me to let it go without further delay.

To account for the seeming neglect of Amy, let me add, that, since the original of that character died, it has been impossible for me to write of her as when she was here to suggest, criticise, and laugh over her namesake. The same excuse applies to Marmee. But the folded leaves are not blank to those who knew and loved them, and can find memorials of them in whatever is cheerful, true, or helpful in these pages.[1]

. . . simple domestic scenes that touch people's hearts, and make them laugh and cry and feel better.[2]

1. Alcott, preface to *Jo's Boys* (Boston: Roberts, 1886). The preface is dated 4 July 1886.

2. Alcott, *Jo's Boys* (Boston: Little, Brown, 1920 [1886]), 231.

D 26
METHODS OF WORK

Louisa May Alcott Describes Her Work Habits to Frank Carpenter, 1 April [1887][1]

My methods of work are very simple. . . . My head is my study, & there I keep the various plans of stories for years sometimes, letting them grow as they will till I am ready to put them on paper. Then it is quick work, as chapters go down word for word as they stand in my mind & need no alteration. I never copy, since I find by experience that the work I spend the least time upon is best liked by critics & readers.

Any paper, any pen, any place that is quiet suit me, & I used to write from morning till night without fatigue when "the steam was up." Now, however, I am paying the penalty of twenty years of over work, & can write but two hours a day, doing about twenty pages, sometimes more, though my right thumb is useless from writer's cramp.

While a story is under way I live in it, see the people, more plainly than real ones, round me, hear them talk, & am much interested, sur-prized or provoked at their actions, for I seem to have no power to rule them, & can simply record their experiences & performances.

Material for the children's tales I find in the lives of the little people about me, for no one can invent anything so droll, pretty or pathetic as the sayings & doings of these small actors. . . . In the older books the events are mostly from real life, the strongest the truest, & I yet hope to write a few of the novels, which have been simmering in my brain while necessity & unexpected success have confined me to juvenile literature.

. . . [I] find my best success in the comfort my family enjoy, also a naughty satisfaction in proving that it was better *not* to "stick to teach-ing" as advised, but to write.

1. Reprinted from the original in the Houghton Library, Harvard University. Frank George Carpenter, journalist, traveler, and author, was Washington corre-spondent for the *Cleveland Leader* when this letter was written.

D 27
METHODS OF WORK

I never had a study. Any pen and paper do, and an old atlas on my knee is all I want. Carry a dozen plots in my head, and think them over when in the mood. Sometimes keep one for years, and suddenly find it all ready to write. Often lie awake and plan whole chapters word for word, then merely scribble them down as if copying.

Used to sit fourteen hours a day at one time, eating little, and unable to stir till a certain amount was done.

Very few stories written in Concord; no inspiration in that dull place. Go to Boston, hire a quiet room and shut myself up in it.[1]

1. Cheney, 399.

D 28
METHODS OF WORK

Concord, October 24.

[J. P. True]

Dear Sir,—I never copy or "polish," so I have no old manuscripts to send you; and if I had it would be of little use, for one person's method is no rule for another. Each must work in his own way; and the only drill needed is to keep writing and profit by criticism. Mind grammar, spelling, and punctuation, use short words, and express as briefly as you can your meaning. Young people use too many adjectives and try to "write fine." The strongest, simplest words are best, and no *foreign* ones if it can be helped.

Write, and print if you can; if not, still write, and improve as you go on. Read the best books, and they will improve your style. See and hear good speakers and wise people, and learn of them. Work for twenty years, and then you may some day find that you have a style and place of your own, and can command good pay for the same things no one would take when you were unknown.

I know little of poetry, as I never read modern attempts, but advise any young person to keep to prose, as only once in a century is there a true poet; and verses are so easy to do that it is not much help to write them. I have so many letters like your own that I can say no more, but wish you success, and give you for a motto Michael Angelo's wise words: "Genius is infinite patience."

Your friend,
L. M. Alcott.

P.S.—The lines you send me are better than many I see; but boys of nineteen cannot know much about hearts, and had better write of things they understand. Sentiment is apt to become sentimentality; and sense is always safer, as well as better drill, for young fancies and feelings.

Read Ralph Waldo Emerson, and see what good prose is, and some of the best poetry we have. I much prefer him to Longfellow.[1]

1. Alcott to J. P. True, Concord, 24 October [n.y.], in Cheney, 399–400. See also J. P. True, "The Advice of Miss Alcott," *St. Nicholas* 15 (May 1888): 545.

Alcott–Redpath Letters

L 1

HOSPITAL SKETCHES, LETTER TO REDPATH, [1863]

I believe the proof is now correct as three pairs of eyes have been over it.

Father thinks it would gratify Miss Stevenson[1] to have the little book inscribed to her as she was the means of my going to Washington & has always been very friendly to me. I enclose his idea of the matter.

"Having consulted the authoress" you *may* decide for yourself about the binding. I like something very neat & plain, & abominate red, blue & gold &c—

The book begins to look quite vast & solid & we all like it.

Yours truly L. M. A.[2]

1. Hannah M. Stevenson arranged for Alcott's appointment as nurse in the Union Hotel Hospital, Georgetown, D.C. Alcott remained there six weeks (December 1862–January 1863) and from there wrote the letters that were published as *Hospital Sketches*. The dedication reads: "These Sketches / Are Respectfully Dedicated / To Her Friend / MISS HANNAH STEVENSON, / By / L. M. A."

2. The letters from Alcott to Redpath are published courtesy of the New-York Historical Society.

L 2

LETTER TO REDPATH, [1863]

Being lamentably stupid about business of all sorts I'm very much afraid I'm not very clear about the compact.[1] But I believe stating it woman-fashion it means—I have five cents on each copy, you have ten to do what you like with & I'm not to meddle. Out of the ten you pay for the cost of the book & give something to the charity to which I heartily wish I could add my share. Is that right? If so I agree with perfect confidence in "my publisher" & all good wishes for his success in the small venture as well as my own.

Father thinks Mr S. E. Sewall[2] would be a good person to arrange the matter as he understands such things, is a friend to both sides, & if he approves I am satisfied.

I have just reread the Memorandum & it seems all right. I dont wish to be grasping but I do wish to have my Hospital attempt pay its own expenses in the way of doctor's bills &c as it was undertaken against the advice of many persons & considered a disastrous failure in one respect.

I send the few notices I have kept, but as I do not see many papers I have not much to offer in the way of vanities, though I often hear others speak of notices they have seen.

I also enclose some of the letters from which extracts can be made if desirable, they at least will give some idea of the various opinions expressed upon this mighty matter.

Will you be kind enough to preserve & return them all when you have made such use of them as you think best as I value some of them very much.

Father wishes me to add that his letter is at your service.

Respectfully yours
"T. P."[3]

1. According to the "Publisher's Advertisement" in Alcott, *Hospital Sketches* (Boston: James Redpath, 1863), "besides paying the Author the usual copyright, the publisher has resolved to devote at least five cents for every copy sold to the support of orphans made fatherless or homeless by the war." From the twenty-five-cent paper printing for army reading, the author received ten percent.

2. Samuel E. Sewall, cousin of Louisa Alcott, lawyer and trusted financial adviser.

3. Nurse Tribulation Periwinkle was the name given herself by the author in her hospital letters.

———

L 3

LETTER TO REDPATH, [1863]

I return your Contract signed, & am sure it is all right. About the dreadful percentage, over which I have puzzled my stupid head till I believe I understand it, I can only say that I too am sure that "he who giveth to the poor lendeth to the Lord" & on that principle devote time & earnings to the care of my father & mother, for one possesses no gift for money making & the other is now too old to work any longer for those who are happy & able to work for her. On this account I often have to deny myself the little I could do for other charities . . . & seem ungenerous that I may be just. All that is rightly mine I prefer to use for them much as I should like to help the orphans, yet wish that you should first entirely repay yourself for all outlays of time, trouble & money in getting up the book.

You ask about any other story I may have. Mr Sanborn[1] spoke to me some time ago on the same subject & advised me to prepare one written several years ago, that you might examine & pronounce judgment. I have partially done so & send the first six chapters for to you [i.e., you to] read if you like. As all my things go by contraries this may come to something as I dont like it myself. Another one which I do like, & for that very reason dont offer though I think it better written & more interesting. This one was begun with the design of putting some [of] my own experiences into a story illustrating the trials of young women who want employment & find it hard to get. From time to time I see articles on the same subject & various people have begged me to finish "Success" as I at first christened the book.[2]

The story is made up of various essays this girl makes, her failures & succes[s]es told in chapters merry or sad, & various characters all more or less from life are introduced to help or hinder her.

Some of the incidents are old now but perhaps may as well stand as the story is the better for them, & slavery troubles are not easily forgotten. These scenes however are at the end of the book & it will be time enough to change them when it is accepted.

I dont know that so small a part is of any use except as a sample, but if you approve I can send more as I rewrite & shorten it, for now it spun out too much.

If this is not a saleable thing Mother thinks a volume of my best, or rather most popular stories, for the best never are popular, might do better, & could easily be arranged as I have printed copies of most all of them. There is one Mr Parker liked, another Mr Emerson praised, & several that have been copied into papers & magazines. This has often been suggested to me but I never cared to do it as so many better books were waiting to be read.

We like the extracts from the letters, & I wait to see my second book in its go abroad gown. Respectfully yrs L. M. A.

I should like to keep the copyright of the book myself.

1. Franklin Benjamin Sanborn, author, journalist, abolitionist, and Alcott family friend. He published "Hospital Sketches" in the Boston *Commonwealth* from 22 May to 26 June 1863 before Redpath's publication in book form.

2. Alcott labored for years upon her autobiographical novel at one time called "Success" and renamed *Work: A Story of Experience,* published in 1873 by Roberts Brothers.

L 4

HOSPITAL SKETCHES, LETTER TO REDPATH, 28 AUGUST [1863]

I have delayed writing both because of company & that I might collect my wits a little for such a burst of new plans & projects rather made my head spin.

Firstly we all like the book very much, & I have the satisfaction of seeing my townsfolk buying & reading, laughing & crying over it wherever I go.[1] One rash youth bought eight copies at a blow, & my dozen would have gone rapidly if I had not locked them up. . . . I as yet have given away but three t[o] my various boys, "Baby B"[2] among them.

I had a visit from an army surgeon the other day who considered my mules striking likenesses, & the book "one to do no end of good both in & out of the army, &c." I didn't quite see how. . . . All is pleasant & looks promising, I hope such a powerful work wont distract the mind of the nation from more useful matters.

I send ten stories & have two more if I can only get them. . . . I suppose I have a right to republish these things without asking leave haven't I? There are many other tales of the "thrilling" style but they are not worth reprinting.

The editorial plan was so like an old dream coming true, that my family shouted over it, as we have had several domestic newspapers conducted by "T. P." I can only say, I know nothing about the real thing nor the requirements needed, but if there is any thing in the way of selections, reading MS, noticing common books I might perhaps do that. . . . I asked a wise lady about salaries, or whatever that sort of wages are called, & was told that they varied from five hundred a year to three or four thousand according to the amount of work done & the ability of the individual. I could not give all my time to it, & had planned to go to Port Royal this winter, but am not positively engaged to do so.[3]

Mother wants me to tell you that Conway[4] & our Consul at Venice shouted over the Sketches in some palace in that mouldy city, & the Consul sent his compliments to "Nurse P"

It will take some time to prepare "Success" as I cannot work very steadily without my poor old head beginning to ache & my family a[ll] predict relapses. If you wish I can go on with it while the tales are coming out (if they come) & be ready in case a discerning public demand further gems from my illustrious pen.

My sister will call on Monday & take the first chapters out of your way if you decide on the tales appearing first, as I like to refer to them now & then while going on with others. Ellery Channing[5] asked her last evening at a party why her sister did not collect & republish her stories, which remark has been made by several others before. Whether they will go is another thing. I dont think much of them being hastily written to suit purchasers. But here they are & some of them has done well in humbler walks of life.

. . . If the stories need any other arranging I can do it at once. I luckily put them hastily together for you to look at.

L. M. A.

1. Alcott wrote in her journal of August 1863: "On the 25th my first morning-glory bloomed in my room,—a hopeful blue,—and at night up came my book in its new dress. I had added several chapters to it, and it was quite a neat little affair. An edition of one thousand, and I to have five cents on each copy" (Cheney, 153).

2. Sergeant Robert Bane, one of Alcott's hospital patients.

3. One of the domestic newspapers was entitled the *Olive Leaf* (see Stern, *Louisa May Alcott*, 62). For her unfulfilled plans about Port Royal, see Document 2, note 4. In her journal of September 1863, she wrote: "Received $40 from Redpath for 'Sketches,'—first edition; wanted me to be editor of a paper; was afraid to try, and let it go" (Cheney, 154).

4. Moncure Daniel Conway (with Sanborn, editor of the *Commonwealth*) wrote of "Hospital Sketches": "The series . . . showed every variety of ability, and excited

much attention" (*Autobiography Memories and Experiences,* vol. 1 [Boston: Houghton Mifflin, 1904], 369).

5. Ellery Channing, Transcendentalist poet and occasional neighbor of the Alcotts in Concord.

———

L 5

LETTER TO REDPATH, 29 SEPTEMBER [1863]

I send you copies of paragraphs from two letters lately recieved [*sic*], one from Wasson to father, the other to myself from Sergeant James, one of the Wagner heroes & son of Henry James.[1] Use them if you like. I am expecting a letter from one of my boys to whom I sent the book, & from Chas Sumner who told father he was intending to write.

I was afraid the price would hurt the sale of the book & think the plan you suggest a good one.[2] About selling the copyright I'm unable to decide knowing so little of such matters, but will inquire & let you know as soon as may be.

If I go to Port Royal "Success" will have to wait, but letters or "Sketches" from there will make a better because truer book &, I think, one that would sell more rapidly than a common romance.

I've written to Mr Judd for information & shall soon know how my winter is to be employed. I've another story for Fields nearly done & when the "Contraband" (or "Brothers" as he insists on naming it) is out next month I'll hand him this & continue doing so till we get enough for our book of Tales.[3]

I should like to tell the Congregationalist some of the pious doings I saw at the Union; the sanctified nurse who sung hymns & prayed violently while stealing the men's watches & money; the much esteemed lady whose devout countenance was abominated by the boys though the chaplain approved of her till it was found that her exhortations ceased when the patients had made their wills in her favor; & sundry other samples of humbug which so disgusted "Nurse P" that she resolved to put her religion into her work rather than her words & save souls in ways of her own, that seemed to suc[c]eed though not of kind to bear telling in a newspaper.

Respectfully yrs
L. M. A.

1. David Atwood Wasson, writer of radical religious works, and Garth Wilkinson James. The clipped paragraphs she enclosed were: from Wasson, "Let me tell you what extreme pleasure I have taken in reading 'Hospital Sketches.' Written with such extraordinary wit & felicity of style, & showing such power to portray character! Surely she has a brilliant literary future before her"; from James, "Your wonderful little book was recieved [*sic*] while suffering much from my wounds. Greatly am I indebted to you for it; it has whiled away several otherwise weary hours & I have enjoyed it exceedingly."

2. A paperbound printing for army reading was priced at twenty-five cents.

3. "My Contraband; or, The Brothers," first called "The Brothers," appeared in the *Atlantic Monthly* for November 1863. No other Alcott story subsequently appeared there.

L 6

MOODS, LETTER TO REDPATH, N.D.

Your letter has quite settled my mind on several points, & now I can comfortably attend to my own affairs without a dozen plans bewildering my mind.

Thank you for so clearly & kindly enlightening me, & be assured I have no intention of changing my publisher. . . . I think the literary laws *are* just & shall abide [by] them, hoping that your faith in my ability may be rewarded, & future books may prove a good investment for us both. It is done except the last Chap—do you want to see it? If so let me know & I will send half by May next Wed—It is such a vast Ms that I'm afraid it will appal[l] you, though I've taken out ever so many pages & simmered it down almost as much as I can. One or two might be omitted if you think best. I should very much value your instruction[?] even if you bundled the book home with "Rubbish" written on the cover.[1]

I'll try not to be spoilt, & think ten or fifteen years of scribbling rather good training for an ambitious body; but people mustn't talk about genius—for I drove that idea away years ago & dont want it back again. The inspiration of necessity is all I've had, & it is a safer help than any other.

I have a sort of feeling that it wasn't quite fair for Fields to offer an engagement after another manager had run all the risks of bringing the new debutante out. He wont have "Moods," unless you get tired of your bargain & send me adrift. I'm not sure that I dont take a little naughty satisfaction in being able to say No—when he asks me, for between him & Ticknor things dont go as freely as F likes & the Atlantic is dreadfully afraid of certain words & ideas which such a big ocean ou[gh]t to be glad to carry into a safe harbor.

Speaking of the Atlantic reminds me of another thing I want to ask you about. F likes my stories & pays promptly & well for them but if I go on writing for him wont he expect to print them if I ever want them in a book?[2] He *has had* the best, & even those you saw may not be mine to give you, at least three or four, Father thinks he would make a fuss if I did it, what do you say? Would not any paper or Magazine do the same?

Now about "Moods"—it is a big thing, thirty chapters long—rather odd, sentimental, & tragical—written for my own amusement at various spare times during the last three years. My family laugh & cry over it, & think it fine—they are no judges—neither am I—Mr Emerson offered to read & give his opinion long ago but I hadn't the courage to let him.

. . . when the notice, or whatever it was, appeared some one said one paper wished I'd write a novel, that is all I know, & I think I'll gratify him.

Very truly yours
L. M. Alcott.

1. *Moods,* to which Alcott refers, was not published until 1865, when A. K. Loring of Boston brought it out. James T. Fields and Redpath were both at one time interested in it (see Cheney, 154, 156).

2. James T. Fields of Ticknor & Fields, publishers of the *Atlantic Monthly,* accepted the following Alcott stories for that periodical: "Love and Self-Love" (March 1860); "A Modern Cinderella; or, The Little Old Shoe" (October 1860); "Debby's Début" (August 1863); and "The Brothers" (November 1863). Of these, "A Modern Cinderella" and "The Brothers" were reprinted in *Hospital Sketches and Camp and Fireside Stories* (Boston: Roberts, 1869).

L 7

LETTER TO REDPATH, CONCORD, 2 DECEMBER [1863]

I prefer not to part with H. S.'s. But will gladly help on the "Camp Fire" series by letting you have as many of my stories as you like. Two or three suitable for such purpose might be put in a small book. I have one "On Picket Duty" which the Atlantic wouldn't take, & other war-like matters simmering in my head. "A Hospital Christmas["] is one & if Ticknor would let us have the brothers these three would do as a beginning perhaps if you want them.[1]

As soon as the Sanitary plays[2] are over I'll work with all my might at Success & let you have it as soon as possible for I want that to come first.

My time seems likely to be pretty fully occupied if I accept all the offers made me. Leslie asks for several more tales, Fields wants another in "The Brothers" style, & Richardson the unknown makes a proposal which I send for you to see,[3] & if you will be so kind to give me your opinion of the enterprize. Are they clever people? & is it worth my while to accept?

I suppose if my stories are printed in the "dime set" they can still be gathered into one volume at some time with others, if we think best?

Respectfully & illegibly
L. M. A.

1. *On Picket Duty, and Other Tales* (Boston: James Redpath, 1864) was the first of Redpath's *Books for Camp and Home* series, also called *Books for the Camp Fires*. It included "On Picket Duty," "The Cross on the Old Church Tower," and "The Death of John," as well as "The King of Clubs and the Queen of Hearts," which had appeared in the *Monitor* for 19 April–7 June 1862.

2. In December 1863, a fair to benefit the Sanitary Commission opened in Boston, and Alcott dramatized *Scenes from Dickens,* managed by George Bartlett, for performance at the Tremont Theatre.

3. Frank Leslie published in his *Frank Leslie's Illustrated Newspaper* the following Alcott tales: "Pauline's Passion and Punishment" (3 and 10 January 1863); "A Whisper in the Dark" (6 and 13 June 1863); and "Enigmas" (14 and 21 May 1864). For Fields's publications of Alcott stories in the *Atlantic Monthly,* see Letter 6, note 2. Charles B. Richardson published Alcott's "Love and Loyalty" in the *United States Service Magazine* for July–December 1864.

L 8

LETTER TO REDPATH, 29 JANUARY [1864]

It strikes me that S. R. Bartlett is making a "coil" about a very small matter, & I know of nothing to be done, on my part, except to repeat what I wrote on sending you the story. It was never wholly paid for though Atlantic prices were promised, or rather more than that as we were to have $5.00 a column. I recieved [*sic*] $30 & no one else any thing as I was told by several of my fellow contributors.[1]

As the paper died in a little while & was not much known nor read while it lasted I fancied my "King of Clubs" was rather wasted on the desert air, & that there would be no harm in republishing it, as I said to Bartlett when I gave it to him that I wished to be at liberty to do so by & by if I chose. He may [made] no objection & as I did not know that the Monitor was copyrighted I never thought of asking his leave to print my own story.

It seems neither neighborly nor necessary to make objections now, & it does not appear to me that we have either of us done any thing unlawful or unjust. I never asked for the rest of the money due me as I knew the Monitor was going down & did not want to add another jolt to the many borne by its commander.

Respectfully

L. M. Alcott.

1. "The King of Clubs and the Queen of Hearts," published by Samuel Ripley Bartlett in the *Monitor* for 19 April–7 June 1862, was reprinted both in *On Picket Duty* and in *Hospital Sketches and Camp and Fireside Stories*, despite Bartlett's "coil."

L 9

LETTER TO REDPATH, 30 JANUARY 1864

The little green backs were *very* welcome & I hardly knew my own scribbles in their new dress. I never liked "Picket Duty" very well for Yankee talk is my abomination, though as the great James professed to like it I thought I'd try to suit him. I didn't, nor myself either. "The King of Clubs" suits me better & the "Cross on the Church Tower["] is pious enough to please any one I hope. It was written so long ago I'd forgotten the whole family.[1]

You ask about errors, there are none of any consequence except in "Picket Duty" where poor Flint is made to talk something that is not even down east Yankee.

On page 21 he swallows a "tub" instead of a "nut"—page 23 needs another *b* in "shabby", the word "loopin" is "loafin"—page 26—*stoxe* is *store*, & *keell* is kill—also omit the "per" in the sentence "offered permotion on the field"—there is an I omitted on page 11 in the 10th line—& Flag substituted for done on the 30th page—which would do very well if the Rebs did not think as much of their flag as we & fight for it more pluckily—

Page 36 poor dear Wilhelmina Carolina Amelia Skeggs suffers the same amputation of a letter as before, & I begin to think no one has ever read the "Vicar of Wakefield." The two Dickens are bad, but I suppose it cannot be helped now unless in the new edition if there is one.

I should like Billings for the Fairy Tales, though Miss Green has a delicate fancy & if she would let me see her designs before engraving I could tell her how to make them suit me better.[2] Several people have urged me to get out "Beach Bubbles"[3] or Songs for the seaside—which were printed but never paid for some years ago—They came out in the Gazette & were copy righted in my name by Mr Clapp so they have never been reprinted & were much liked. There are a dozen I believe, & perhaps if prettily illustrated would make a good summer book.

Respectfully L. M. Alcott.

"Success" is just where I left it for though I have tried a dozen times I cannot get on with it, so must wait for inspiration. Writing books is too hard work for one who likes to finish soon.

1. For the publication and contents of *On Picket Duty, and Other Tales*, see Letter 7, n. 1. Henry James, Sr., had written of his pleasure in Louisa Alcott's "charming pictures of hospital service" (clipping, Alcott Papers, Harvard University).

2. Redpath published Alcott's *The Rose Family. A Fairy Tale* in 1864. The volume of fairy tales was never published as such, though the manuscript had a strange history; see *Louisa's Wonder Book: An Unknown Alcott Juvenile*, ed. Madeleine B. Stern (Mount Pleasant: Central Michigan University, 1975), 10–12. The artists referred to are Hammatt Billings, who probably illustrated *Little Women*, part 2, and Elizabeth B. Greene, illustrator of Alcott's *Morning-Glories, and Other Stories* (Boston: Horace B. Fuller, 1868).

3. The poems entitled "Beach Bubbles" had appeared in William Warland Clapp, Jr.'s *Saturday Evening Gazette*, Quarto Series, for 21 June–23 August 1856.

LETTER TO REDPATH, CONCORD, 2 FEBRUARY [1864]

I have written to my amiable townsman S. R. Bartlett & hope he will feel satisfied. One thing has escaped your memory I find, & that is that I told you in one of my notes about the stories that "King of Clubs" had been printed in the Monitor but not paid for &c. I did not mention copyrights because I did not know any thing about them. It's of no consequence probably, but I am quite sure I told you that much.[1]

I dont know what to say about "H. S.'s." My wise friends say "Dont sell it," so I hold on as I'm bid, though I cannot find any great wisdom in it. The high price killed the sale of it, one literary party said, & many have complained. But *I* think it is done with now so why bewail any mistake at the outset?

Suppose you make me an offer for it, & then we will see.[2]

I send a corrected copy of "P. D." The first story contains about all the mistakes I believe.

I should like to see what the Post & Traveller say if its worth the trouble of slipping into a note sometime. I dont agree with L. S. & never shall. I hate Yankees. Leslie & Richardson still send for stories & "Success" still remains in a muddle.   L. M. A.

I have nothing but the Fairy Tales. If you want to do any thing about them for next Christmas you can have them. I have added a new one.

1. See Letter 8, note 1.
2. From payments on all editions of *Hospital Sketches,* including the twenty-five-cent army printing in paper, Alcott received two hundred dollars.

LETTER TO REDPATH, "REDPATH ROOMS," [1864]

I recieved [*sic*] a note from Roberts Brothers this morning enclosing one from you to them. They say—"If you (meaning me) are under any engagement to Mr Redpath which we are obliged to purchase we cannot think of making any proposals with reference to publishing. We also decline to purchase his plates."

I had no intention of doing anything with "Rose Family" which is your property, but I *did* wish to have the Brothers get up my book of fairy tales, & think they are still mine to do as I like with as you told me when I saw you some time ago that you did not feel able to get them up in the expensive way they should be done, also that such books were not very profitable, & let the whole thing rest after I had hurried to get them ready as you said it took a good while for illustrations.

I have signed no contract about them & as you have no new books or tales of mine in hand, or any still unsettled for I believe I am at liberty to dispose of the fairy tales to whom so ever will do them to suit me.[1]

I desired father to enquire if the Bros. got out fairy books, & he entered into the matter more than I meant he should till I had seen you. I wish to be honorable & right in my dealings all round, & as I find my things will go elsewhere to do the best I can. You spoke of not publishing any more for a time—"Camp-Fire" books at least[2]—& as I am not able to write new stories I want to make the old ones profit-able & think a Christmas book might do well if finely gotten up.

I shall do nothing further till I hear from you as I still have the fear of some dreadful breach of etiquette before my eyes, tho I *dont* fear any Bartlett transactions this time I assure you.

I came in from Medford where I was going when I last saw you, & shall be in town till tomorrow P.M. so any message or letter from you I will call for tomorrow morning when father will be in town.

I was sorry to hear that you were ill, & send the sympatting [*sic*] regards of a fellow sufferer to your typhoid son.

Respectfully yours
L. M. Alcott.

1. For the fairy tales, see Letter 9, note 2.
2. Redpath's last advertisement appeared in the *American Publishers' Circular* for 15 April 1864, ending his brief career as a publisher.

Alcott-Dodge Letters

———

L 12

LETTER TO MARY MAPES DODGE, CONCORD,
8 OCTOBER [1874?]

I am so busy with home affairs just now that I have no time even to think of stories. If I can get any leisure this winter I will try to send one or two.[1]

The state of my mother's health forbids my making any very binding engagements this year, so I can only say I will if I can.[2]

I do not know Miss Greene's[3] address since her return from the South. Revd Cyrus Bartol[4] is the only person who can give it, & I dont know if he is in town yet. His address is 17 Chestnut St. Boston.

I am very lame & tied to my sofa for some weeks I fear & therefore pretty helpless, or I would go & look up little Betsey.

I like Mrs Innis' drawing better than Miss Greene's. Mrs I. is illustrating a book for me now. She did Sallie Windham's "K. & D." & some other stories. Her children are altogether charming, thier [*sic*] little fat legs captivate me entirely.

But I love E. B. G. & dont mind her infant's dropsical heads very much.

Yrs truly

L. M. Alcott.

1. "Roses and Forget-Me-Nots," Alcott's first contribution to Dodge's new juvenile magazine, *St. Nicholas,* had appeared in the March 1874 issue; "The Autobiography of an Omnibus" appeared in the October 1874 number. Alcott's next contribution would be the serial "Eight Cousins," which began in the January 1875 issue. The original of this letter is in the Louisa May Alcott Collection, Brigham Young University.

2. Mrs. Alcott's final illness had begun by the beginning of 1874.

3. Elizabeth B. Greene, the artist who had illustrated Alcott's *Morning-Glories, and Other Stories,* and provided a few illustrations for *Merry's Museum* (see Stern, *Louisa May Alcott,* 170, 172).

4. Dr. Cyrus Augustus Bartol, a Unitarian clergyman.

L 13

EIGHT COUSINS, LETTER TO DODGE, BOSTON,
2 DECEMBER [1874?]

I infer from Scribner's last voluminous epistle that you are troubled about thier [*sic*] & my allusion to your tears.

Of course I understood what they meant, but as the whole affair has seemed like a tempest in a teacup to me I did not want any more time wasted over it.

The excellent gentlemen have evidently "got a bee in their bonnet" on this point, & I cannot find out just what it is in spite of the many explanations so kindly given me.

To me the matter appears thus. I make an agreement with S. & Co. about Eight Cousins exactly as I have always done with other serials. Reserving all rights to the tale outside of thier [*sic*] magazine. Among these rights is that of selling it as a serial in England which gives me my copyright there & secures the book hereafter. Of course I protect S. & Co. by forbidding the tale to appear in this country in any English magazine, & if it *does* I have the power to stop it.

If I do not secure myself in England S. & Co. as well as myself are at the mercy of [whoever] chooses to take the story.

S. & Co. agree as a matter of courtesy, & proceed to put so many obstacles in the way & make so many stipulations that the English publisher is perplexed, & I shall probably lose the sum he offered me for the tale in order that he might keep control of the serial. I telegraph, write, explain, & try to be as obliging as I can. Change the name of the tale to suit others, put in babies to suit the artist, & endeavor to go on writing with the whole affair in such a coil that my genius refuses to burn & the story is put away till calmer times.

I value peace & good will much more than money & would gladly give away the whole Eight or put them in the fire if it were fair to others. As it is not I still wait & hope.

I am not well, & with little relief from pain day & night worry wears upon me more than I like to have it. If it were not for the blessed fact that everything has its comic as well as tragic side I should have lost my wits long ago with three publishers thundering at me all at once. As a sister woman you can understand this, & know that neither tears nor laughter can keep one from losing patience & spirits sometimes

Yrs truly   L. M. Alcott.[1]

I should like to see the pictures if I may, before they are posted [to] change if need be. R. & Bros. will like to have them if they suit

1. This letter concerns the serialization of "Eight Cousins" in the British periodical *Good Things: A Picturesque Magazine for the Young of All Ages* for 5 December 1874–27 November 1875, in *St. Nicholas* for January–October 1875, and the book publication by Roberts Brothers in 1875. Prior to publication, Roberts Brothers, Sampson Low of London, and Scribner, publishers of *St. Nicholas*, outbid each other; see Cheney, 274–75, and Stern, *Louisa May Alcott*, 239. Complications also

attended publication of the sequel, *Rose in Bloom*. According to Raymond L. Kilgour: "There was a legal dispute between Sampson, Low and Son and a Swiss firm, H. Mignot, of Lausanne, over the European rights to *Rose in Bloom*. Sampson, Low asserted that the book appeared *first* in England and thus had European copyright, whereas Mignot claimed that the American edition appeared first and hence Sampson, Low had no rights" (*Messrs. Roberts Brothers, Publishers* [Ann Arbor: University of Michigan Press, 1952], 296 n. 157). This letter is printed from the original in the Louisa May Alcott Collection, Brigham Young University.

L 14

UNDER THE LILACS, LETTER TO DODGE, CONCORD, 3 JUNE [1877]

The tale goes slowly owing to interruptions, for summer is a busy time, and I get few quiet days. Twelve chapters are done, but are short ones, and so will make about six or seven numbers in "St. Nicholas."

I will leave them divided in this way that you may put in as many as you please each month; for trying to suit the magazine hurts the story in its book form, though this way does no harm to the monthly parts, I think.

I will send you the first few chapters during the week for Mrs. Foote,[1] and with them the schedule you suggest, so that my infants may not be drawn with whiskers, and my big boys and girls in pinafores, as in "Eight Cousins."

I hope the new baby won't be set aside too soon for my illustrations; but I do feel a natural wish to have one story prettily adorned with good pictures, as hitherto artists have much afflicted me.

I am daily waiting with anxiety for an illumination of some sort, as my plot is very vague so far; and though I don't approve of "sensations" in children's books, one must have a certain thread on which to string the small events which make up the true sort of child-life.

I intend to go and simmer an afternoon at Van Amburg's great show,[2] that I may get hints for the further embellishment of Ben and his dog. I have also put in a poem by F. B. S.'s small son,[3] and that hit will give Mrs. Foote a good scene with the six-year-old poet reciting his verses under the lilacs.

I shall expect the small tots to be unusually good, since the artist has a live model to study from. Please present my congratulations to the happy mamma and Mr. Foote, Jr.

Yours warmly,
L. M. A.[4]

1. Mary Anna Hallock Foote, author and illustrator. She provided illustrations of "Bab and Betty" and "The Blue Beard Group" for the *St. Nicholas* serialization of "Under the Lilacs."

2. I. A. Van Amburgh's Mammoth Menagerie and New Great Golden Menagerie, Boston, featured a performing elephant, a waltzing Shetland, Jocko the monkey ponyrider, Hannibal, Jr., King and Queen Lori Grandi, and a black spaniel. Alcott visited the menagerie to get suggestions for *Under the Lilacs* (see H. Barnum, *Illustrated and Descriptive History of the Animals . . . in Van Amburgh and Company's . . . Menagerie* [New York: Booth, 1869], passim, and Stern, *Louisa May Alcott*, III, 268–69).

3. The poem by F. B. Sanborn's third son, Francis Bachiler Sanborn, born 5 February 1872, appears in *Under the Lilacs*, 78.

4. This letter is reprinted from Cheney, 301–2.

L 15

JACK AND JILL, LETTER TO DODGE, 21 AUGUST 1879

I have not been able to do anything on the serial. . . . But after a week at the seaside, to get braced up for work, I intend to begin. The Revolutionary tale does not seem to possess me. I have casually asked many of my young folks, when they demand a new story, which they would like, one of that sort, or the old "Eight Cousin" style, and they all say the latter. It would be much the easier to do, as I have a beginning and a plan all ready,—a village, and the affairs of a party of children. We have many little romances going on among the Concord boys and girls, and all sorts of queer things, which will work into "Jack and Jill" nicely. Mrs. Croly[1] has been anxious for a story, and I am trying to do a short one, as I told her you had the refusal of my next serial. I hope you will not be very much disappointed about the old-time tale. It would take study to do it well, and leisure is just what I have not got, and I shall never have, I fear, when writing is to be done. I will send you a few chapters of "Jack and Jill" when in order, if you will, and you can decide if they will suit. I shall try to have it unlike the others if possible, but the dears *will* cling to the "Little Women" style.

I have had a very busy summer, but have been pretty well, and able to do my part in entertaining the four hundred philosophers.[2]

Your truly,
L. M. A.[3]

1. Jane Cunningham Croly ("Jenny June"), journalist and magazine editor, was editor of *Demorest's Monthly Magazine,* where Alcott's "Victoria. A Woman's Statue" appeared in March–May 1881.

2. The Concord School of Philosophy. In her journal, Alcott wrote: "The town swarms with budding philosophers, and they roost on our steps like hens waiting for corn. Father revels in it, so we keep the hotel going, and try to look as if we liked it" (Cheney, 321; see also *The Letters of Bronson Alcott,* 772).

3. This letter is reprinted from Cheney, 302–3.

L 16

LETTER TO DODGE, 17 SEPTEMBER [1879]

. . . Don't let me *prose.* If I seem to be declining and falling into it, pull me up, and I'll try to prance as of old. Years tame down one's spirit and fancy, though they only deepen one's love for the little people, and strengthen the desire to serve them wisely as well as cheerfully. Fathers and mothers tell me they use my books as helps for themselves; so now and then I like to slip in a page for them, fresh from the experience of some other parent, for education seems to me to be *the* problem in our times.

Jack and Jill are right out of our own little circle, and the boys and girls are in a twitter to know what is going in; so it will be a "truly story" in the main.

Such a long note for a busy woman to read! but your cheery word was my best "starter;" and I'm, more than ever,

Yours truly,
L. M. A.[1]

1. This letter is reprinted from Cheney, 303.

L 17

JACK AND JILL, LETTER TO DODGE, 5 MARCH [1880]

Some days ago Mr Niles sent the last chapters of "J. & J."[1] in corrected proof, to save me the trouble of copying. Hope they went safely, & that you are as much relieved to see the end as I am.

People told me to make the tale "a little pious," so I have here & there tried to suit them without being too preachy.

The Concord children enjoy the numbers as they come out, & my other infants seem satisfied, so I trust the delay & dark days have not done any great harm.

"Molly & her cats" was a funny picture & "Boo" very good.[2]

I hope your invalid is up & out again. My regards to him.

Yrs truly
L. M. Alcott[3]

1. Alcott's "Jack and Jill" was serialized in *St. Nicholas* for December 1879–October 1880 before book publication as *Jack and Jill: A Village Story* (Boston: Roberts, 1880).

2. A reference to the illustrations of the characters Molly Loo and Boo.

3. This letter is published courtesy the New-York Historical Society.

L 18

LETTER TO DODGE, CONCORD, 29 MAY 1880

I was away from home, so your letter did not reach me till I got back yesterday.

Thanks for your kind thought of me, and recollections of the pleasant week when the L. L.'s[1] had a lark. I should like another; but in this work-a-day world busy folk don't get many, as we know.

If I write a serial, you shall have it; but I have my doubts as to the leisure and quiet needed for such tasks being possible with a year-old baby.[2] Of course little Lu is a *very* remarkable child, but I fancy I shall feel as full of responsibility as a hen with one chick, and cluck and scratch industriously for the sole benefit of my daughter.

She may, however, have a literary turn, and be my assistant, by offering hints and giving studies of character for my work. She comes in September, if well.

If I do begin a new story, how would "An Old-Fashioned Boy" and his life do? I meant that for the title of a book, but another woman took it.[3] You proposed a revolutionary tale once, but I was not up to it; for this I have quaint material in my father's journals, letters, and recollections. He was born with the century, and had an uncle in the war of 1812; and his life was very pretty and pastoral in the early days. I think a new sort of story wouldn't be amiss, with fun in it, and the queer old names and habitats. I began it long ago, and if I have a chance will finish off a few chapters and send them to you, if you like.

Yours cordially,

L. M. Alcott.[4]

1. Possibly a reference to Lucy Larcom (and her family), author and magazine editor, whose verses appeared in *St. Nicholas* and elsewhere.

2. Lulu Nieriker arrived in America on 19 September 1880.

3. Alcott's "An Old-Fashioned Boy" was never written; Martha Finley, author of *Elsie Dinsmore*, who used the pen name of Martha Farquharson, was the author of *An Old-Fashioned Boy* (Philadelphia: William B. Evans, 1871) (see Kilgour, *Messrs. Roberts Brothers*, 103).

4. This letter is reprinted from Cheney, 333.

L 19

LETTER TO DODGE, NONQUITT, 6 AUGUST [1881]

I am sorry for the children's disappointment, & dont delay for want of urging as the twenty boys & girls here at the beach clamor for more stories & suggest many plans.

None seem to think that a Revolutionary one would be interesting, & I fear that patriotism is not natural to the youthful soul.

Next Fall I will see what I can do. Meantime I will try to get a little story done if the hot weather will let me work.

As I lead the life of an oyster just now I fear it wont be a very thrilling tale, but it may appease the little people till we can promise something better.

Baby[1] is well, thank you, & has just tumbled down stairs for the first time, frightening me out of my wits but not hurting herself a bit.

She is so fat she rolled down like a ball & had not a bruise to show after the exploit.

Yrs truly

L. M. A.[2]

1. Louisa May Nieriker, daughter of May Alcott Nieriker, who died in December 1879 in Paris, was sent to America to be raised by her aunt. She was the "Lulu" of *Lulu's Library.*

2. This letter is printed from the original in the Louisa May Alcott Collection, Brigham Young University.

SPINNING-WHEEL STORIES, LETTER TO DODGE, CONCORD,
15 AUGUST [1883?]

I like the idea of "Spinning-Wheel Stories," and can do several for a
series which can come out in a book later.[1] Old-time tales, with a thread
running through all from the wheel that enters in the first one.

A Christmas party of children might be at an old farm-house and
hunt up the wheel, and grandma spins and tells the first story; and
being snow-bound, others amuse the young folks each evening with
more tales. Would that do? The mother and child picture would come
in nicely for the first tale,—"Grandma and her Mother."[2]

Being at home and quiet for a week or so (as Father is nicely and has
a capable nurse), I have begun the serial, and done two chapters; but
the spinning-tales come tumbling into my mind so fast I'd better pin a
few while "genius burns." Perhaps you would like to start the set Christmas. The picture being ready and the first story can be done in a week,
"Sophie's Secret"[3] can come later. Let me know if you would like that,
and about how many pages of the paper "S. S." was written on you
think would make the required length of tale (or tail?). If you don't
want No. 1 yet, I will take my time and do several.

The serial was to be "Mrs. Gay's Summer School,"[4] and have some
city girls and boys go to an old farmhouse, and for fun dress and live as
in old times, and learn the good, thrifty old ways, with adventures and
fun thrown in. That might come in the spring, as it takes me longer to
grind out yarns now than of old.

Glad you are better. Thanks for kind wishes for the little house; come
and see it, and gladden the eyes of forty young admirers by a sight of
M. M. D. next year.

Yours affectionately,

L. M. A.[5]

1. The stories reprinted in *Spinning-Wheel Stories* (Boston: Roberts, 1884) appeared in *St. Nicholas* for January 1884–January 1885.

2. The first of the *Spinning-Wheel Stories* was "Grandma's Story," in *St. Nicholas*
for January 1884.

3. "Sophie's Secret" appeared in *St. Nicholas* for November and December 1883. It was reprinted in *Lulu's Library*, vol. 3 (Boston: Roberts, 1889).

4. "Mrs. Gay's Summer School" was never written.

5. This letter is reprinted from Cheney, 374–75.

_____

L 21

JO'S BOYS, LETTER TO DODGE, 13 APRIL [1886]

I am glad you are going to have such a fine outing; may it be a very happy one.

I cannot promise anything, but hope to be allowed to write a little, as my doctor has decided that it is as well to let me put on paper the tales "knocking at the sauce pan lid & demanding to be taken out," (like "Mrs Cratchet's" potatoes[1]), as to have them go on worrying me inside. So I'm scribbling at "Jo's Boys" long promised to Mr Niles & clamored for by the children. I may write but one hour a day so cannot get on very fast, but if it is ever done I can think of a serial for St N.

I began one & can easily start it for 88 if head & hand allow.

I will simmer on it this summer & see if it can be done. Hope so, for I dont want to give up work so soon.

I have read "Mrs Null,"[2] but dont like it very well. Too slow & color-less after Tolstoi's "Anna Karanina."[3] I met Mr & Mrs S. at Mrs Ald-rich's this winter.[4] Mr Stockton's child's stories I like very much; the older ones are odd but artificial.

Now good by & God be with you, dear woman, & bring you safely home to us all.

Affectionately yrs

L. M. Alcott.[5]

1. The reference is to the Cratchits of Charles Dickens's *A Christmas Carol.*

2. Frank R. Stockton, *The Late Mrs Null* (New York: Charles Scribner's Sons, 1886).

3. Published in New York by Crowell in 1886; see Mott, *Golden Multitudes,* 183.

4. Frank R. Stockton and his wife, Marian Edwards Tuttle Stockton. Thomas Bailey Aldrich and his wife Lilian Woodman Aldrich were then living in Boston.

5. This letter is printed from the original in the Louisa May Alcott Collection, Brigham Young University. It was also printed in Cheney, 377.

L 22

"TRUDEL'S SIEGE," LETTER TO DODGE, 22 DECEMBER 1887

I send you the story your assistant editor asked for.[1] As it is needed at once I do not delay to copy it, for I can only write an hour a day & do very little.

You are used to my wild Mss. & will be able to read it. I meant to have sent the Chinese tale, but this was nearly done, & so it goes, as it does not matter where we begin.

Do you have the bound volumes of St N. now?

If so will you kindly send me the one for last year. My Lulu adores the dear book, & has worn out the old ones. I want to give it her for New Year Any time will do, however.

I hope you are well & full of the peace work well done gives the happy doer.

I mend slowly but surely, & my good Dr. says my best work is yet to come. I will be content with health if I can get it.

With all good wishes,

Yrs affectionately

L. M. A.[2]

1. "Trudel's Siege" was published in *St. Nicholas* for April 1888.

2. This letter is printed from the original in the Louisa May Alcott Collection, Brigham Young University. It was also printed, with omissions, in Cheney, 384.

L 23

LETTER TO DODGE, BOSTON, 31 DECEMBER [N.Y.]

A little cousin, thirteen years old has written a story & longs to see it in print. It is a well-written bit & pretty good for a beginning, so I send it to you hoping it may find a place in the children's corner. She is a grandchild of S. J. May,[1] & a bright lass who paints nicely & is a domestic little person in spite of her budding accomplishments. Good luck to her.

I hoped to have had a Xmas story for some one but am forbidden to write for six months after a bad turn of vertigo. So I give it [i.e., in] & take warning. All good wishes for the New Year from

yrs affectionately

L. M. Alcott.[2]

1. Samuel Joseph May, Unitarian clergyman and reformer, was Louisa Alcott's uncle.

2. This letter is printed from the original in the Louisa May Alcott Collection, Brigham Young University. It was also printed in Cheney, 375.

Alcott–Niles Letters

L 24

LITTLE WOMEN, LETTER TO NILES, [1878]

. . . I was very glad Mr B. gave you credit for the immortal Little Women, for you evolved the book from chaos & made my fortune, & deserve much more honor & thanks than you get. *I* dont forget ten years of kindness & hope a day will come when I can in some way prove my appreciation of that which is better than money or fame.

Very truly your friend

L. M. A.[1]

1. This letter is printed from the original at the Boston Public Library, by courtesy of the Trustees of the Boston Public Library.

L 25

LITTLE WOMEN, PART TWO, LETTER TO NILES, [1869]

I can only think of the following titles. "Little Women Act Second". "Leaving the Nest. Sequel to Little Women".[1]

Either you like. A jocose friend suggests "Wedding Marches" as there is so much pairing off, but I don't approve.

Suggestions gratefully received.

Yrs. truly

L. M. A.[2]

1. The second part of *Little Women*, published in April 1869, was entitled simply *Little Women or Meg, Jo, Beth and Amy Part Second.*

2. This letter is printed from the original in the Houghton Library, Harvard University. The editor is grateful to Jennie Rathbun for the transcription.

L 26

ILLUSTRATED *LITTLE WOMEN,* LETTER TO NILES, YORK, 20 JULY 1880

The drawings are all capital, and we had great fun over them down here this rainy day. . . . Mr. Merrill[1] certainly deserves a good penny for his work. Such a fertile fancy and quick hand as his should be well paid, and I shall not begrudge him his well-earned compensation, nor the praise I am sure these illustrations will earn. It is very pleasant to think that the lucky little story has been of use to a fellow-worker, and I am much obliged to him for so improving on my hasty pen-and-ink sketches. What a dear rowdy boy Teddy is with the felt basin on!

The papers are great gossips, and never get anything quite straight, and I do mean to set up my own establishment in Boston (D.V.). Now I have an excuse for a home of my own, and as the other artistic and literary spinsters have a house, I am going to try the plan, for a winter at least.

Come and see how cosey we are next October at 81 Pinckney Street. Miss N. will receive.[2]

Yours truly,

L. M. A.[3]

1. Frank Merrill's two hundred illustrations appeared in *Little Women* (Boston: Roberts, 1880), issued by Thomas Niles as a holiday book (see Kilgour, *Messrs. Roberts Brothers,* 176, and Stern, *Louisa May Alcott,* 291).
2. Lulu Nieriker.
3. This letter is reprinted from Cheney, 334.

L 27

LETTER TO NILES, 23 JUNE 1883

Thanks for the Goethe book. I want everything that comes out about him. "Princess Amelia"[1] is charming, and the surprise at the end well done. Did the author of "My Wife's Sister"[2] write it?

I told L. C. M. she might put "A Modern Mephistopheles" in my list of books.[3] Several people had found it out, and there was no use in trying to keep it secret after that.

Mrs. Dodge begged me to consider myself mortgaged to her for tales, etc., and as I see no prospect of any time for writing books, I may be able to send her some short stories from time to time, and so be getting material for a new set of books like "Scrap-bag," but with a new name. You excel in names, and can be evolving one meantime. . . .

Yours truly,

L. M. A.[4]

1. Elizabeth W. Latimer's *Princess Amélie* appeared in Roberts Brothers' third No Name Series in 1883.

2. Elizabeth W. Latimer's *My Wife and My Wife's Sister* appeared in the second No Name Series in 1881.

3. Louise Chandler Moulton wrote the article on Louisa May Alcott for *Our Famous Women* (Hartford: A. D. Worthington, 1883).

4. This letter is reprinted from Cheney, 351.

———

L 28

LETTER TO NILES, 15 JULY 1884

I wish I might be inspired to do those dreadful boys ["Jo's Boys"]; but rest is more needed than money. Perhaps during August, my month at home, I may take a grind at the old mill.[1]

1. This letter is reprinted from Cheney, 351–52.

———

L 29

LULU'S LIBRARY, LETTER TO NILES, NONQUITT, 13 JULY 1885

I want to know if it is too late to do it and if it is worth doing; namely, to collect some of the little tales I tell Lulu and put them with the two I shall have printed the last year and the "Mermaid Tale"[1] to match the pictures we bought, and call it "Lulu's Library"? I have several tiny books written down for L.; and as I can do no great work, it occurred to me that I might venture to copy these if it would do for a Christmas book for the younger set.

I ache to fall on some of the ideas that are simmering in my head, but dare not, as my one attempt since the last "Jo's Boys" break-down cost me a week or two of woe and $30 for the doctor. I have lovely long days here, and can copy these and see'em along if you want them. One has gone to "Harper's Young People,"[2] and one is for "St. Nicholas" when it is done,—about the Kindergarten for the blind.[3] These with Lulu's would make a little book, and might begin a series for small folks.[4] Old ladies come to this twaddle when they can do nothing else. What say you? . . .

Yours truly,

L. M. A.[5]

1. The "Mermaid Tale" may be a reference to "Josie Plays Mermaid," which appeared as Chapter 8 of *Jo's Boys* in 1886, or to "Mermaids" in *Lulu's Library*, vol. 2.

2. "Baa! Baa!" appeared in *Harper's Young People* for 15 and 22 September 1885, and was reprinted in *Lulu's Library*, vol. 1 (Boston: Roberts, 1886).

3. "The Blind Lark" appeared in *St. Nicholas* for November 1886, and was reprinted in *Lulu's Library*, vol. 3 (Boston: Roberts, 1889).

4. In September 1885 Alcott wrote in her journal: " 'Lulu's Library' as a 'pot-boiler' will appease the children, and I may be able to work on 'Jo's Boys' " (Cheney, 357; see also Stern, *Louisa May Alcott*, 313–14, 316, 318).

5. This letter is reprinted from Cheney, 360–61.

L 30

LETTER TO NILES, 18 SEPTEMBER 1885

I send you some funny sketches by Mrs. L.[1] She seems to be getting on. How would it do to ask her to illustrate the fairy book? She has a pretty taste in elves, and her little girl was good. I hope to touch up the other stories this winter, and she can illustrate, and next Christmas (or whenever it is ready) we can have a little book out.[2] This sort of work being all I dare do now, I may as well be clearing the decks for action when the order comes to "Up, and at 'em!" again, if it ever does.

I'd like to help Mrs. L. if I could, as we know something of her, and I fancy she needs a lift. Perhaps we could use these pictures in some way if she liked to have us. Maybe I could work them into a story of our "cullud bredren."

Thanks for the books. Dear Miss —— is rather prim in her story, but it is pretty and quite *correct*. So different from Miss Alcott's slap-dash style.

The "H. H." book [*Ramona*] is a noble record of the great wrongs of her chosen people, and ought to wake up the sinners to repentance and justice before it is too late. It recalls the old slavery days, only these victims are red instead of black. It will be a disgrace if "H. H." gave her work and pity all in vain.[3]

Yours truly,

L. M. A.[4]

1. Possibly Addie Ledyard, who illustrated many books for Roberts Brothers, including *Aunt Jo's Scrap-Bag. My Boys* (Boston: Roberts, 1872).
2. The first volume of *Lulu's Library* appeared in 1886.
3. See Document 24, n. 1.
4. This letter is reprinted from Cheney, 361, 364.

L 31

A GARLAND FOR GIRLS, LETTER TO NILES, [1886]

My doctor forbids me to begin a long book or anything that will need much thought this summer. So I must give up "Tragedy of To-day," as it will need a good deal of thinking to be what it ought.

I can give you a girls' book however, and I think that will be better than a novel. I have several stories done, and can easily do more and make a companion volume for "Spinning-Wheel Stories" at Christmas if you want it.

This, with the Lulu stories, will be better than the set of novels I am sure. . . . Wait till I can do a novel, and then get out the set in style, if Alcott is not forgotten by that time.

I was going to send Mrs. Dodge one of the tales for girls, and if there is time she might have more. But nearly all new ones would make a book go well in the holiday season. You can have those already done now if you want them. "Sophie's Secret"[1] is one, "An Ivy Spray: or Cinderella's Slippers"[2] another, and "Mountain Laurel"[3] is partly done. "A Garland for Girls"[4] might do for a title perhaps, as they are all for girls.

Yours truly,

L. M. A.[5]

1. "Sophie's Secret" appeared in *St. Nicholas* for November and December 1883 and was reprinted in *Lulu's Library,* vol. 3.
2. "An Ivy Spray" appeared in *St. Nicholas* for October 1887, and was reprinted

as "An Ivy Spray and Ladies' Slippers" in *A Garland for Girls* (Boston: Roberts, 1888).

   3. *Mountain-Laurel and Maidenhair* (Boston: Little, Brown, 1903).

   4. *A Garland for Girls* was listed for publication on 10 December 1887.

   5. This letter is reprinted from Cheney, 365.

L 32

JO'S BOYS, LETTER TO NILES, 1886

The goodly supply of books was most welcome; for when my two hours pen-work are over I need something to comfort me, and I long to go on and finish "Jo's Boys" by July 1st.

My doctor frowns on that hope, and is so sure it will do mischief to get up the steam that I am afraid to try, and keep Prudence sitting on the valve lest the old engine run away and have another smash-up.

I send you by Fred[1] several chapters, I wish they were neater, as some were written long ago and have knocked about for years; but I can't spare time to copy, so hope the printers won't be in despair.

I planned twenty chapters and am on the fifteenth. Some are long, some short, and as we are pressed for time we had better not try to do too much.

. . . I have little doubt it will be done early in July,[2] but things are so contrary with me I can never be sure of carrying out a plan, and I don't want to fail again; so far I feel as if I could, without harm, finish off these dreadful boys.

Why have any illustrations? The book is not a child's book, as the lads are nearly all over twenty, and pretty pictures are not needed. Have the bas-relief if you like, or one good thing for frontispiece.

I can have twenty-one chapters and make it the size of "Little Men." Sixteen chapters make two hundred and sixteen pages, and I may add a page here and there later,—or if need be, a chapter somewhere to fill up.

I shall be at home in a week or two, much better for the rest and fine air; and during my quiet days in C[oncord]. I can touch up proofs and confer about the book. Sha'n't we be glad when it is done?

Yours truly,

L. M. A.[3]

1. Frederick Alcott Pratt, Louisa's nephew, worked for Roberts Brothers.

2. *Jo's Boys* was completed in July 1886 (Cheney, 359) and published the same year by Roberts Brothers.

3. This letter is reprinted from Cheney, 372–73.

L 33

JO'S BOYS, LETTER TO NILES, 3 OCTOBER [1886]

The first gun fired seems to object to "Jo's Last Scrape"[1] after much twaddle about Thackary [*sic*] &c.

Now you remember I asked you if it should go in, & you said, "By all means, it[']s very good, & ends Jo, the favorite, off in a natural way."

That was one reason for letting it stand, as the success of L. W. comes from just that same use of real life & one's own experience. Another reason is that in no other way can the rising generation of young autograph fiends be reached so well & pleasantly, & by a little good natured ridicule be taught not to harass the authors whom they honor with thier [*sic*] regard.

If it is not good taste to put this part of Jo's life in print all the rest is a mistake also, for the best liked episodes are the real ones.

I had my doubts, as people are particular about these small matters, but the young folks are the only critics I care for, & if they like it I'm satisfied. So far they enjoy that bit much & find no fault.

If there is much fault found with this bit, you might, later, print my reasons, as I cannot appear. But I fancy there wont be any trouble made except by the old quiddles who expect perfection, & that I never even *try* to attain.

Yrs truly

L. M. A.[2]

1. Chapter 3 of Alcott's *Jo's Boys and How They Turned Out* (Boston: Roberts, 1886), entitled "Jo's Last Scrape," concerns Jo March Bhaer's aversion to lion hunters and autograph fiends.

2. This letter is printed from the original in the Louisa May Alcott Collection (#6255–b), Manuscripts Department, University of Virginia.

L 34

LETTER TO NILES, 7 MAY 1887

Yours just come. "A Whisper" is rather a lurid tale, but might do if I add a few lines to the preface of "Modern Mephistopheles," saying that this is put in to fill the volume, or to give a sample of Jo March's necessity stories, which many girls have asked for.[1] Would that do?

It seems to me that it would be better to wait till I can add a new novel, and then get out the set. Meantime let "Modern Mephistopheles" go alone, with my name, as a summer book before Irving comes.[2]

I hope to do "A Tragedy of To-day"[3] this summer, and it can come out in the fall or next spring, with "Modern Mephistopheles," "Work," and "Moods."

A spunky new one would make the old ones go. "Hospital Sketches" is not cared for now, and is filled up with other tales you know. . . .

Can that plan be carried out? I have begun my tragedy, and think it will be good; also a shorter thing called "Anna: An Episode," in which I do up Boston in a jolly way, with a nice little surprise at the end. It would do to fill up "Modern Mephistopheles," as it is not long, unless I want it to be.

I will come in next week and see what can be done.

Yours truly,
L. M. A.[4]

1. *A Modern Mephistopheles and A Whisper in the Dark* was published by Roberts Brothers in 1889. For the author's attitude about her "necessity stories," see also Document 8.

2. Henry Irving played Mephistopheles in William Gorman Wills's version of *Faust* in New York between December 1886 and April 1887; he toured America with that play and others between November 1887 and March 1888.

3. Neither "A Tragedy of To-day" nor "Anna: An Episode" was published.

4. This letter is reprinted from Cheney, 379, 382.

L 35

LULU'S LIBRARY, LETTER TO NILES, [23 JUNE 1887]

Is it too late to put this dedication into Lulu's Library? The tales were mostly written for E. E. & I think it would please her to be so remembered.[1]

Judge Brook has settled the adoption, & John Sewall Pratt is now my "legal son."[2] A very easy process. I think I'll take a few more nice boys as mine. Cant have too much of a good thing.

Judge B. did not know much about copyrights, but said we had no state law, only a U. S. law, & under that he was not *sure* that an *adopted* child could use the copyrights.

Who is your lawyer? There are men who are posted on this point, & will know about that & the name. Do let us be sure if we can.

Has Mrs Dodge sent to you for the "Flower's Story" out of L. L.?[3] She wanted a short one as one of the three months left open in St N. for this year is free, & my other tale too long for a single number. I told her she could use that tale if you liked as it was all ready.

I have had no proof of "Pansies"[4] yet. After Friday direct me W. Bullard Mountain House Mt. Wachusett, Mass.

Till then care B. F. Wheeler Concord Mass.

If John should die after me & unmarried what can he do about the copyrights? Adopt a child I suppose. Fred may have provided a few by that time. What a funny muddle a little money makes!

I'm doing nicely & hope to come home almost as good as new.

Yrs truly   L. M. A.[5]

1. Volume 2 of Alcott's *Lulu's Library* (Boston: Roberts, 1887) contained reprints from the author's first book, *Flower Fables*, originally narrated to Ellen Emerson. Hence, the volume was appropriately dedicated to her.

2. In June and July 1887, Louisa Alcott completed the plan to adopt her nephew John Sewall Pratt, whose name was changed to John Sewall Pratt Alcott. She bequeathed to him her copyrights in trust, the income to be divided among her sister Anna, her other nephew Fred, her niece Lulu, and himself (see Stern, *Louisa May Alcott*, 331–33).

3. "The Flowers' Story" was included in *Lulu's Library*, vol. 2, but apparently not in Mrs. Dodge's *St. Nicholas*.

4. "Pansies" appeared in *St. Nicholas* for November 1887, and was reprinted in *A Garland for Girls* (Boston: Roberts, 1888).

5. This letter is printed from the original in the Louisa May Alcott Collection (#6255–b), Manuscripts Department, University of Virginia.

Louisa May Alcott Had Her Head Examined

Madeleine B. Stern and Kent Bicknell

For most of the nineteenth century the phrenological firm of Fowler (or Fowlers) and Wells attracted many illustrious personages to its depot of skulls.[1] Having sat for their phrenological examinations, subjects received, in exchange for a few dollars, a marked chart or lengthier written analysis that appraised the faculties of their minds and described their characters and temperaments. Some—like Walt Whitman—kept their phrenological readings all their lives and even had them printed. Others—such as Mark Twain—had their skulls phrenologized but scoffed at the so-called science of bumpology. A recent discovery by Alcott collector-scholar Kent Bicknell now reveals that Louisa May Alcott was among the illustrious who had their heads examined and kept the manuscript of the examination. The document just recently found by Kent Bicknell is of interest on several counts, but principally because it forms a brief but most astute analysis of the author of such diverse works as *Hospital Sketches*, "Behind a Mask," *Little Women*, and *A Modern Mephistopheles*.

In 1875 Louisa May Alcott enjoyed a winter in New York City, residing at Dr. Eli Peck Miller's Bath Hotel at 29 West 26th Street.[2] The hotel was centrally located near Madison Square, whence she could easily make journeys of exploration. On Monday, 22 November, a week before her forty-third birthday, her explorations took her downtown near Union Square. 737 Broadway—a memorable number since it read the same both ways—was the address of the Fowler phrenological headquarters now known as S. R. Wells and Company. There, between her numerous engagements, dinners, and sight-seeing trips, Louisa Alcott entered and had her head examined.

She found herself surrounded by the symbols of phrenology: skulls and busts, plaster casts, paintings, and minerals—the accumulation of some forty years of collecting. Neither of the Fowlers who had founded the business was on hand in the New York establishment. Partner Samuel R. Wells had died in April, and the business, now named S. R. Wells and Company, was carried on by his widow, Charlotte. The chief examiner was Nelson Sizer, who had been with the firm twenty-five years and, "built to endure," would last another twenty-five.

It was Nelson Sizer who now examined the skull of Louisa May Alcott. His examination, like all phrenological examinations, was predicated upon the belief that, since the brain was the organ of the mind and shaped the skull, an examination of the exterior skull would disclose the nature of the mind that lay beneath it. The examination included measurement of the head with a tape and tactile study of the various areas of the skull that housed the so-called faculties. The examiner sized those areas from two for small to seven for very large, and the faculties numbered about forty, among them Amativeness and Friendship, Inhabitiveness and Conjugality, Cautiousness and Self-Esteem, Benevolence and Ideality. The assumption was that once a subject learned that a desirable faculty was small, he or she would endeavor to enlarge it; and once aware that an undesirable faculty was large, he or she would struggle to diminish it. Self-improvement was entirely attainable if the injunction "Know Thyself" was heeded.

Whether Louisa Alcott was aware of all these details when she submitted her head for analysis is conjectural. She may not even have known that her father had, in 1838, when she was six, similarly submitted his head to Fowler's exploring fingers.[3] At all events, she had something in common with the phrenologists, who endorsed, as she did, reforms tending to improve the lot of her sex, especially temperance, the rights of women, and anti-lacing (that is, anti-corsets). It is unlikely that she had met Nelson Sizer before 22 November 1875, and it is also unlikely that he recognized her or that she identified herself when she entered the phrenological cabinet at 737 Broadway. Many subjects enjoyed testing the testers by appearing for their examinations anonymously or pseudonymously.

In his customary anecdotal style and salty language, chief examiner Sizer proceeded to explore Louisa Alcott's head, size its organs, and discuss his findings. Her skull measured twenty-two inches, and most of her faculties were unusually large. She rated the highest number, seven, for Friendship as well as for Conjugality (although she never married); she reaped a six for most of the faculties appraised: from Vital Temperament to Conscientiousness, Spirituality to Ideality, Mirthfulness to Language, and Hope to Human Nature.[4]

Alcott's chart as marked by the examiner, Sizer, was an extraordinary one. From its figures he made his deductions in a remarkable summation. Apart from the emphasis upon Conjugality, the analysis is quite accurate in its estimation of Alcott's character. Louisa May Alcott valued the reading, and although she failed to mention it in a long letter to her father about her New York activities, clearly she was intrigued.

The manuscript recording her phrenological reading—copied out in her own hand—was inserted into the book she doubtless acquired at the Cabinet: *How to Read Character: A New Illustrated Hand-Book of Phrenology and Physiognomy for Students and Examiners; with A Descriptive Chart.* Alcott's character analysis, either verbatim from Sizer or modified somewhat by the famous author with tongue in cheek, reads:

L. M. A.   Age 43

Head examined Nov. 22nd 1875

Faith hope & charity very large, especially the latter. Friendship remarkable, has more friends than she wants, bears others' burdens, & lets them impose on her through her strong sympathy & generosity. *Conjugal love* very marked, capable of all things for the man she loved. A devoted wife & mother. Adores children & wins thier hearts at once. Loves praise but can go without it if her will or principle makes it seem right. Leans to the *ideal,* yet from certain motives can be very practical. A good nurse through her magnetic & sympathetic power. Has the gift of language, is dramatic & witty. Strong passions but can control them. Dual nature very marked, but the higher predominates through culture & moral sentiment. Great powers of observation & mimicry. A good talker but not a speaker. Intellectual faculties developed largely, but great benevolence prevents entire devotion to intellectual pursuits. Conscientiousness large, will also, & the two conflict. Great vitality & a fine constitution, yet liable to overdo as the spirit is ardent & sometimes headstrong.

A person who can row *against* the tide & like it. If she wrote a story no one could tell how it was coming out as it would be sure to take an unexpected &

unusual turn. Love of nature, reads character well & has great intuitive perception, understands without study & knows things by instinct.

A remarkable head.[5]

Except for its reference to the "devoted wife and mother," the analysis is highly perceptive. Alcott was inclined to bear the burdens of others; indeed, she assumed the role of family breadwinner all her life. She did win the hearts of children, especially through her writings. She was assuredly a good nurse, both for the soldiers in the Civil War and for the members of her family. All who know her or her life must agree that she possessed the gift of language, that she was dramatic to the extent of being stagestruck, that she was a good talker but never a platform speaker, that she was often headstrong and inclined to overdo.

Most interesting are Sizer's conclusions about Alcott's "dual nature": the ideal versus the practical; the intellectual faculties in conflict with great benevolence; conscientiousness at war with will. "If she wrote a story," the analyst commented, "no one could tell how it was coming out as it would be sure to take an unexpected & unusual turn." Does not the extraordinary corpus of her secret gothic thrillers testify to the dual nature not only of Alcott as writer but of Alcott as persóna?

Having tucked the document that described her "remarkable head" into her copy of *How to Read Character*, Alcott on 1 January 1876 gave the volume to her older sister Anna Pratt ("Nan"), mother of two young boys, Frederick and John (ages twelve and ten). On the first flyleaf she inscribed a poem "To Nan" in which she recalled a phrenological doll from days when phrenological fervor had extended even to the nursery:

To Nan.

> I remember, I remember
>   A doll which once you had
> A plaster head with numbered bumps
>   In long clothes sweetly clad.
> And how you loved the funny thing
>   And bore it in your arms,
> A tender mother even then
>   And proud of baby's charms.
>
> Now living idols fill your heart
>   And be in your embrace;

Two yellow heads, bright eyed & fair
  Smile up in mother's face.
So here's a book to help you read
  There pates from brow to crown.
Which bumps are made by growing up
  And which by tumbling down.
                Jan. 1st 1876.[6]

Eventually, Anna Alcott Pratt's son Frederick Alcott Pratt inherited the copy of *How to Read Character* that his aunt Louisa had obtained from the phrenological Cabinet on New York's Broadway in 1875.[7] In 1959 the Pratt family deposited the volume with its inserted manuscript leaf in Harvard's Houghton Library. There Kent Bicknell found it. Thanks to his discovery, we have an intriguing character analysis of the author of *Little Women* and can speculate productively on which of *her* bumps were made by growing up and which by tumbling down.

As with so much of Alcott's career, the episode of the phrenological reading had a sequel. Among the serial publications issued by the firm of S. R. Wells and Company was the long-lasting *Phrenological Journal.* In its April 1881 issue it carried an article on Louisa Alcott consisting of a biographical sketch and character analysis. The analysis, however, was not based upon the actual phrenological examination to which she had submitted over five years before, but upon a profile photograph.

The published estimate of her character stated:

Miss Alcott's portrait shows her to be a woman of unusual force. The profile is strong and distinct in its markings. Nose, mouth, and chin have characteristics of energy, purpose, and resolution. She is tall and spare in frame—the Motive temperament of her father being impressed upon the bodily contours, and conspicuously influencing her mental organism. She is more powerful in thought, more earnest and thorough-going as a worker, than she is delicate and symmetrical. Her convictions are deep and controlling, giving her character for independence. Her intellectual faculties are generally active, and being strong and well disciplined, she has a much broader comprehension of the matters relating to life than the average. Few persons . . . are more steadfast in opinion than she. Firmness contributes emphasis and positiveness to her conduct, supporting the impressions or conclusions obtained through the intellect.

As a member of society, judging from the portrait, she is not known for an easy disposition to conform to fashion and custom, but rather for originality of view and practicality of motive. She believes in being true to one's impressions of truth and duty; admires spirit and zeal in those who have work to perform for themselves or the world. . . . As for formalism in Church, State, or social life she has comparatively little time or regard to give in that direction.[8]

Though Alcott may not have been aware of the published analysis of her photograph, she would no doubt have agreed with it. It amplifies, without altering, the earlier reading of her skull. Both in life and in picture, both in manuscript and in print, Louisa May Alcott had "a remarkable head."

NOTES

1. For the history of the firm, see Madeleine B. Stern, *Heads & Headlines: The Phrenological Fowlers* (Norman: University of Oklahoma Press, 1971).

2. For Alcott's stay in New York, see Stern, *Louisa May Alcott* (Norman: University of Oklahoma Press, 1950).

3. For Bronson Alcott's phrenological examination in 1838, see Odell Shepard, *Pedlar's Progress: The Life of Bronson Alcott* (Boston: Little, Brown, 1937), 235. For an earlier analysis of Bronson, see Madelon Bedell, *The Alcotts: Biography of a Family* (New York: Clarkson N. Potter, 1980), 16, 342. For an account of the influence of this "science of the mind" upon Bronson's observations about his eldest daughter, see Frederick C. Dahlstrand, *Amos Bronson Alcott: An Intellectual Biography* (Rutherford, N.J.: Fairleigh Dickinson University Press, 1982), 81–91.

4. The chart was an integral part of the phrenological manuals. Alcott's chart, with her name, that of the examiner, and the date written in pencil, appears in part 2 of *How to Read Character:* "A Delineation of the Character, Physiological Development, and Present Condition of *Louisa M. Alcott* as given by *Nelson Sizer, Nov 22, 1875.*"

5. The analysis has been reproduced here through the courtesy of the Houghton Library of Harvard University.

6. The poem has been reproduced here through the courtesy of the Houghton Library of Harvard University.

7. In her own copy of *How to Read Character* (New York: Samuel R. Wells, 1870), Alcott made several marginal signs and comments, some of them significant. For example, on page 55 near a portrait (figure 55) showing "Destructiveness Small" she wrote: "Alcott whopper jaw," referring to the large lower jaw that characterized in physiognomy "one who prefers vegetable food, and is adverse to the shedding of blood." Surely she was reminded of the "vegetarian wafers we used at Fruitlands" such as "Vegetable diet and sweet repose." On page 162 of *How to Read Character,* in the section that describes Inhabitiveness or Love of Home (indicated for her as "Large"), she scribbled "Ah! ha!" in the margin and underlined three words in the following passage: "*You* are very strongly attached to home; love your native land

with a pure devotion; leave your place of abode with great reluctance, and are *home-sick* and *miserable* if compelled to remain long away from it." Her restlessness and consequent residencies in many different dwellings in the Boston area are well documented; she fled Concord only to return again and again to take care of family concerns. In similar self-dialogue in the section on Continuity she marked with a cross and wrote "yes" beside the passage, "You love variety; change readily from one thing to another; commence many things that you never finish; think clearly, perhaps, but not always consecutively; lack connectiveness and application, and should aim at more fixedness of mind and steadiness of character. *Cultivate*" (163). Such marginalia indicate not only Alcott's attention to the book's phrenological observations, but her own self-knowledge. She had long since obeyed the phrenological injunction "Know thyself."

Alcott's copy of *How to Read Character* bears the ownership stamp of F. Alcott Pratt on the front flyleaf, and below it the presentation inscription: "For Frederic Wolsey Pratt/Keep this book."

8. "Louisa May Alcott," *Phrenological Journal* 72 (April 1881): 186–88; rpt. in Madeleine B. Stern, *A Phrenological Dictionary of Nineteenth-Century Americans* (Westport, Conn.: Greenwood, 1982), 3–5.

Louisa May Alcott
& Frank M. Lupton

I t is something of a literary shock to realize that the author of *Little Women* who played the role of youth's companion to generations of readers, also deserves a place in the history of the dime novel.

In 1867, a year before publication of her masterpiece, Louisa May Alcott submitted to the Boston firm of Elliott, Thomes and Talbot two sensational concoctions: "The Skeleton in the Closet," a page-turner in which the heroine, a kind of involuntary femme fatale, lives in seclusion guarding her secret, the curse of heriditary madness; "The Mysterious Key," an amalgam of feigned sleepwalking, a touch of bigamy, and a silver key that opens a grisly tomb—in short, a suspenseful fabric of gothic devices. Both narratives were published by Elliott, Thomes and Talbot in their Ten Cent Novelettes series of Standard American Authors, *Skeleton* in number 49 as a trailer to Perley Parker's *The Foundling*, and *The Mysterious Key* on its own as number 50.[1]

What Louisa Alcott could not know, since the events occurred after her death, is that both these narratives would be republished by the New York cheap book publisher F. M. Lupton. Moreover, Lupton did not confine his Alcott publications to sensational narratives. At least six Alcott titles, in various genres, can be traced to him, all between 1900 and 1906, when he headed one of the largest cheap reprint establishments.

Alcott, just beginning her literary career, had two published stories to her credit when Frank Moore Lupton was born in 1854 to a comfortable and well-established family in Mattituck, Long Island, New York. By the time he was apprenticed at age fifteen, to the printer of the

Suffolk Weekly Times in Greenport, Alcott had published *Little Women*. The next year he was employed in the printing company of S. W. Green in New York City, and in 1875, when Alcott had become nationally known, Lupton published a monthly journal, *Cricket on the Hearth*. During the 1880s, when Alcott, weary and ill, was struggling to complete the last volume of her March family saga, *Jo's Boys*, Lupton came into his own. Founder of the F. M. Lupton Publishing Company, he launched the *People's Home Journal* and *Good Literature*, repositories for serial fiction. In addition, he was owner of William J. Brown & Company, a printing and binding house, and part owner of the Manhattan Typesetting Company. Thus, he was expert in many phases of book manufacture—typesetting, printing, binding—as well as in publishing.[2]

Between the 1880s and his death in 1910, Lupton expanded his publishing concern until it could boast some fifteen hundred paper-covered titles and an extensive list of series: the Leisure Hour, the Idle Hour, the Bijou, the Acme, the Windsor, the Golden Rod, the Elite, the Aldis, the Southworth, and the Violet. With the aid of his manager, J. M. Ruston, he issued hundreds of paper-bound and cloth-bound books, including the Boys' Own Library, the Girls' Popular Library, the Jack Harkaway Library, and the Mary J. Holmes Series. He was part of the revolution in publishing that brought to the masses books cheaply produced and cheaply priced. Located successively on Murray Street, Reade Street, Duane Street, and finally City Hall Place, New York, in the Lupton Building, the F. M. Lupton Publishing Company—its name changed in 1903 to the Federal Book Company—was a giant supplier of cheap books for mass entertainment.

The books offered by Lupton were for the most part not original publications but reprints of the tried and tested, writings of authors many of whom were deceased. Thus the publisher eliminated the need for author contracts and advance payments. His risks were few, and by 1904 he could boast, "The number and variety of Books published by us have increased to such an extent that we have been obliged to issue A Separate Catalogue of Paper Covered Books (containing over 1500 Titles) Which we shall be pleased to mail upon application."[3]

One of the authors in Lupton's stable was the creator of *Little Women* who, revered as the "Children's Friend," had died in 1888. The publisher had an interest in at least six Alcott titles. He obtained some of them, as he obtained much of his list, from a colorful personality, a jack-of-all-trades relating to publishing who also became an effective agent in the distribution of books for mass consumption.

Tall, dark, slender, William James Benners, Jr., encompassed many lives in one, all of them touching upon some phase of the publishing business.[4] Born in Philadelphia in 1863, he became poet, traveler, writer, editor, literary agent, aficionado of pseudonyms, collector and historian of the dime novel. Indeed, his interest in dime novels began when he was eight and continued all his life. He not only read and collected them; he added to the literature.

Among the narratives traced to him are such delectable titles as: *Curse of the Opals, The Rajah's Jewels, Magdalene's Mystery,* and *The Quest of the Golden Skull.* Moreover, Benners adopted several pseudonyms for his stories: Eric Braddon, Wyne Winters, and the already familiar pen name of Bertha M. Clay previously used by Charlotte M. Brame. Benners's expertise in pseudonyma extended to the detection of frauds in publishing—an investigation for which he was employed by such mass-oriented houses as Street & Smith and George Munro's Sons.

Benners could change his literary caps with ease. As an agent, he traveled abroad and "made the personal acquaintance of a number of the most celebrated English authors," from whom he purchased the American rights to their narratives. His familiarity with the tribe of writers was perhaps even greater among those deceased. Benners not only knew "every story published by many writers" but collected files of their appearances in popular story papers such as the *New York Ledger, New York Weekly, Fireside Companion,* and *Chimney Corner.* Those files were originally intended for use in the preparation of a comprehensive history of the dime novel and an encyclopedia of popular writers—projects never completed.

From the empire founded by the New York publishing magnate Frank Leslie, Benners acquired in 1902 reprint rights to several juvenile periodicals along with certain serials from *Frank Leslie's Chimney Corner* which he sold in turn to the Maine publisher William H. Gannett. There is no doubt that Benners was an operator. Many of the stories he amassed, along with publishing rights to the serials, he sold to Street & Smith, Norman L. Munro—and Frank Moore Lupton.

By his own admission, Frank Lupton did business with Benners "for years." A small collection of their correspondence in 1904 and 1906 reveals much of their methods and trade relations.[5] In addition, it indicates that that prolific writer whose pen made her the family breadwinner was posthumously involved in the exchanges between a literary operator who was selling and a publisher of cheap books who was buying.

On 11 January 1904, William J. Benners, writing from Hicks Street in Philadelphia to Frank M. Lupton at City Hall Place, New York, announced that he was "sending . . . by express" a number of "manuscripts." The price list that followed cited twenty-seven titles by Charlotte M. Brame, including one that "has a perplexing mystery . . . is full of love and is written in Mrs. Brame's best vein." Among other stories and serials appear the following:

| "The Belle of Santiago" | By Louisa Alcott | 10.00 net |
| "Lost in a Pyramid" | By Louisa Alcott | 10.00 ″ |

Once Lupton had examined "the large amount of material submitted," he hastened to reply on 23 February to his supplier, whom he chastised on several counts. "It is not a pleasant thing," he wrote, "to find that a man with whom I have been dealing for years, to whom I have paid considerable sums of money, will make a deliberate attempt to impose upon and injure me." Benners, Lupton alleged, had sent him one story that he (Lupton) had already refused and another that he had previously purchased from Benners; one story was under copyright to Street & Smith and another was already in Lupton's Arm Chair Library. After citing his objections, Lupton settled upon eleven stories he would be willing to purchase, "provided you will reduce the prices to such figures as the material is worth." Among the items were "The Belle of Santiago" and "Lost in a Pyramid."

Two years later, on 26 March 1906, Lupton again wrote to Benners requesting four stories, one of which was by Louisa M. Alcott, "and if after I see them I want the lot for $50.00 . . . I will send you a check." On 2 April Lupton enclosed his check in that amount and, in a brief note, named the Alcott story included in the purchase—"The Skeleton in the Closet." And so, to the known canon of Alcott tales published by Lupton these extant letters add three possible titles: "The Belle of Santiago," "Lost in a Pyramid," and "The Skeleton in the Closet."

Earlier, around 1900, F. M. Lupton had reprinted as number 38 in his Leisure Hour Library Louisa May Alcott's narrative "The Mysterious Key," which had made its initial appearance as an Elliott, Thomes and Talbot dime novel over thirty years before. Out of copyright, it was an eminently suitable title for the Leisure Hour Series whose books, originally priced at five cents each, were subsequently reduced to two cents. The next two Lupton Alcotts appeared in the publisher's Chimney Corner Series: *Moods* as number 162 around 1900, and *Flower Fables* as number 185 around 1901. Both books, listed at twenty five cents each, were later reduced to ten cents. Both were cheaply printed quarto paperbacks, two columns to a page, with pictorial covers.

Thus, for the Alcott items in his Chimney Corner Series the astute publisher had selected Alcott's first novel, *Moods,* and her first published book, *Flower Fables.* Like "The Mysterious Key," both were out of copyright. Alcott had embarked upon her first experiment in the novel, *Moods,* in August 1860, when she was twenty-seven. In it, she wrote, "I've freed my mind upon a subject that always makes trouble, namely, Love." The result was a kind of fictional disquisition on wrong marriages, "unmated pairs trying to live their legal lie decorously to the end at any cost."[6] Published late in 1864 by Aaron K. Loring of Boston, the book never quite satisfied the author, who years later wrote a revised version published in 1882 by Roberts Brothers. It was not the revision but the original 1864 *Moods,* then out of copyright, that Lupton reprinted, the version ending with the heroine's death. To enlarge his edition to the usual 128 pages, Lupton added two stories by H. Rider Haggard, "A Tale of Three Lions," and "The Wreck of the *Copeland,*" tacked on his catalogue of books, and published the paperback with its pictorial cover in his Chimney Corner Series.

About a year later, in 1901, Lupton turned to Alcott's first published book, *Flower Fables,* a series of romantic fables about flowers, which she had composed in her teens.[7] Published in December 1854 by George Briggs of Boston, it provided F. M. Lupton nearly half a century later with another of his Chimney Corner paperbacks. Illustrated and enlarged with three other Alcott stories, "The Autobiography of an Omnibus," "Roses and Forget-Me-Nots," and "Helping Along," all originally published in *St. Nicholas,* along with Ian Maclaren's "Beside the Bonnie Brier Bush, and Other Stories," the volume ended with

Lupton's catalogue and price list of paper-covered books. That catalogue now listed three Alcott titles at reduced prices: *Moods, Flower Fables,* and *The Mysterious Key.*

In addition to those three, Lupton apparently increased his Alcott list a few years later with three purchases from William James Benners, Jr.: "The Skeleton in the Closet," in the same sensational genre as *The Mysterious Key,* "Lost in a Pyramid," and "The Belle of Santiago."

Louisa May Alcott had been in the habit of listing the titles of her stories and the fees paid for them in her yearly notes and memoranda. For 1869 her earnings included $228 for *Little Women,* vol. 1, $250 for *Little Women,* vol. 2, and $25 for "Mummy."[8] A narrative entitled "Lost in a Pyramid; or, The Mummy's Curse" may be found in the first issue of *The New World,* a periodical launched on 16 January 1869 by the dynamic New York publisher Frank Leslie. After only six months, *The New World* was merged with *Frank Leslie's Chimney Corner,*[9] that family paper from which William James Benners, Jr., apparently acquired some serial rights. Having made its bow in 1869 in a Leslie story paper, Alcott's "Mummy," via a Benners transaction, joined the extensive holdings of Frank M. Lupton.

"The Belle of Santiago," acquired by Lupton at the same time as "Lost in a Pyramid," is less easily traced. There is no mention of that title or of any comparable title in Alcott's journals, letters, or notes and memoranda. Is it possible that William J. Benners, Jr.—that expert in literary pseudonyma who did not hesitate to appropriate the pseudonym Bertha M. Clay previously adopted by Charlotte M. Brame—is it possible that Benners was the author of "The Belle of Santiago," cloaking his secret under a name-turned-pseudonym: Louisa M. Alcott!?

The real Louisa M. Alcott has almost as firm a place in the history of sensational stories and cheap reprints as she has in the annals of juvenile literature. Had she survived into the twentieth century, the fact would probably not have surprised her.

Lupton himself died in 1910, a suicide because of ill health, and at his death he was described as "head of a big publishing house at 23 City Hall Place, Manhattan."[10]

Benners survived Lupton by thirty years, continuing his pursuit of literature and subliterature, and continuing to earn the title of "the world's greatest authority on old story papers and their writers."[11]

The writer who had earned quite a different title—that of America's best-loved author of juveniles—also played a role in a revolution that provided cheap books for the millions. Benners and Lupton were both agents in the conversion of popular literature into mass merchandise, and in that conversion Louisa May Alcott became a profitable commodity.

NOTES

1. "The Mysterious Key, and What It Opened" was most recently reprinted in *Behind a Mask: The Unknown Thrillers of Louisa May Alcott*, ed. Madeleine B. Stern (New York: William Morrow, 1975); "The Skeleton in the Closet" was most recently reprinted in *Plots and Counterplots: More Unknown Thrillers of Louisa May Alcott*, ed. Madeleine Stern (New York: William Morrow, 1976).

2. For Frank M. Lupton and his firm, see Frank Luther Mott, *A History of American Magazines 1885–1905* (Cambridge: Belknap Press of Harvard University Press, 1957), 366; *New York Times* (7 October 1910): 5; *Publishers Trade List Annual*, 1901 and 1904; Madeleine B. Stern, ed., *Publishers for Mass Entertainment in Nineteenth Century America* (Boston: G. K. Hall, 1980), 215–19 (chapter on F. M. Lupton Publishing Company, by Marie Olesen Urbanski, to whom the writer is grateful for additional information). The writer is also, as usual, deeply indebted to Victor A. Berch, who brought to her attention two Lupton imprints.

3. *Publishers Trade List Annual*, 1904.

4. For William James Benners, Jr., see the articles on him in *Dime Novel Roundup* (July 1940; August 1941), and especially those by Ralph Adimari in issues of 15 September 1958 and 15 February 1959. The writer is deeply indebted to Edward T. LeBlanc for copies of those issues.

5. The letters cited are deposited in Fales Library, Elmer Holmes Bobst Library, New York University, and the writer is most grateful to Frank Walker for permission to quote from them.

6. For *Moods*, see *Louisa May Alcott: Selected Fiction*, ed. Daniel Shealy, Madeleine B. Stern, and Joel Myerson (Boston: Little, Brown, 1991), xxi–xxii.

7. For *Flower Fables*, see *Alcott: Selected Fiction*, xiii–xiv.

8. *The Journals of Louisa May Alcott*, ed. Joel Myerson, Daniel Shealy, and Madeleine B. Stern (Boston: Little, Brown, 1989), 172.

9. Madeleine B. Stern, *Purple Passage: The Life of Mrs. Frank Leslie* (Norman: University of Oklahoma Press, 1970), 191.

10. *New York Times* (7 October 1910): 5.

11. *Dime Novel Roundup* (15 September 1958): 124.

Louisa May Alcott at 150

On 29 November 1832, Bronson Alcott, teacher and philosopher, wrote the following letter from Germantown, Pennsylvania, to his father-in-law, Colonel Joseph May:

> It is with great pleasure that I announce to you the *birth of a second daughter.* She was born at half-past 12 this morning, on my birthday (33), and is a very fine healthful child, much more so than Anna was at birth,—has a fine foundation for health and energy of character. . . . Abba [Bronson's wife] inclines to call the babe *Louisa May,*—a name to her full of every association connected with amiable benevolence and exalted worth. I hope *its present possessor* may rise to equal attainment, and deserve a place in the estimation of society.[1]

While Louisa May Alcott could never be characterized as a woman of "amiable benevolence," her "place in the estimation of society" 150 years after that letter was written is indeed secure. She is recognized the world over as "a natural source of stories . . . the poet of children" who "knows their angels."[2] Her books, especially the most famous of all, *Little Women,* and the so-called Little Women Series, have been translated into French, German, Italian, Spanish, Swedish, Norwegian, Polish, Portuguese, Finnish, Hungarian, Czech, and Japanese. By 1947, when Frank Luther Mott compiled his *Golden Multitudes, Little Women* had sold some two million copies in America and was thus entitled to a place among his Over-All Best Sellers in the United States.[3] As early as 1885, the Indianapolis Public Library showed considerable prophetic acumen by classifying all her books as "adult fiction,"[4] and now dissertations are being written on such subjects as "Concepts of Child-rearing and Schooling in the March Novels of Louisa May Alcott" and "An Examination of Louisa May Alcott as 'New Woman.'"[5]

Today, on her 150th birthday, her books are no longer regarded simply as primers for childhood but as works that display the New England family in compassionate versions of the domestic novel. As she moves from the nursery to the study, Louisa Alcott is at last attaining a niche in American literary history long owed to her.

Louisa Alcott's extraordinary skill in creating a family portrait did not materialize overnight. It was, as most masterly writing is, the result of experimentation in diverse literary fields. Here was a writer who wove her fiction fabric not only from the threads of her own life but from the exercises of her experimenting pen. In the case of Louisa May Alcott, the stages by which she elevated herself to mastery and professionalism have long been overlooked, so intent has been the interest in the work of her literary maturity. Yet those stages are, to the critical explorer, transparent and revealing. More than most writers, Alcott essayed a variety of genres and tried many techniques with her ink-stained fingers. To trace her development, as the Brigham Young University exhibit now makes it possible to do, is to trace the development of a writer from feeble beginnings through a labyrinth of failures and successes to professional mastery. The stages in her progress as a writer can be followed, step by step, in a literary adventure story.

Louisa May Alcott was not always the "Children's Friend." Indeed, she began her writing career as many writers do, as a child herself. Little Louy Alcott, age eight, penned four couplets addressed "To the First Robin."[6] Her childhood years were shaped by her extraordinary, perceptive, imperturbable, and exasperating father, Bronson Alcott, whose ultra-modern pedagogical theories were tried out on Louy and her three sisters. They were also shaped by her understanding, progressive, long-suffering, and beloved mother, Abba, and by the radical tenets applied in her father's Temple School in Boston, where the pioneer kindergartner Elizabeth Peabody was a teacher, along with the redoubtable feminist Margaret Fuller. Louisa Alcott's childhood was molded also by her experiences such as that unique sojourn in the community of Fruitlands in Harvard, Massachusetts, where her father and his associates proposed to establish a New Eden but where cold baths, linen tunics, and solar diet were not compatible with a New England winter. As Emerson put it after a summer visit to this consociate family in Paradise: "In July they looked well. He would see them in December."

Then, too, little Louy Alcott's childhood was fashioned, after the family move to Hillside Cottage in Concord, Massachusetts, by her father's neighbors, especially Emerson, whom she worshiped, becoming the Bettine to his Goethe. For him and other neighbors, the Channings and the Hosmers, the Hillside barn was converted into a theater, and Louisa and her sisters enacted original scripts of melodramas, among them "Norna; or, The Witch's Curse," "The Unloved Wife," and "The Captive of Castile." These plays invariably included desertions, suicides, and several elaborate speeches, not to mention daggers, love potions, and death phials.

Louisa Alcott's childhood was enriched by excursions to the woods with neighbor Henry David Thoreau and by much reading in Charles Dickens. By the time she reached her teens, the author was scribbling fairy stories for Emerson's daughter Ellen. Those *Flower Fables* would become her first published book in 1855. She filled her scrapbook with lines from Goethe and Wordsworth. Her mother wrote: "I am sure your life has many fine passages well worth recording. . . . Do write a little each day, . . . if but a line, to show me how bravely you begin the battle, how patiently you wait for the rewards sure to come when the victory is nobly won."

Still another influence was exerted upon the nineteen-year-old Louisa Alcott, a much less beneficent influence than any she had thus far experienced, but one that would also prove grist for her literary mill. At midcentury the family poverty was extreme. Mrs. Alcott opened an intelligence office, or employment agency, in Boston, and when the Honorable James Richardson of Dedham, Massachusetts, applied for a companion for his sister, Louisa decided to take the position herself. Richardson proved somewhat less than honorable, and Louisa Alcott as domestic servant was expected not only to dig paths through the snow, fetch water from the well, split kindling, and sift ashes but also to play audience to her employer who invited her into his study for oral readings and metaphysical discussions. At the end of seven weeks of drudgery, the nineteen-year-old Alcott was paid four dollars. Eventually she would write a bowdlerized account, "How I Went Out to Service," and eventually she would find in James Richardson a prototype for certain of her fictional villains.

The year of this humiliating experience at Dedham—1851—was also the year of Louisa Alcott's first appearance in print. Her poem "Sunlight" was published in *Peterson's Magazine* in September, and it was signed "Flora Fairfield."[7] This was the first but by no means the last of the Alcott pseudonyms. "Sunlight" was followed by bolder attempts at narrative, among them "The Rival Painters. A Tale of Rome," which adorned the pages of the *Olive Branch* in May 1852, and "The Rival Prima Donnas," a tale of vengeance. Again under the name of Flora Fairfield, this exuberant piece of prose illuminated the pages of the *Saturday Evening Gazette* in 1854. Louisa Alcott, who was writing now both from experience and from imagination, was also crafting her narratives to suit a particular audience and was thus taking the first step toward professionalism. As a result, she soon became the mainstay of the *Saturday Evening Gazette,* in which her contributions in verse and prose appeared until 1859.

The following year a different type of work by the young author was published in the pages of an altogether different type of periodical. "With a Rose, That Bloomed on the Day of John Brown's Martyrdom" was printed in *The Liberator* and would subsequently be reprinted in James Redpath's *Echoes of Harper's Ferry*. With the outbreak of the Civil War, Louisa Alcott entered upon yet another phase in her progress as a writer, and for that phase she assumed still another name, half amusing, half pathetic. Her experience as a nurse in the Union Hotel Hospital in the Georgetown section of Washington, D.C., transformed "Flora Fairfield" into "Nurse Tribulation Periwinkle."

Louisa Alcott clearly fulfilled most of the regulations laid down for army nurses by Dorothea Dix. She was thirty years old, of strong health, good conduct, and serious disposition. Her five feet six inches gave her a matronly appearance; her long chestnut hair could be neatly braided. And if her gray eyes sparkled a bit too freely, that would do no harm to a wounded soldier. Having prepared herself by studying Florence Nightingale's *Notes on Nursing* and Dr. Home's *Report on . . . Gunshot Wounds,* Louisa Alcott enlisted for service. Bronson Alcott had, as he put it, sent his only son to war.

Nurse Alcott remained in the Union Hotel Hospital only six weeks.

She carried out her duties faithfully, tended the newly arrived wounded who had survived the Battle of Fredericksburg, and ministered not only poultices but patience to her favorites, Robert Bane, a nineteen-year-old sergeant from Michigan who had lost his right arm, and John Suhre, a Virginia blacksmith who was dying of a chest wound. As she gave, she received—impressions, recollections, observations, anecdotes—all of which she reported in letters home and would later interweave into more public narratives. The midnight vigils in the hospital took their toll finally, and Nurse Alcott, having succumbed to a severe case of what was called typhoid-pneumonia, was forced to leave her post and return home. Being already a writer, she would extract even from the delirium and fever of her prolonged illness colorful strands for stories she would tell.

Meanwhile, Frank Sanborn of Concord, editor of *The Commonwealth*, suggested that Alcott turn her hospital letters into sketches appropriate for publication. And so she relived the scenes she had lived, reconstructed scraps of talk she had heard, and painted full-length portraits of characters she had known in a wartime hospital. Truth and fact, rather than romance and fiction, dominated these sketches and, signing her Civil War plunge into realism with the name Tribulation Periwinkle, she contributed to *The Commonwealth* four sketches that ran in May and June 1863. As a result both of current interest in the war and of her own precise but human handling of her theme, two publishers sought permission to reprint the *Commonwealth* sketches in book form: Roberts Brothers, whom she turned down, and James Redpath, who had accepted her poem on John Brown for his *Echoes of Harper's Ferry*. In return for five cents on each copy sold of the one thousand printed, Redpath published Tribulation Periwinkle's *Hospital Sketches* in August. Louisa Alcott's first truly successful book, it reaped praise from the press as a work "graphically drawn," "fluent and sparkling," with "touches of quiet humor." The writer who had at last tried her hand at realism was aware that truth might well be the fountainhead from which the best of her stories would one day flow.

She was still, however, experimenting. She had attempted both the roses of fairyland and the realism of hospital scenes. Now, under the compulsion not merely of her own desires but of publishers' demands, she dipped her pen into a gall-like brew. Louisa Alcott's blood-and-thunder stories, published between January 1863 and February 1869, appeared for the most part either anonymously or under the pseudonym not of Flora Fairfield or Tribulation Periwinkle but of A. M. Barnard.[8]

After *Hospital Sketches,* Redpath had published *The Rose Family* in 1864, Loring had published *Moods* in 1865, and her shockers had punctuated the late 1860s. Louisa Alcott had tried her hand at fiction and at fact. The time had come for her to combine the two in a tale that would "live in the memory" and win the reader forever.

Little Women, her "girls' story," turned out to be a domestic novel set in nineteenth-century New England. In it she recovered her recollections of childhood and found in the biography of a single family the miniature paraphrase of the hundred volumes of universal history. Her characters were her own family: her sister Anna, transformed into Meg, beautiful of course, for there must be one beauty in the book; her artistic sister May, transmuted into Amy, afflicted with a nose not quite Grecian enough, and struggling in laborious attempts at elegance; Lizzie, metamorphosed into Beth, glorified a bit, the cricket on the hearth who sat in corners and lived for others. Beth was Jo's conscience. And Jo of course was Louisa—Flora Fairfield, Tribulation Periwinkle, A. M. Barnard all in one—tall and thin, with sharp gray eyes and long thick hair, odd blunt ways and a fiery spirit. Her father, addicted as he was to fads and reforms, was softly adumbrated, a mere shadow, but her mother shone forth as Marmee, whose gray cloak and unfashionable bonnet adorned a staunch defender of human rights.

Now in her midthirties, Louisa Alcott assembled the experiences and observations of her life and reproduced them in a book as vibrant and fresh today as it was in 1868. Louisa took up her pen, but the Marches wrote her story. Its background was the Concord, Massachusetts, where her family lived. Its episodes include a composite melodrama entitled "The Witch's Curse, an Operatic Tragedy," alarmingly like the plays of the Hillside barnstorming days. The American home was here, reanimated in these pages, the good times, the tableaux, the sleigh rides, the skating frolics. By mid-July the author had finished what would become part 1 of *Little Women.* Toward the end of August she read the proofs, writing in her journal: "It reads better than I expected. Not a bit sensational, but simple and true, for we really lived most of it; and if it succeeds that will be the reason of it."[9]

The reception was favorable, notices and letters indicated much interest in the four little women, and the publisher demanded a sequel or second volume for the spring. It was part 2 of *Little Women* that sealed its destiny. There, the sisters, three years older, were brought into young womanhood, Meg marrying John, Amy making a plaster cast of her own foot, Jo March re-enacting Louisa's checkered literary career even to the inclusion of the *Blarneystone Banner* and the *Weekly Volcano*. The American countryside of the midnineteenth century was unfolded here, historic notes of life and letters in New England were written, and under the roof of a single New England home could be discovered all the homes of America. A tale embodying the simple facts and persons of the family had been written. As one reader would observe: "She unlatches the door to one house, and . . . all find it is their own house which they enter." At the time of her death the *Boston Herald* would declare: "When the family history, out of which this remarkable authorship grew, shall be told to the public, it will be apparent that few New England homes have ever had closer converse with the great things of human destiny than that of the Alcotts."[10]

The publication of part 2 of *Little Women* in 1869 divided Louisa Alcott's life and profoundly influenced the course of her progress as a writer. While its tremendous success relieved her from economic anxiety, it placed upon her the onus of persisting in the genre she had so enriched. Flora Fairfield, Tribulation Periwinkle, and A. M. Barnard were discarded, and in their place emerged the world-famous author of *Little Women*, the "Children's Friend," who had to place upon the altar of her reputation the literary sacrifices of sequel after sequel.

The first of them—*An Old-Fashioned Girl*, published in 1870—was not literally a sequel, except that it adapted the style of *Little Women* to a different concept. Here Louisa Alcott simply inverted her household portrait of *Little Women* and created a domestic drama in reverse. The Shaw home, unlike the March home, provided glaring examples of the fashionable follies and absurdities against which the "Children's Friend" crusaded: the wad on top of Fanny's head, the fringe of fuzz around her forehead, her huge sashes, and little panniers. From prevalent attacks of "nerves" to Grecian bends, from the giddy lives of fourteen-year-olds to the silly orthography that placed an *ie* after a jumble of *Netties, Nellies,* and *Sallies,* she sent the stab of satire. And, set against this erring family shone the Old-Fashioned Girl, Polly, who hailed from a home similar to the Marches', whose hearty goodwill and honest realism saved her from the fate of becoming a prig in a storybook. Despite her own ailing health, the author of *Little Women* completed her new book for Roberts Brothers. With her left hand in a sling, one foot up, head aching, and no voice, she continued her crusade against the absurdities of a time when doctors flourished and everyone was ill, when switches and waterfalls adorned the hair of the fashionable, and when the fear of what people would think dominated polite society. It is in *An Old-Fashioned Girl* that the author reveals the reasons for her adoption of a mannerless manner, a styleless style:

> I deeply regret being obliged to shock the eyes and ears of such of my readers as have a prejudice in favor of pure English . . . but, having rashly undertaken to write a little story about Young America, for Young America, I feel bound to depict my honored patrons as faithfully as my limited powers permit.

That ambition was filled not only in *An Old-Fashioned Girl* but in the stories about Young America and for Young America that followed. From memories of her father's Temple School in Boston she portrayed the Plumfield School in *Little Men*. The book was written while the world-famous author was touring Rome, and it was written to provide funds for her sister Anna, whose husband had died. Since the story was told for Anna's two boys, she called it after them, *Little Men*. Alcott selected her "little men" carefully, choosing boys ripe for the methods of Plumfield, where Latin and Greek were considered all very well but self-knowledge, self-help, and self-control far better. To each of her characters she gave some fault awaiting help and, as she sat on a balcony overlooking the Piazza Barberini, she wove from her memories of Bronson Alcott's methods and Dio Lewis's musical gymnastics, from lessons at Fruitlands and the Hillside theatricals, from recollections of Dickens and neighbor Thoreau, from Walden woods and Tremont Temple the delightful episodes of *Little Men*. It was published on the day of her return home. Bronson Alcott and publisher Thomas Niles of Roberts Brothers appeared at the wharf, and a great red placard announcing the new book, fifty thousand copies of which had been sold in advance of publication, was posted on the carriage.

The attitudes of *An Old-Fashioned Girl* and of *Little Men* reappeared in the next volume of the so-called Little Women Series—*Eight Cousins: or, The Aunt-Hill.* Here the author's gospel on the education of American children was proclaimed, a gospel that included the discarding of medicine and the use of brown-bread pills instead, the substitution of new milk for strong coffee, and brown bread for hot biscuits. Dress reform that loosened tight belts and suggested the loose attire called freedom suits was championed, along with the three great remedies of sun, air, and water. As at Plumfield, less Greek and Latin and more knowledge of the laws of health were recommended. As usual, Alcott was able to depict her dramatis personae with the broad strokes used in her thrillers, and so she made not merely palatable but exciting her advocacy of the new enlightenment in food, clothing, and schooling. As Henry James remarked of her protagonist Uncle Alec, she had ridden atilt at the shams of life.

That crusader's ride was continued in the sequel to *Eight Cousins, Rose in Bloom.* So too was the author's skill in extracting from the mine of memory the beads to string upon a thin thread of plot. Two themes—autobiography and reform—were combined. Touches reminiscent of *Little Women*—the gifts four sisters had given one another, May's casts and easels, Lizzie's fever—reappeared in a new guise, along with gems from Thoreau's *Week on the Concord and Merrimack Rivers,* Emerson's *Self-Reliance,* and Dickens's *Nicholas Nickleby.* Upon her thread the author also strung the beads of temperance, woman's rights, and philanthropy, and, since her characters were strong and credible, her message reached its target. In 1876 *Rose in Bloom,* the fifth of the Alcott full-length juveniles, joined its predecessors on the bookshelf.

Between 1877 and 1886 only three more would follow. Like *Eight Cousins, Under the Lilacs* was serialized before book publication in the pages of *St. Nicholas,* and there a new type of Alcott hero made his appearance: a performing poodle, Sancho, who wore a tassel at the end of his tail and ruffles around his ankles. Research for her leading character was conducted at Van Amburgh's Menagerie, and once again, partly to forget the anxieties of her mother's illness and partly to embellish her story, Louisa plumbed the depths of the past. The result was a waltzing, parading poodle who, with a whisk of his tasseled tail, leapt straight into the hearts of all readers of *Under the Lilacs.*

In a sense, *Jack and Jill*, which appeared over the Roberts Brothers imprint in 1880, was an expansion of *Little Women*. Here, not a single family but an entire village takes the stage. A boy and girl in an upset sled are discovered at the rise of the curtain, and from then on Concord, Massachusetts, transmuted into Harmony Village, is spotlighted. The clubs and skating excursions, the Milldam stores, the hemlocks, the river are all here. The fairground and yearly apple picking, the school festival in Town Hall, the performances of the Dramatic Club, the whole quiet life of a New England village are reanimated in these pages. So too are the children.

The last of the Little Women Series was not published until 1886. A sequel to *Little Men, Jo's Boys, and How They Turned Out* catches a thread dropped more than a decade before and follows the little men to maturity. Partly because of her ill health, partly perhaps because she sensed the book would bring down the final curtain on the Marches, Louisa Alcott tarried over its writing. Working only one or two hours a day, she once again drew the threads of her life into the fabric of a book. The Plumfield plays were the theatricals of her youth; a scene depicting a ward in an army hospital was modeled directly upon Georgetown; again the trumpet of reform sounded clarion calls for women's rights, temperance, and the freedom dress. If some of those calls sounded like echoes and if certain of the incidents were stereotyped, there were still enough simple domestic scenes left to touch the hearts of readers. The weary historian was strongly tempted to close her tale with an earthquake that would engulf all of Plumfield. Instead, having, as she put it, endeavored to suit her readers with many weddings, few deaths, and as much prosperity as the eternal fitness of things would permit, she simply let the music stop, the lights die out, and the curtain fall forever on the March family.

If none of the books that followed *Little Women* quite attained the stature of that masterpiece, the eight books of the series form a composite picture of life in nineteenth-century New England. The March family and the families in companion volumes are, however, also touched with universality. In a simple and enduring way, Louisa Alcott created a saga of nineteenth-century America that is unbounded by time or place. The door she unlatched to one home unlatched the doors of every home.

During the almost twenty years when those books were written, the author, "a natural source of stories," composed an abundance of minor works. Hundreds of her tales appeared in periodicals and were reprinted in collections—the six volumes of *Aunt Jo's Scrap-Bag, Spinning-Wheel Stories,* and the three volumes of *Lulu's Library,* named for May's daughter after May's tragic death. Unequal as these stories may be, they all reflect the facile skill of the professional writer who, after diverse experimentations, had learned the art of painting character to the life and the art of extracting from the exigencies of the installment the triumph of suspense.

Experimenter that she was, Louisa Alcott understandably wearied of the task of supplying the books expected by her avid public. Upon a few occasions she deviated from the pattern set in her Little Women Series and wrote to please herself and indulge her "natural ambition . . . for the lurid style." One of the most interesting of those deviations is *A Modern Mephistopheles.*

Opportunity to give vent to her "gorgeous fancies" came to her when her publishers, Roberts Brothers, launched a No Name Series to which well-known authors were to contribute anonymously. Louisa Alcott's anonymous contribution was a novel in which she analyzed the "psychological curiosity" that penetrates and violates "the mysterious mechanism of human nature." Interspersed through *A Modern Mephistopheles* are metaphysical borrowings from Goethe and Hawthorne, as well as themes dredged up from the days of her thrillers: mind control and the lure of drugs.

When it was published in 1877, reviewers gratifyingly asked: "Who wrote this story? Whose hand painted these marvellous pictures of the angel and the demon striving for the mastery in every human soul?"[11] As for the author, she commented in her journal: " 'M.M.' appears and causes much guessing. It is praised and criticised, and I enjoy the fun, especially when friends say, 'I know *you* didn't write it, for you can't hide your peculiar style.' "[12]

Yet Louisa Alcott's style was far less limited in its applications than her friends believed. That she is indeed entitled to a high place in the hierarchy of American writers is only recently becoming apparent. The bowdlerized and uncritical work of her first biographer, Ednah D. Cheney, did nothing to advance such a conviction. The delightful picture of *Invincible Louisa* by Cornelia Meigs was painted for a juvenile market, while the *Louisa May Alcott* drawn by Katharine Anthony in 1938 suffered from the limitations of the genre known as psychological biography. My own biography of Alcott, which was first published in 1950, was an attempt to provide a full-length portrait with extensive documentation, and it has been described as marking "the beginning of serious modern study of the subject." So-called modern studies have included two recent biographies, one by Martha Saxton, who, inspired by publication of the Alcott blood-and-thunder stories, viewed their author "through a glass darkly," suggesting that she was the guilt-ridden victim who hailed from a house of horrors. Madelon Bedell's *The Alcotts*, scholarly and authoritative, is rather the biography of an entire family than of any one of its members.

As for Louisa Alcott bibliography, at least three useful works are available: the first by Lucile Gulliver, which is limited to the writer's publications in book form; my own, which includes 291 numbered items of books and contributions to periodicals; and a recent reference guide by Alma J. Payne, which is particularly useful for its secondary bibliography of writings about Alcott.[13]

A careful study of that secondary bibliography indicates that gradually Louisa May Alcott is coming into her own. *Little Women* has been compared with *Pride and Prejudice*, and Alcott's educational concepts, her attitudes toward feminism, her relations with her father, her novels as commentary on the American family are all being analyzed. The few unpublished stories still available in manuscript form—such as *A Free Bed*, which was acquired by Brigham Young University—and the letters that occasionally appear on the market—such as the group of eight remarkable ones now on exhibition, which discuss her literary problems and techniques as well as her relations with publishers—are the object of avid collection and eager study. *Critical Essays on Louisa May Alcott* is part of a series that concerns itself with the outstanding authors of nineteenth- and twentieth-century America. And here today, on the occasion of the writer's 150th birthday, this exhibition mounted by Brigham Young University must surely help to place Louisa May Alcott in the literary niche to which she is entitled. From an examination of this display, if from nothing else, it must become clear to all that, although Louisa Alcott was indeed the "Children's Friend," she was far more. As

Flora Fairfield, Tribulation Periwinkle, A. M. Barnard, and author of *Little Women*, she made her writer's progress. The multifaceted career of this experimenting author may at last be traced in all its fascinating phases, and the mastery to which it led may now be recognized.

NOTES

1. Richard L. Herrnstadt, ed., *The Letters of A. Bronson Alcott* (Ames: Iowa State University Press, 1969), 19 f.

2. The description, by Emerson, is quoted in Madeleine B. Stern, *Louisa May Alcott* (Norman: University of Oklahoma Press, 1971), preliminary page.

3. Frank Luther Mott, *Golden Multitudes: The Story of Best Sellers in the United States* (New York: Macmillan, 1947), 102, 309.

4. John Tebbel, *A History of Book Publishing in the United States*, vol. 2 (New York and London: Bowker, 1975), 600 f.

5. Alma J. Payne, *Louisa May Alcott: A reference guide* (Boston: G. K. Hall, 1980), 73, 75.

6. Ednah D. Cheney, ed., *Louisa May Alcott: Her Life, Letters, and Journals* (Boston: Roberts, 1889), 16. For biographical references to Louisa May Alcott throughout, see Cheney, and Stern, *Louisa May Alcott*.

7. For this and further bibliographical Alcott references, see Madeleine B. Stern, ed., *Louisa's Wonder Book: An Unknown Alcott Juvenile* (Mount Pleasant: Central Michigan University, 1975), 25–52.

8. For the Alcott blood-and-thunder stories, see Leona Rostenberg, "Some Anonymous and Pseudonymous Thrillers of Louisa M. Alcott," reprinted in this collection; Madeleine B. Stern, ed., *Behind a Mask: The Unknown Thrillers of Louisa May Alcott* (New York: William Morrow, 1975); Madeleine B. Stern, ed., *Plots and Counterplots: More Unknown Thrillers of Louisa May Alcott* (New York: William Morrow, 1976).

9. Cheney, 199.

10. These comments, the first by Cyrus Bartol, the second from the *Boston Herald* (7 March 1888), are quoted in Stern, *Louisa May Alcott*, preliminary page.

11. Louisa May Alcott, *A Modern Mephistopheles and A Whisper in the Dark* (Boston: Roberts, 1889), advertisement at end, quoting from review in *The New Age*.

12. Cheney, 297.

13. Lucile Gulliver, *Louisa May Alcott: A Bibliography* (Boston: Little, Brown, 1932); Payne, *Louisa May Alcott: A reference guide*; Stern, *Louisa's Wonder Book*, 25–52.

Index

Abolition, 5, 24, 34, 116, 117, 150, 168, 181
Adams, Mildred: "When the Little Angels
    Revolted," 89
Alcott, Abby May (sister), 8, 16, 18, 19, 21, 24,
    28, 41, 118, 120, 184, 213, 258, 261
    See also Nieriker, May Alcott
Alcott, Abigail May (mother), 15, 28, 37, 41,
    48, 49, 54, 94, 130, 136, 144, 145, 146, 152,
    154, 175, 189, 204, 209, 211, 220, 253, 254,
    255, 258, 261
    Petition . . . on Equal Political Rights of
        Woman, 145, 152–54
Alcott, Amos Bronson (father), 9, 15, 34, 49,
    51, 54, 94, 130, 144–46, 147, 149, 151, 154,
    162, 182, 185, 189, 193, 208, 209, 212, 214,
    219, 227, 240, 241, 243, 253, 254, 255, 256,
    258, 260, 264
    Tablets, 185
Alcott, Anna (sister), 13, 14, 16, 17, 18, 19, 21,
    28, 32, 33, 46, 50, 51, 63–64, 65, 96, 114,
    119, 120, 253, 258
    See also Pratt, Anna Alcott
Alcott, Elizabeth (sister), 18, 20, 41, 55, 63,
    66, 258, 261
Alcott, Louisa May
    bibliographies of, 107, 131, 138–39, 264
    biographies of, 42, 107, 131, 263–64
    birth of, 253
    domestic novels, 4, 5, 40, 120, 123, 254, 258–
        59, 262
    domestic service, 55, 94–95, 122, 130, 255–56
    feminist letters, 3, 4, 138, 144–72
    interest in theater, 5, 7–8, 13–31, 47, 63, 64,
        66, 68, 96, 97, 122, 255

and Merry's Museum, 2, 6, 57, 109, 110, 111,
    127–29, 132–33, 136, 137, 138, 179, 195
and "Mrs. Jarley's Waxworks," 8, 24–25, 28
phrenology of, 3, 4, 239–45
professionalism, 4, 5, 58, 68, 91, 175, 179–
    80, 181, 184, 186, 254, 256, 263
pseudonyms, 1, 3, 7, 9, 21, 38, 40, 75, 76, 77,
    80, 85–86, 88, 94, 97, 98, 115, 131, 132,
    138, 256, 258
sensation narratives, 2–3, 4, 5, 6, 7, 9, 26,
    39, 40, 52–53, 57, 63–69, 73–82, 83–92,
    93–103, 115–16, 117, 127, 132, 138, 144,
    175–76, 190–93, 246, 251, 257–58, 263,
    264
Alcott, Louisa May, works of
    "Abbot's Ghost, The," 78, 86, 88, 93, 97,
        176
    "Agatha's Confession," 51, 53, 54, 58, 59
    Aunt Jo's Scrap-Bag, 136, 137, 148, 186, 232,
        263
    "Autobiography of an Omnibus, The," 250
    "Baron's Gloves, The," 176, 193
    "Beach Bubbles," 59, 217
    "Behind a Mask" and Behind a Mask, 2,
        40, 68, 77, 80, 86, 87, 88, 90, 91, 93–
        103, 144, 176, 239
    Belle of Santiago, The, 249, 251
    "Bertha," 8, 49, 51, 59
    "Blue and the Gray, The," 117
    "Captive of Castile, The," 26, 27, 255
    Comic Tragedies, 26, 114, 122
    "Country Christmas, A," 177, 202
    "Cross on the [Old] Church Tower, The,"
        51, 54–55, 56–57, 59, 216

"Defence of Woman's Suffrage," 57

"Double Tragedy, A," 68

Eight Cousins, 27, 136, 137, 138, 146, 176, 179, 180, 182, 183, 184, 185, 198–200, 220–21, 222, 223, 261

"Enigmas," 73, 74

Flower Fables, 3, 4, 6, 9, 32–45, 47, 48, 75, 97, 107, 112, 114, 127, 175, 188, 250, 251, 255

"Flower's Story, The," 238

Free Bed, A, 264

Garland for Girls, A, 186, 234

"Greek Slave, The," 26

"Happy Birthday, A," 136

"Happy Women," 134

"Helping Along," 250

"Hospital Christmas, A," 117, 118, 215

Hospital Sketches, 9, 25, 51, 75, 97, 107, 109, 119, 120, 127, 128, 134, 175, 181, 189, 207–13, 214, 218, 237, 239, 257, 258

"Hour, An," 117

"How I Went Out to Service," 95, 255–56

Inheritance, The, 4

"Ivy Spray, An," 234

Jack and Jill, 136, 137, 182, 183, 223, 224–25, 262

"Jamie's Wonder Book," 107–13

"Jeune, La," 57, 68

"Jimmy's Cruise in the 'Pinafore,' " 137, 182

Jo's Boys, 27, 147, 177, 183, 185, 186, 204, 228, 232, 233, 235–36, 247, 262

Journals, 6, 8

"King of Clubs and the Queen of Hearts, The," 121, 216, 218

"Lady and the Woman, The," 50, 51, 56, 57, 58, 59

"Little Genevieve," 49, 54, 59

Little Men, 40, 48, 68, 179, 197–98, 235, 260, 261, 262

"Little Sunbeam," 51, 55, 59

Little Women, 2, 5, 6, 9, 19, 25, 27, 40, 41, 48, 55, 56, 57, 67, 68, 73, 78, 84, 85, 88, 89, 90, 91, 93, 98, 99, 102, 108–9, 112, 120, 122, 123, 127–29, 131, 133, 134–35, 136, 144, 148, 176, 177, 181, 184, 185, 186, 196, 223, 230–31, 236, 239, 243, 246, 247, 251, 253, 258–59, 260, 261, 262, 264, 265

"Living in an Omnibus," 128

Long Fatal Love Chase, A, 4

Lost in a Pyramid, 249, 251

"Love and Self-Love," 115, 134

Lulu's Library, 40, 41, 42, 136, 186, 232, 237, 238, 263

"Mabel's May Day," 49, 59

"Marble Woman, A," 40, 76, 77, 80, 85, 86, 88, 93, 97, 102, 176

"Marion Earle; or, Only an Actress!," 5, 63–69

"Mark Field's Mistake," 51, 59

"Mark Field's Success," 51, 59

"Mermaids," 232

"M. L.," 116

"Modern Cinderella, A," 119, 120, 123, 134

Modern Mephistopheles, A, 176, 202, 231–32, 236–37, 239, 263

"Monk's Island, The," 51, 54, 59

Moods, 5, 25, 26, 108, 122–23, 176–77, 179, 181, 194–95, 213–14, 237, 250, 251, 258

Morning-Glories, 127, 184

Mountain-Laurel and Maidenhair, 234

"Mrs. Podgers' Teapot," 51, 59

"Mrs. Vane's Charade," 57

"My Contraband," 117, 118, 178, 188, 212, 215

"My Girls," 148

"My May Day among Curious Birds and Beasts," 111

Mysterious Key, The, 13, 26, 86, 88, 97, 246, 250, 251

"Mysterious Page, The," 7, 13

"Nat Bachelor's Pleasure Trip," 8, 23–24

"New Way to Spend Christmas, A," 201

"New Year's Blessing, A," 49, 54, 59

"Norna," 26, 27, 255

"Nurse's Story, A," 57

Old-Fashioned Girl, An, 48, 68, 137, 179, 196–97, 259–60, 261

"On Picket Duty" and *On Picket Duty,* 181, 215, 216–17, 218

"Pansies," 238

"Pauline's Passion and Punishment," 2, 26, 73, 85, 87, 93, 97, 101, 176

"Perilous Play," 88, 97, 102

Plots and Counterplots, 87, 102, 144

"Prince and the Peasant, The," 7

Proverb Stories, 176

"Recollections of My Childhood," 138

"Reminiscences of Ralph Waldo Emerson," 136

"Rival Painters, The," 48, 50, 114, 130, 256

"Rival Prima Donnas, The," 8, 21–23, 27, 38, 48, 49, 52–53, 59, 131–32, 256

Rose Family, The, 181, 218, 258
Rose in Bloom, 27, 146, 200, 201, 261
"Roses and Forget-Me-Nots," 136, 250
"Ruth's Secret," 50, 59
Selected Letters, The, 6
"Silver Pitchers," 135
"Sisters' Trial, The," 27, 49, 56–57, 59, 119, 120, 134
Skeleton in the Closet, The, 26, 67, 86, 88, 97, 102, 246, 249, 251
"Sophie's Secret," 227, 234
Spinning-Wheel Stories, 137, 185, 186, 227, 234, 263
"Sunlight," 256
"Thrice Tempted," 54, 59
"Trudel's Siege," 229
Under the Lilacs, 136, 137, 182, 183, 184–85, 222–23, 261
"Unloved Wife, The," 27, 255
"V.V.; or, Plots and Counterplots," 26, 68, 76–77, 78, 79, 80, 85, 86, 88, 93, 97–98, 102
"What the Bells Saw and Said," 51, 57, 59
"Whisper in the Dark, A," 88, 93, 97, 102, 236–37
Will's Wonder Book, 2, 107–13, 133
"With a Rose, That Bloomed on the Day of John Brown's Martyrdom," 181, 256
"Woman's Part in the Concord Celebration," 59, 138, 147, 155–59
Work (first called "Success"), 5, 27, 116, 121–22, 137, 181, 209, 211, 212, 215, 217, 218, 237
Aldrich, Lilian W., 228
Alger, Horatio, 89, 176
American Antiquarian Society, 86
American Catalogue, 2
American Literary Gazette, 108
American Revolution, 152, 183, 226
American Union, 63, 66–67, 74, 76, 79
American Woman Suffrage Association, 137–38, 151, 154, 168
Anthony, Katharine: *Louisa May Alcott*, 264
Atlantic Monthly, 73, 97, 115, 116, 134, 139, 181, 188, 214, 215, 216
Auerbach, Nina, 91
Austen, Jane, 89
  Pride and Prejudice, 33, 91, 264
Austin, Jane G., 26

Ballou, Maturin Murray, 74
Baltimore, 96

Bane, Robert, 257
Barnard, A. M. (Alcott pseudonym), 1, 40, 75, 76, 77, 78, 79, 80, 85, 86, 88, 94, 95, 97, 101, 102, 115, 132, 138, 258, 259, 265
Barnard, Henry, 75
Barrow, Julia, 22, 23, 53
Barry, Thomas, 20, 22, 53
Bartlett, George B., 18, 19, 21, 26
Bartlett, Samuel Ripley, 215–16, 218, 219
Bartol, Cyrus Augustus, 220
Beaufort, S.C., 188
Bedell, Madelon
  Alcotts, The, 264
  "Beneath the Surface: Power and Passion in *Little Women*," 89
Bellows Falls and Vicinity Illustrated, 6
Bellows family, 15
Benners, William James, Jr., 248–49, 251, 252
Berch, Victor A., 66, 67
Bernard, Bayle: *Dumb Belle, The*, 19
Bibliographical Society of America, *Papers*, 86, 100
Bicknell, Kent, 4, 239, 243
Blackwell, Henry B., 137, 147
Blish, Ariadne, 199–200
Bond, Henry May, 109
Bond, Louisa, 41, 42
Bonner, Robert, 134
Boston, 4, 8, 19, 20, 21, 22, 24, 25, 28, 33, 34, 35, 36, 37, 38, 39, 42, 46, 47, 48, 49, 50, 51, 52, 57, 58, 59, 64, 66, 67, 73, 74, 78, 79, 84, 85, 92, 94, 97, 107, 108, 115, 121, 130, 132, 133, 134, 137, 145, 147, 155, 176, 180, 181, 198, 201, 206, 220, 229, 231, 237, 246, 250, 254, 255, 260
Boston Advertiser, 46, 140
Boston [Daily] Evening Transcript, 6, 37, 140
Boston Herald, The, 74, 259
Boston Journal, 57
Boston Public Library, 75
Brame, Charlotte M., 248, 249, 251
Briggs, George Ware, 34
Briggs, George Washington, 33–34, 37, 38, 39, 42, 250
Briggs, George W., & Co., 33, 34, 35, 37, 39
Briggs, Oliver L., 39
Brigham Young University, 3, 7, 254, 264
Brook Farm, 18
Brooklyn, N.Y., 146
Brown, John, 181, 256, 257
Brown, William J., & Company, 247

Browning, Elizabeth Barrett: *Aurora Leigh*, 63–69
Burdick, William, 36, 47

Cambridge, Mass., 24, 36
"Car-Hook" Tragedy, The, 40
Carpenter, Frank George, 178, 182, 183, 205
Channing, Ellery, 211
Channing family, 255
Cheney, Ednah Dow Littlehale, 149, 160, 263
Christian Union, 137, 141
Cincinnati, 151
Civil War, 4, 39, 51, 57, 91, 92, 93, 95, 116, 117, 119, 120, 134, 180, 181, 242, 256, 257
Clapp, William Warland, 36, 46
Clapp, William Warland, Jr., 4, 8, 46–47, 48, 49, 50, 51, 52, 53, 54, 56, 57, 58, 114, 135, 217
   My Husband's Mirror, 47
Clarke, James Freeman, 24
Clemens, Samuel Langhorne (Mark Twain), 176, 239
Commonwealth, The, 117, 118, 134, 139, 181, 257
Concord, Mass., 1, 4, 7, 8, 13, 18, 19, 20, 21, 22, 24, 25, 26, 34, 35, 36, 64, 83, 85, 87, 92, 94, 96, 102, 119, 120, 121, 123, 130, 134, 136, 137, 138, 147–48, 149, 150, 154, 155–59, 160, 161, 163, 164–65, 166, 167, 168, 181, 182, 188, 192, 193, 206, 214, 218, 219, 222, 223, 225, 227, 235, 238, 255, 257, 258, 262
   Anti-Slavery Society, 24
   Dramatic Union, 18, 19, 21, 26, 28
Conway, Moncure Daniel, 134, 211
Cricket on the Hearth, 247
Croly, Jane Cunningham ("Jenny June"), 223
Curtis, George William, 156
Cushman, Charlotte, 64

Daily Republican (Springfield), 108
Dall, Caroline Healey, 199
Dance, Charles: *Naval Engagements*, 17, 19
Davenport, Edward L., 23
Dedham, Mass., 55, 94, 95, 255, 256
Degen & Co., 39, 42
Demorest's Monthly Magazine, 68, 141
Detroit, 154
Dickens, Charles, 8, 19, 24–25, 27, 54, 115, 118, 217, 255, 260
   David Copperfield, 19–20
   Dombey and Son, 115
   Nicholas Nickleby, 261

Old Curiosity Shop, The, 115
   Scenes from Dickens, 19
Dirigo Series, 2, 107, 110, 111
Dix, Dorothea, 256
Dodge, Mary Mapes, 136, 137, 181–82, 183–84, 185, 186, 198, 219–30, 232, 234, 238
   Hans Brinker or the Silver Skates, 181
Dollar Monthly, 74
Douglas, Ann: "Mysteries of Louisa May Alcott," 90

Edgeworth, Maria, 193
Elliott, James R., 4, 7, 67, 74, 75, 76, 77, 78–80, 84, 85, 92, 98, 99, 101, 135
Elliott, Thomes and Talbot, 3, 6, 7, 66, 67, 74, 75, 86, 97, 115, 180, 246, 250
   Ten Cent Novelettes, 67, 76, 86, 97, 246
Emerson, Edith, 18
Emerson, Edward, 18
Emerson, Ellen, 32, 34, 35, 36–37, 40, 41, 42, 114, 237, 255
Emerson, Lidian, 34, 37
Emerson, Ralph Waldo, 9, 32, 34, 94, 115, 136, 145–46, 193, 207, 209, 214, 254–55
   Self-Reliance, 261
   Wood-Notes, 36
Estes, Dana, 39, 42
Estes and Lauriat, 39

Fairfield, Flora (Alcott pseudonym), 21–22, 38, 48, 49, 59, 131, 132, 256, 258, 259, 265
Famous Dogs (M. G. Sleeper), 110
Federal Book Company, 247
Feminism, 2, 3, 4, 5, 57, 58, 63, 65, 66, 67–68, 88, 91, 93, 94, 95, 101, 102, 115, 137–38, 144–72, 240, 261, 262, 264
Fetterley, Judith: "*Little Women*: Alcott's Civil War," 89, 91
Field, Joseph M., 23
Fields, James T., 5, 108, 110, 116, 133, 188, 212, 213–14, 215
Fields, Osgood & Company, 109
Flag of Our Union, The, 2, 3, 4, 6, 74–75, 76, 77, 78, 79, 84, 85, 86, 88, 97, 108, 127, 132, 138, 139
Foote, Mary Anna Hallock, 184, 185, 222
Ford, Daniel Sharp, 135, 136, 180, 201
Forrest, Edwin, 22
Foster, William, 39–40
Fowler (or Fowlers) and Wells, 239–40
Frank Leslie's Chimney Corner, 54, 57, 88, 97, 140, 248, 251

Frank Leslie's Illustrated Newspaper, 2, 3, 4, 6, 53, 73, 74, 85, 87, 101, 115, 127, 132, 139
Fredericksburg, Va., 119, 257
Freud, Sigmund, 43
Fruitlands (Harvard, Mass.), 254–55, 260
Fuller, Horace B., 2, 107, 108, 109, 110, 111, 127, 129, 132–33
Fuller, Margaret, 145, 150, 254

Gannett, William H., 248
Garrison, William Lloyd, 24, 145
Georgetown, 25, 57, 119, 120, 121, 256, 262
Germantown, Pa., 253
Gleason, Fred, 74
Goethe, Johann Wolfgang von, 135, 231, 255, 263
  Faust, 202
  Wilhelm Meister, 120
Good Literature, 247
Good Things: A Picturesque Magazine, 136, 138, 141, 184
Graves & Weston, 66, 67, 79
Green, S. W., 247
Greene, Elizabeth B., 107, 108, 109, 110, 111, 133, 184, 217, 220
Gulliver, Lucile: *Louisa May Alcott: A Bibliography*, 264

Haggard, H. Rider
  "Tale of Three Lions, A," 250
  "Wreck of the *Copeland*, The," 250
Harper's Young People, 137, 141, 233
Harrington, Stephanie: "Does *Little Women* Belittle Women?," 89
Harvard, Mass., 254
Harvard University, 16, 18
  Divinity School, 34
  Houghton Library, 6, 7, 8, 84, 86, 243
  Widener Library, 75
Hawthorne, Nathaniel, 94, 263
Hayward, John, 15
Hayward, Louisa, 15, 16
Hayward, Louisa Bellows, 15
Hayward, Waldo, 15, 16, 17
Hayward family, 15
Higginson, Thomas Wentworth, 145, 161, 178, 188–89
Hillside Cottage (Concord, Mass.), 13, 14, 17, 26, 27, 28, 34, 96, 114, 115, 120, 255, 258, 260
Hoar, Ebenezer Rockwood, 149–50, 157, 162
Hoar, George Frisbie, 161

Home, William: *Report on . . . Gunshot Wounds*, 256
Hosmer, Alfred, 16
Hosmer family, 255
How to Read Character, 241, 242, 243
Howard Athenaeum (Boston), 8, 23, 24
Howe, Julia Ward, 148, 149, 165
  Battle Hymn of the Republic, The, 148
Howland, Alfred, 15–16
Howland, Henry, 16, 17

Independent, The, 129, 134, 135, 139, 146
Indianapolis Public Library, 253
Innis, Mrs., 184, 220
Irving, Henry, 237

Jackson, Helen Hunt, 203, 234
  Ramona, 234
James, Garth Wilkinson, 212
James, Henry, 89–90, 261
James, Henry, Sr., 134, 212, 216
Janeway, Elizabeth, 91

Kemble, Fanny, 117
Keyes, Annie, 26
Kittredge family, 15

Latimer, Elizabeth W.
  My Wife and My Wife's Sister, 231
  Princess Amélie, 231
Lawrence, D. H., 89
Ledyard, Addie, 233
Leslie, Frank, 3, 4, 53, 57, 66, 73, 74, 77, 86, 88, 98, 99, 115, 135, 215, 218, 248, 251
Leslie's Illustrated Newspaper. See Frank Leslie's Illustrated Newspaper
Lewis, Dio, 260
Liberator, The, 139, 181, 256
Library of Congress, 75
  Rare Book Division, 86
Lincoln, M. V., 74
Lind, Jenny, 52
Livermore, Mary, 148, 149
Loggers, The, 110, 111, 133
London, 184
Longfellow, Henry Wadsworth, 207
Loring, Aaron K., 7, 108, 176–77, 180, 250, 258
Low, Sampson, 184
Lupton, Frank Moore, 42, 246–52
Lupton, F. M., Publishing Company, 246–52

Manhattan Typesetting Company, 247
Mattituck, N.Y., 246
May, Col. Joseph, 189, 253
May, Samuel, Jr. (of Leicester), 145, 156
May, Samuel Joseph, 229
Meigs, Cornelia: *Invincible Louisa*, 264
Merrill, Frank, 184, 186, 231
Merry's Museum, 2, 6, 57, 109, 110, 111, 127–29, 132–33, 135, 136, 137, 138, 140, 179, 195
Miller, Eli Peck, 239
Miller, James, 111
Milton, John, 114
Mink Curtiss (Emerson Bennett?), 110, 111
Mitchell, Maria, 148, 149
Mobile, Ala., 23
Moers, Ellen: "Money, Job, Little Women: Female Realism," 89
Monitor, 139, 216, 218
Monthly Novelette, 74
More, Hannah, 193
Morrow, William, 87
Morton, John M.
  Two Bonnycastles, The, 16, 17
  Two Buzzards, The, 8, 17, 19
Mott, Frank Luther: *Golden Multitudes*, 253
Moulton, Louise Chandler, 231
Moulton, W. U., 74
Munro, Norman L., 248
Munro's Sons, George, 248
Myerson, Joel, 3, 4

New England Woman Suffrage Association, 147
New World, The, 140, 251
New York, 7, 23, 39, 40, 42, 43, 53, 66, 73, 83, 111, 134, 145, 182, 239, 240, 241, 243, 246, 247, 248, 249, 251
New York Atlas, 66, 67
New York Graphic, 48
New York Herald Tribune, 1
New-York Historical Society, 86
New York Ledger, 134, 140, 248
New York Public Library, 76, 86
New York Review of Books, 90
New York Times, 102
Nieriker, Louisa May (Lulu), 40, 41–42, 151, 183, 225, 226, 229, 231, 232, 233, 234, 263
Nieriker, May Alcott, 40, 41–42, 151, 204, 263
  See also Alcott, Abby May
Nightingale, Florence: *Notes on Nursing*, 256
Niles, Thomas, 5, 41, 109, 118, 123, 128, 132, 150, 177, 180, 185–86, 224, 228, 230–38, 260

Nonquitt, Mass., 183, 226, 232
Norris, Thomas F., 49, 50, 114
Northeastern University Press, 3

Old Corner Bookstore, 185
Olive Branch, 48, 49, 114, 130, 139, 256
Orchard House, 1, 6, 7, 23
Osgood, James, 109

Paris, 40
Parker, Perley: *Foundling, The*, 246
Parker, Theodore, 51, 145, 209
Payne, Alma J., *Louisa May Alcott: A reference guide*, 264
Peabody, Elizabeth Palmer, 254
People's Home Journal, 247
Periwinkle, Tribulation (Alcott pseudonym), 128, 138, 210, 256, 257, 258, 259, 265
"Perry Mason," 135
Peterson's Magazine, 139, 256
Pforzheimer, Arthur, 7
Philadelphia, 42, 247, 249
Phillips, Wendell, 24, 145, 151
Phrenological Journal, 243
Phrenology, 3, 239–45
Pickett, LaSalle C., 176
Planché, J. R.: *Jacobite, The*, 15–17, 19, 20–21, 24
Plymouth, Mass., 34
Pratt, Anna Alcott, 150, 151, 242, 260
Pratt, Frederick Alcott, 154, 235, 238, 242, 243, 260
Pratt, John Bridge, 18, 19, 20, 21, 28, 64, 65, 119, 120, 260
Pratt, John Sewall (John S. P. Alcott), 237, 238, 242, 260
Pratt, Minot, 18, 21
Pratt, Theodore, 20, 21
Providence, R.I., 34, 40
Provo, Utah, 3
Publishers Weekly, 102
Putnam, Austin G., 33, 38–39, 42
Putnam, Avery D., 33, 39, 40, 42
Putnam & Brother, 33, 38, 39

Radcliffe, Anne, 132
Random House, 4
Redpath, James, 115, 178, 180, 181, 207–19, 257, 258
  Echoes of Harper's Ferry, 181, 256, 257
  Public Life of Captain John Brown, The, 181
Reed, Mary Ann Williams, 50

Richardson, Charles B., 215, 218
Richardson, Hon. James, 94, 95, 255–56
Ripley, Ezra, 156, 157
Roberts, Lewis A., 185
Roberts Brothers, 5, 28, 41, 109, 129, 132, 136,
    150, 180, 181, 184, 185, 218–19, 221, 250,
    257, 260, 262, 263
  No Name Series, 263
Robinson, Harriet H.: *Massachusetts in the
    Woman Suffrage Movement*, 150–51
Rome, III, 260
Rostenberg, Leona, 1, 7, 9, 90
  discovery of Alcott pseudonym, 1, 2, 3, 7,
    9, 83–92, 100
  "Some Anonymous and Pseudonymous
    Thrillers of Louisa M. Alcott," 1, 73–
    82, 86, 100
Rostenberg, Leona, and Madeleine Stern—
    Rare Books, 7, 100–101
Ruston, J. M., 247

St. Nicholas, 129, 136, 137, 138, 141, 146, 180,
    181–82, 183–84, 185, 198, 222, 228, 229,
    233, 238, 250, 261
Sanborn, Francis B., 222
Sanborn, Franklin Benjamin, 18, 19, 20, 134,
    135, 209, 222, 257
Saturday Evening Gazette (Boston), 3, 4, 6, 8,
    21, 22, 36, 38, 46–62, 73, 97, 114–15, 127,
    131–32, 134, 139, 217, 256
Saxton, Martha: *Louisa May: A Modern Bi-
    ography of Louisa May Alcott*, 42–43, 90,
    264
Scott, Walter, 15
Scribner & Company, 181, 184, 220–21
Sewall, Samuel E., 145, 208
Shattuck, Harriette Robinson, 160
Shealy, Daniel, 3, 4
Sheridan, Richard B.: *Rivals, The*, 8, 17
Sherwood, Mrs., 193
Siddons, Sarah Kemble, 14
Sizer, Nelson, 240–42
Smith, Roswell, 136
Smith, Mrs. William H., 23, 24
Sontag, Henriette, 52
Stern, Madeleine B.: *Louisa May Alcott*, 1, 7,
    83–84, 101, 264
Stern, Madeleine B., edited works
  Behind a Mask, 2–3, 87, 93–103, 144
  Critical Essays on Louisa May Alcott, 89,
    264

Feminist Alcott, The, 3
Louisa May Alcott Unmasked, 3
Louisa's Wonder Book, 2, 107–13, 133, 139,
    264
Plots and Counterplots, 87, 102, 144
Stevens, Wealthy, 32, 35, 36, 42, 47
Stevens, William Burdick, 35–36, 42, 47
Stevenson, Hannah M., 207
Still River, Mass., 14
Stockton, Francis R., 180, 183, 198, 228
  Late Mrs. Null, The, 228
Stockton, Marian, 228
Stone, Lucy, 68, 137, 145–46, 147, 149, 151, 154,
    159
Story without an End, The, 35
Street & Smith, 248, 249
Suhre, John, 257
Sumner, Charles, 212
Sweet, Jannette E. Sykes, 7, 178–79, 202–4
Syracuse, N.Y., 19, 148

Talbot, Emily Fairbanks, 160
Talbot, Newton, 74
Temple School (Boston), 254, 260
Thomes, William H., 74
Thoreau, Henry David, 35, 43, 89, 94, 255,
    260
  *Week on the Concord and Merrimack Rivers,
    A*, 261
Ticknor, Howard M., 16, 108, 109–10, 214,
    215
Ticknor & Fields, 33, 108, 109, III
Tilton, Theodore, 134
Tolstoi, Lev: *Anna Karenina*, 228
Trowbridge, J. T., *Coupon Bonds*, 25–26
True, J. P., 179, 206–7
True Flag, The, 74
Twain, Mark. *See* Clemens, Samuel Lang-
    horne

Union Hotel Hospital (Georgetown), 51, 119,
    134, 212, 256
United States Sanitary Commission, 121
University of Virginia, Alderman Library, 86

Van Amburgh, I. A., 129, 222, 261
Van Buren, Jane: "Louisa May Alcott: A
    Study in Persona and Idealization," 90
Venice, 211
Verne, Jules: *Michael Strogoff*, 28
Vevey, Switzerland, 77

Vincent, Elizabeth: "Subversive Miss Alcott," 89

Walker, Fuller & Company, 109, 111, 132
Walker, Wise & Company, 107–8, 109, 111, 132
Walpole, N.H., 6, 7, 14, 15, 16, 17, 21
    Amateur Dramatic Company, 6, 7, 14, 15, 16, 17, 28
Walpole as It Was and as It Is, 6
Warren, William, 20, 23
Warwick, R. I., 33
Washington, D.C., 178, 188, 191, 207, 256
Wasson, David Atwood, 212
Wells, Charlotte Fowler, 240
Wells, Samuel R., 240
Wells, S. R., and Company, 239, 240, 243
Whitman, Alfred, 8, 18–19, 20, 100
Whitman, Walt, 239

Whittemore, Niles and Hall, 185
Willis, Benjamin, 6, 14–15
Willis, Hamilton, 46, 47, 51
Willis, Llewellyn, 48
Willis, Nathaniel Parker, 135
Wilson, Carroll A., 83, 84, 85, 86
Wilson, Henry, 156
Windship, Dr. Charles, 22, 23, 24
Winter, William, 33
Wollstonecraft, Mary, 150
Woman Suffrage, 57, 137–38, 145–72
Woman's Journal, 137–38, 141, 147–51, 160, 161, 164, 166, 167–68
Wood, Mrs. John, 22, 53
Wordsworth, William, 255
World War II, 1, 100
Wroth, Lawrence C., 1

Youth's Companion, 129, 135, 136, 137, 138, 140, 146, 180